"The market is flooded with books on personal finance. However, it's rare to come across a resource that deals with all the major issues in this area. Whether you're single, married with young kids, or at mid-life or retirement age, the principles Mary Hunt shares in *Debt-Proof Living* will absolutely put you on solid financial ground."

—Kent S.

"I found Mary Hunt when I was staying at home with my two young children. I bought her book and read it in two days. It changed my family's future. I have raised two daughters, now 30 and 32, and my husband retired early. Due to Mary's advice and my freedom account we are right on target for me to retire in August 2014. Our house is paid off and I feel in control of our future and finances. THANK YOU, Mary, your book was the best thing I ever picked up."

—Mary A.

"I am happy to say that reading *Debt-Proof Living* several years ago made it possible for me to decide to get rid of any debt and stay out of it. Learning to buy when I had cash rather than depending on plastic has made all the difference in the world. If I do have to use plastic for any reason, that is paid in full the next month. I think this is the most sensible plan for anyone to live with and it makes it so much easier to live within your means."

—Doris H.

"It has been four years since I really took to heart all of the information in *Debt-Proof Living*. I am happy to report today that we have paid back over $35,000 of 'toxic debt' and are currently saving like crazy for a house. I would have had no idea where to start if I had not read this book."

—Denise J.

"*Debt-Proof Living* was our salvation and now it is our daily living reference. We had a lot of toxic debt (over $40,000) about three years ago. We have now paid off each and every credit-card account. What a weight was lifted from our shoulders. We used this book every step of the way. I hope many people will read this book—it's wonderful. We are living proof that it works."

—Kathy W.

"When I bought your book I did not know how it would change my life in so many ways. Thank you."

—Joan B.

Books by Mary Hunt

Cheaper, Better, Faster
Debt-Proof Your Christmas
Debt-Proof Your Marriage
The Financially Confident Woman
Live Your Life for Half the Price
Raising Financially Confident Kids
7 Money Rules for Life
The Smart Woman's Guide to Planning for Retirement

Debt-Proof Living

How to Get Out of Debt and Stay That Way

Mary Hunt

Revell

a division of Baker Publishing Group
Grand Rapids, Michigan

© 1999, 2014 by Mary Hunt

Published by Revell
a division of Baker Publishing Group
P.O. Box 6287, Grand Rapids, MI 49516-6287
www.revellbooks.com

Printed in the United States of America

Library of Congress Cataloging-in-Publication Data is on file at the Library of Congress, Washington, DC.

ISBN 978-0-8007-2145-9 (pbk.)

This book is designed to provide accurate and authoritative information on the subject of personal money management. It is sold with the understanding that neither the author nor the publisher is engaged in rendering legal, accounting, or other professional services by publishing this book. As each individual situation is unique, questions relevant to personal finances and specific to the individual should be addressed to an appropriate professional to ensure that the situation has been evaluated carefully and appropriately. The author and publisher specifically disclaim any liability, loss, or risk that is incurred as a consequence, directly or indirectly, of the use and application of any of the contents of this work.

14 15 16 17 18 19 20   7 6 5 4 3 2 1

For Harold
and all the joys that money cannot buy

Contents

Contents

Acknowledgments

It is only right that I disclose my personal debts of gratitude, which are considerable.

First, my heartfelt thanks to the untold numbers of people who shared their hearts and their lives with me as a result of having read this book since its original release. Over the past two decades, I have received thousands of letters and messages from people whose lives have been changed. That connection has been my lifeline.

Debt-Proof Living staff: Thank you for keeping my office and professional life together against tremendous odds and for holding back the world so I could check myself into book jail from time to time. You are invaluable to the work we do. By taking care of all the technical stuff—the website, the mail, fulfillment, shipping, and inventory—you free my life considerably. You have no idea how much I depend on you.

Harold, my husband: Thank you for keeping everything balanced. Our boat would have capsized long ago had it not been for your steady ways, constant support, and unconditional love.

Jeremy, Tawny, Josh, and Wendy, my kids: You're the air I breathe, my reason for living. I cannot imagine my life without you. You are the hope I have that DPL will go on after I'm gone.

Eli, my grandson: You are the light in my life that shines so brightly and lifts me higher than anything I could have ever imagined. You make Friday my favorite day of the week and the best reason I've ever had to get my work done so we can play.

Vicki Crumpton, my editor: Who would have ever predicted that we'd still be together after all these years? Thank you a million times over for using what I write to make me look so good. I never cease to be amazed by your organization, intelligence, and kindness. And punctuality. I aspire to your level of excellence. Your friendship means the world to me.

Dr. James Dobson: Our first broadcast in 1994 was a defining moment for me, the newsletter, and the books I would write. Thank you for knowing that my story would touch so many lives in a positive way and for your unwavering support and encouragement through the years.

The organizations, corporations, and churches that have hosted Debt-Proof Living seminars: Thank you. You may never know the full extent of the good you have done to help people learn to manage their resources effectively. It is immense.

My dear reader: Thank you for giving me the reason to write this book and the next one too.

Introduction

Welcome to the updated, revised, and "even more all-new" edition of my book *Debt-Proof Living*. The first edition of this book rolled off the press in December 1999. It began . . .

> The median income for a U.S. four-person household has just hit an all-time high of $62,228. Unemployment continues to decline while inflation is minuscule. And Americans are deeper in debt than ever before. What is wrong with this picture?

Since then the economy has gone through major upheavals as a result of the terrorist attack of September 11, 2001, the wars in Iraq and Afghanistan, the tsunami of 2004, Hurricanes Katrina and Sandy, United States presidential elections, and on and on it goes. Gasoline prices have more than tripled, the cost of food has increased by more than 60 percent, and United States residential real estate values shot skyward then crashed.

In 2005, so many things had changed that I updated, revised, and expanded this book for an "all-new" edition and posed the question, So where are we six years later? The economy was on track, and the median income for a United States four-person household had climbed to $67,019. Unemployment was on the decline, while inflation remained low. But Americans were far more deeply in debt than ever before. Revolving unsecured, non-mortgage consumer debt totaled $735.3 billion, about 31 percent higher than it had been six years earlier.

So here we are in 2014. The economy plummeted in 2008 and has struggled ever since. Promises of a recovery have not materialized. The median income for a United States four-person household is $65,000, a *decrease* of 4.3 percent.[1] Unemployment has increased to 7.7 percent, and inflation is ticking higher. While consumer debt dropped significantly after the financial crash of 2008, it has taken a startling turn upward. As of January 2013, United States credit card debt stood at $851 billion on top of $1 trillion in student loan debt.[2]

Again I ask, What is wrong with this picture? You could be wondering why, given such a dismal report, I would even think about revising, updating, and republishing this book. One might conclude that, with the overall picture becoming decidedly worse since this book's first and second releases, this book was not successful. But that would be a very wrong conclusion.

While it is important to look at the big picture, it is too general, too depressing. What matters are individual lives. I measure effectiveness and progress by the mail I receive from people whose lives have been forever changed because they learned how to manage their money following the debt-proof living principles you will find in this book.

I measure success by the thousands of people I've heard from who have followed the steps and repaid all their unsecured debts, are well on their way to paying off their mortgages, and have learned how to fund their own emergencies—to not depend on credit cards when the unexpected happens. They have debt-proofed their lives and continue to do so one day at a time!

So why revise and update this book if it was and continues to be effective in its prior releases?

Many things have changed over the years. Take credit scores, for example. In 1999, individuals were not allowed to know their credit scores. Lenders were sworn to keep that proprietary information secret. That's no longer true. Not only does the law now allow us to know our credit scores, but we can also know to what extent our scores affect our lives (hint: it's huge). In this updated edition, you will find the latest information available on what contributes to your scores and how to improve them.

You will also find other information that did not appear in the original book. And I hope that the knowledge, insight, and maturity I've gained over the years are reflected in the following chapters as well. Readers have taught me a lot.

Take student debt. I've learned it is a far bigger concern to far more people than I realized in the past. In the first edition, I gave a strong warning about the dangers of taking out student loans. Now I have added information on how to deal with and conquer your educational loans. Of course, avoiding them in the first place is most ideal, but reality is what it is, and this is a subject I cannot ignore.

Even with all the new content, let me be quick to say that some things have not and probably will never change.

The consumer credit industry will forever want us to believe that credit cards are necessary to bridge the gap between our pitiful incomes and the lifestyles we deserve. Lines of credit have become the socially acceptable means of survival in this gotta-have-it-now world. Everywhere we turn we're told that no matter our income we deserve to be several levels higher.

We don't need more credit or more stuff. What we need is the courage to think for ourselves, the maturity to tailor our lifestyles to fit within our incomes, and the willingness to find contentment where we are and with what we have.

We need to understand that money is not just for spending. It is for managing first and then for spending. We need to see money not as power or prestige but as provision—God's provision for our physical and material needs.

Contrary to the financial pressures and stress we might feel from time to time, generally the problem is not that we don't have enough money. The problem is that we don't know how to manage what we do have. We see money as a qualifier. It is a down payment on what we want. It is the lever we use to lift ourselves to economic privileges we have not earned.

Since 1992 I have devoted my life to learning about money and personal finance. At first it was a matter of survival. It took twelve years for me to plunge my family into the pit of financial despair. It appeared there was no way out. But appearances are not always what they seem. Slowly but surely we began to fight, scratch, and work our way out.

By 1992 we'd been working on our horrendous mountain of debt for nearly ten years. About $12,000 of the debt remained. I desperately wanted to find an additional source of income so we could pay off those last remaining credit accounts. It was time to close the chapter on that part of our lives. It was time to move on.

About that time I had a wild idea. What if I created a forum? One in which I could help others help themselves, and I could help myself in the process? It seemed plausible and a way I might be able to speed the pay-back process. I had nothing to lose by trying, so I went for it.

My number one reason for starting a subscription newsletter was not a secret: I was in it for the money. I came clean in the first issue of Cheapskate Monthly (it has since undergone a name change to Debt-Proof Living and gone from a subscription newsletter to a full membership at DebtProofLiving.com). I told anyone who would listen that, for pocket change, I would provide them with information and motivation to get out of debt just as my family was doing. We would take the journey together.

Two decades later, the newsletter continues in full publication and has become a regular part of tens of thousands of people's lives.

I am smarter now than I was in 1992. I've proven that teaching teaches the teacher. Naively, I thought I knew it all—at least enough to fill the few issues of the newsletter I planned to publish. But I was wrong. I never dreamed I could become so passionate about a subject I had heretofore considered hopelessly boring. And I continue to learn.

I did raise the funds we needed to reach our goal. We used the profits from the newsletter to finish repaying our whopping unsecured debt, and in a relatively short period. According to my original plan, it was time to move on. But I'd developed such a bond with so many readers that my new passion transcended that plan. I was hooked, and pulling the plug on the newsletter was not an option. It didn't cross my mind.

I also noticed that something weird was going on. My new knowledge was intoxicating; I couldn't get enough. I was driven to learn more and more. Every week I'd receive stacks of letters from readers. Some were filled with questions; others were cries for help. Some were testimonials about how this person or that couple was understanding for the first time the principles and specific steps they needed to follow to take charge of their finances and become effective money managers.

The more I wrote, the more I developed a burning desire to know more. As I learned, I watched as my family's personal financial picture began to improve—significantly. As I taught my readers to anticipate the unexpected, we became better prepared. As I waded into the waters of beginning investing, our portfolio experienced amazing growth. I actually learned the definition of *portfolio*. I could hardly believe the confidence I felt in the knowledge I was gaining.

Often I would step back and look at myself through eyes of astonishment. "Look at you! What an unlikely development for someone who was so financially ignorant, so downtrodden by debt, and so unwilling to change." I liked what I saw. My husband liked it too.

There is no doubt in my mind that getting out of debt is the important first step in gaining control of your personal finances.

But then what? The only way to stay out of debt and keep moving toward a secure financial future is to manage your income effectively. That means adopting a new way of living. It may require giving up old ways of thinking, changing your attitudes about money, and rejecting the notion that you are entitled to more than you can afford now, even when the credit industry says you are more than qualified.

It's only fair that I warn you: I am seriously opinionated on this matter of money, credit, and consumer debt. I refuse to pull punches or take the soft approach. I lived far too many years in financial bondage to see that condition as tolerable. I paid back more than $100,000 in unsecured debt and lived to tell about it. I've been there. I know what it takes. I know the temptations and challenges that hit you every day.

I am the first to admit that the countless offers of entitlement and promises of happiness that appear online and on our television screens day after day are more than just enticing. They are downright seductive. And I know the pain and personal devastation of cashing in on those promises only to find that having it now and paying for it later is not the path to contentment and peace of mind. Rather, it leads to self-centeredness and defeat.

I have written this book to present my case, in the most powerful way I know, that it is possible to live a rich, fulfilling life without consumer debt.

One of the most gratifying aspects of what I do is having readers tell me I've changed the direction of their lives. If that has been true for even one person, I am blessed, because I know my passion has found purpose. In that, I have found unspeakable fulfillment.

Wherever you are on your financial journey, consider this my personal invitation to join me and thousands of others on the road to a debt-proof life.

1

Debt-Proof Living

What It Means, What to Expect

Knowledge is the difference between really living and just existing. Existing is instinctual; living is the exercise of certain learned skills, attitudes, and abilities that you have acquired and honed to a sharp and focused edge.

Dr. Phil McGraw,
clinical psychologist and television host

Like graduation, becoming debt-free is not the end—it's the beginning of a new adventure. To drop out at your debt-free "graduation" and fall back into debt would be to turn your back on everything for which you have been preparing. It would be to close the door on your dreams of financial ease. In some way, it would diminish the importance of what you accomplished. Who would be so foolish as to do the difficult work and then not stick around to enjoy the rewards?

Not long ago I heard from someone who dropped out. In her letter, Bonnie described how she and her husband had gotten into quite a debt mess during the early years of their marriage. It took them three years to unload $18,000 of credit card debt, but they did it! They were debt-free. And they assumed they were finished. That is when they dropped out.

Bonnie and her husband bought a home and soon welcomed their first child. Of course, they needed all kinds of things for this new chapter in their lives. The baby needed a new crib; they needed a new sofa. It all seemed so logical and necessary.

Apparently, they needed many other things too, because by the time Bonnie wrote, they were in debt again—this time they owed more than $26,000. Bonnie described how she and her husband make good money, live fast-paced lives, have no savings, and spend thousands each year eating out. Every nickel that comes in goes out to keep the bills at bay.

I could feel Bonnie's panic as I read her closing paragraph:

> We did it once. We know we can do it again. But how do we avoid falling back into the cycle of debt the next time? There must be some way for us to cure ourselves of this disease once and for all. I'm afraid that if we become debt-free this time, the way we think about money might lead us right back into debt again . . . and again . . . and again. How can we win over debt for a lifetime? Help!

I must have stared at that letter for a full hour as a million thoughts raced through my mind. Over and over, I kept coming back to the simple truth that getting out of debt is only the first step. That is how you get to the starting point. Staying out of debt and moving forward to financial independence—that's the bigger challenge. And that's where the big rewards await.

I thought about the thousands of people I had met or communicated with over the years who had made it to the starting line. Are they progressing, I wondered, or did they, like Bonnie, mistake the starting line for the finish line? How many of them grabbed the prize and went back to their old ways of living and thinking, putting the lessons they learned in "boot camp" far away from their daily lives? Did they go through the steps to get out of debt hoping they wouldn't have to think about money again? That somehow they'd have so much money they would not need to care for it?

Bonnie's letter brought to mind my own situation and how I repaid a boatload of debt, how the temptation to fall back into the old ways of incurring debt becomes less intense and certainly manageable but never really goes away. What keeps me from going back? How can I encourage people not to stop but to move on to the next level and beyond? Is it possible to win over debt for a lifetime?

I startled myself when I jumped to my feet and answered Bonnie as if she were sitting across the desk. Yes, it is possible, and no, I will never go back! You have to get to the starting line, establish your long-term goal of reaching financial freedom, define that goal in terms of steps, and then change gears from debt recovery to debt prevention. You have to think specifically, not generally, about how you're going to get there and then rejoice because each step from now on will be one of progress, not repair.

I continued pontificating, in the privacy of my office, on this matter of maintenance—a way of living I would soon call debt-proof living. It was a defining moment as I described to myself what a debt-proofed life looks like: You spend less than you earn; you give, save, and invest confidently and consistently; your financial decisions are purposeful; you turn away from impulsive behavior; you shun unsecured debt; you borrow cautiously; you anticipate the unexpected; you scrutinize your purchases; and you reach your goals by following a specific plan.

Perhaps you've heard of a weather condition known as El Niño. An El Niño makes meteorologists giddy because it gives them a very unusual type of weather to report.

I can't help but think back to the El Niño of 1998. Where I lived in California, it washed sections of the beach out to sea and took a few homes along for the ride. It was amazing to watch as certain other structures were pounded relentlessly but remained intact. Was El Niño selectively cruel, targeting some homes and for no apparent reason sparing others? No, El Niño slammed the entire area with equal force and showed no mercy. What made the difference was how the homes were constructed. Those tied to bedrock weathered the storms just fine; those built on shifting sand did not.

I never could have predicted which homes would survive such an ordeal. Foundations aren't exactly out there for everyone to see. Often it was the more showy, ostentatious homes that flunked the test. They looked good, but they did not remain standing when things got rough.

In the same way that Laguna Beach homes must be tied to something immovable, the way you manage your money must be tied to unchanging truths and principles. If your financial behaviors are based on shallow thoughts and fickle feelings, the storms of life will wipe you out. And there will be storms—I guarantee it.

Bonnie and her husband were washed out to the sea of debt because they did not tie themselves to a solid foundation of unchanging truth. Once they fixed the initial problem, they tossed aside the principles that had served them so well in getting out of debt. They handled debt recovery well but failed to kick into debt-prevention mode. They got to the starting line, and then they quit.

Truth be told, you may not have a clue what you believe about money and its role in your life. Or you might firmly believe things that are not true. No matter what you've done or believed in the past about money and how to take care of it, now is the time to tie yourself to a foundation that will not change, one that will withstand the storms of life. In the same way you would insist on a sturdy, well-built foundation on which to build your dream house, you need a strong foundation on which to build your financial life. In the coming chapters, we are going to create that solid foundation using sound yet simple financial principles that will stand the test of time.

Don't be surprised if at first you find some of this information overwhelming. There's a lot to learn and a lot to do even if your finances are not in terrible shape. You won't be able to do everything at once, so relax and learn all you can. Take it one step at a time, and you will find that you can begin immediately to improve your personal financial picture.

I am confident that you will find a sense of enjoyment and personal satisfaction as you get your debts and spending under control, as you learn specific strategies, and as you let go of the hit-or-miss method of money management. Everything will not change overnight, but as you take the first steps and then commit to steady progress, you will be well on your way to achieving the financial security you desire.

What Is Debt-Proof Living?

To debt-proof means to live without reliance on consumer credit. Debt-proof living is:

A *lifestyle*. Debt-proof living is a way of life in which you spend less than you earn, you give and save consistently, your financial decisions are purposeful, you strive to live below your means and free of consumer debt, and you work toward your goals by following a specific plan.

A *system of personal money management*. Debt-proof living is a specific money-management method that makes it possible to debt-proof your life and is presented in its entirety in this book.

A *newsletter*. Debt-Proof Living (formerly Cheapskate Monthly) newsletter is a monthly publication that picks up where this book ends and is a monthly source of encouragement, information, and entertainment in your quest to debt-proof your life.

A *website*. DebtProofLiving.com was established in 1997 and has grown into a member community. The website is where members access the monthly newsletter and its archives, use DPL's calculators and money-management tools, and interact with other DPLers in lively community forums.

A book. This method is presented in its entirety in the book titled, not surprisingly, *Debt-Proof Living*—a copy of which you hold in your hands (for which I thank you very much).

Five Reasons to Debt-Proof Your Life

You will never find success in turning your money life around until you are thoroughly convinced it needs to happen. Here are five reasons you need to make that turn and debt-proof your life.

1. *To survive lean times.* If you have a load of debt, even the slightest shift in your economic picture can plunge you into financial despair. Debt represents a heavy load and makes the journey nearly unbearable. Debt offers few, if any, options. If you are debt-free, you are traveling light. When you live without debt, you have alternatives to help you survive times of challenge and struggle.

2. *To reduce your stress.* Financial stress comes in many forms: worry, sleeplessness, communication breakdown, depression, and anxiety. The medical community reminds us that stress takes a terrible toll on our health. We are less immune to disease and illness. Our bodies bear the consequences of the heavy loads our minds carry when we place our lives in financial jeopardy. Debt-proof living can turn stress into joy, peace of mind, and rest.

3. *To protect your future.* Revolving debt forces you to transfer your future wealth to your creditors' bank accounts. Debt-proof living is an insurance policy for your future income. It builds a protective shield that creditors cannot penetrate.

One woman I spoke with recently brought this truth home to me in a poignant way. Only months before our encounter, her mother had died, leaving her a sizable inheritance. How comforted she should have felt knowing she was so important to her mother that she had purposely blessed her daughter in this way. Although the mother would never know, this woman had run up such significant debt that it was going to take every penny of her inheritance to bring her current and back into favor with her creditors. Through tears, she finally understood what it means to transfer your future wealth to your creditors.

4. *To protect your marriage.* Whether you are married now or hope to be one day, you need to understand just how devastating debt can be to the relationships you hold most dear.

The number one killer of marriages in the United States is unresolved conflicts.[1] And what do couples argue about the most? An impressive study published by the Center for Marital and Family Studies at the University of Denver reported how couples rated their problem areas over an extended period of time.[2] The study tracked couples from before they married to many years after. People before marriage, people after marriage, people with a lot of money, people with little money—all rated their number one area of conflict as money.

Divorce is expensive, but more than that, it is devastating for all parties, especially the children. If strengthening your marriage were the only reason to debt-proof your life, it would be reason enough.

5. *To teach your children.* If your kids read magazines, go to school, watch television, listen to the radio, know what a fast-food restaurant is, or have ever been inside a store or supermarket, they already know something about entitlement and instant gratification. Right under your nose they are developing into world-class consumers. They may be well on their way to becoming future debtors of America.

If you do nothing to intervene, statistics indicate your kids are headed for a life that will be severely and negatively impacted by consumer debt. By debt-proofing your life, you will affect your children's lives as well because families reproduce themselves. Kids learn through observation and imitation, and when all the smoke clears, they usually turn out like their parents.

Principles for Debt-Proof Living

There are only five things you can do with money. You can give it away, save it, invest it, lend it, and spend it. I purposely put "spend it" last on the list. Spending should never be the first thing you do with your money. The proper management of money is specific and orderly. If we short-circuit the system by spending it first, we create fiscal disorder and eventually financial chaos.

These are the never-changing principles upon which you can build your financial life—whether you live on a fixed income, are self-employed, rely on commissioned sales for your livelihood, or have huge sums of money at your disposal.

Principle 1: Never keep it all. The first thing you must do when money flows into your life is give some of it away.

You have two enemies that will do all they can to make sure you do not live below your means—that you spend all the money you have now and hope to have in the future. The first enemy is greed. The antidote for greed is giving.

Greed is that voice whispering in your ear that insists you are entitled to have anything you want and everything you like. Greed keeps you from being satisfied. Giving away some of your income brings balance to your life. It is a remarkable antidote for a condition that has the potential to ruin your life.

Giving connects you to something greater than yourself; it takes your eyes off your situation. How much you give away is a personal decision; however, I suggest that 10 percent is a good amount.

Giving is the tangible expression of gratitude and proves the condition of your heart. Giving easily defeats the enemy named greed.

Principle 2: Always save some. Your second financial enemy is fear—fear of poverty, fear of running out of money, fear of losing your job, or any number of money-related fears. The antidote for fear is saving.

Diligently save 10 percent of your paycheck—over and above any contributions you are making to retirement plans. You must always save without fail before you pay your bills and before you spend your paycheck.

The money you save is money that will be there to carry you through times when your income stream is cut off. And that will happen sometime in the future. Get prepared. Always pay yourself before anyone else. Always.

Principle 3: God is the source. If you see your employer, your spouse, your investments, your trust account, your parents, or any other entity as the source of your income, you are setting yourself up for a great deal of worry. Employers go away, parents and spouses die, investments can turn sour overnight. The truth is that all of these are only the conduits in the delivery system. They are the channels through which you receive money, but they are not the ultimate source.

God, who gave you the talents, intelligence, and ability to think and work, is the source of your money. Once you see yourself as the manager or "steward" of your resources, you will also understand your responsibility to be trustworthy and reliable, to care for what you've been given to manage. Believing this truth will bring a sense of peace and calm to your life. No longer will you fear a drop in the stock market or the plunging of real estate values. No longer will you lie awake worrying about losing your job.

The way your money is delivered may change radically and frequently, but the source never changes. It is the same yesterday, today, and forever.

Principle 4: Pay with cash. ATM cards, debit cards, and credit cards are all stand-ins for money. They are not the real thing; they are just representatives, and often very poor representatives if they enable debt.

Using cash in your day-to-day living whenever prudent may require lifestyle changes and sacrifices, but it will keep you from drowning in a sea of red ink on your journey to financial freedom.

Paying cash promotes contentment because you can see the value in the things you buy. Paying cash makes spending difficult and uncomfortable. And that is exactly the way it should be.

Principle 5: No new debt. Unsecured debt is like cancer. At first it is not life-threatening because it involves only a cell or two. But it never stays small. It begins to grow, and then it takes over. It becomes the master; you become its slave. A little cancer is never okay. Neither is a little debt.

Note that "no new debt" is not the same as not using a credit card to make a purchase. As you will learn, a credit card used properly can be a very helpful tool. The way you pay that credit card bill determines whether the debt becomes unsecured debt. If you are unable to pay your credit card in full within the grace period, you will incur new debt, and each new purchase added to that amount only increases that debt.

Principle 6: You need a specific strategy. Hope is not a strategy. Hope is an emotion. Without a specific plan for getting from where you are to where you want to be, reaching your goal of financial freedom will remain a dream. A plan turns a dream into a goal.

Having a plan liberates you from depending on willpower, which is unreliable emotional fuel. Willpower can get you going at break-neck speed, but once the emotion is gone, you fizzle. You should not rely on willpower. A written plan stands firm whether you're on an emotional roller coaster or an even keel.

Principle 7: More money is not the answer. I used to believe that if I had more money, everything would be fine. Then we'd get a raise, and we'd have more money, but it wasn't enough. And that made things worse because we turned more money into more debt.

Sometime ago I heard from Lynn. Sadly, her story illustrates this point perfectly:

> I am thirty years old and have worked since I was fifteen. I married straight out of high school. I have always been good at selling any product I represented, and that is where my nightmare begins.
>
> While working at my first "real" job in a bank, a customer recruited me to become a copier salesperson. I was hesitant until he showed me his commission check for that month. I got really

26

excited about my potential to make good money too. So I resigned my position and started selling office products.

My first commission check was $1,500; the next one was even better. After a couple of months I began to see just how much I could make, so I leased a new BMW for myself and a fully loaded Nissan Pathfinder for my husband. I needed many other things as well to demonstrate to people just how successful I was. I began incurring debt, all the while thinking I'll just pay it off with my next commission check.

As the months went by, meeting my quota became more difficult. I worried about where I would find my next customer. The stress became unbearable, so I quit that job after three years. But that did not stop the car payments and the unsecured debts that were breathing down our necks.

Lynn's letter went on for many more pages to describe how the situation worsened. She closed by announcing their plans to file for bankruptcy.

Lynn's train began to derail the day she impressed herself with her newfound wealth, failing to see that first $1,500 commission check as $1,500 cash. She wrongly viewed it as a harbinger of things to come. To her, it represented a life of luxury, where she could have anything she wanted and where money was no object. She assumed the checks would continue to roll in and, of course, in ever-greater amounts.

Lynn's situation is a perfect example of why, for most people who carry revolving consumer debt, more money will never be enough. Unmanaged money has a way of creating more debt. Then the unrelenting nature of more debt requires more money, and a vicious cycle begins—one in which more money is never enough.

Principle 8: Money is not just for spending. Money must be managed first, spent later. In a coming chapter, you are going to learn exactly how to manage money according to a plan that will profoundly change your life.

Attempting to hold on to money that you have not managed specifically is like trying to hold a handful of water: No matter how hard you try or how tight your grip, the water leaks out. Money that is not managed will disappear. That's just a fact of life that most of us have proven many times over, much to our humiliation. Knowing how to manage money allows you to respond intelligently, not just emotionally. When you spend first, emotions take over and the results are, at best, unpredictable.

In your lifetime, you will have the opportunity to manage a lot of money. Let's say you and your mate are twenty-five, and your combined income is the United States median, last reported to be about $49,103.[3] If you both work until you're sixty-five, even if you never get a raise, you're going to bring home over $1.8 million. If your salary goes up just 3 percent a year, you'll earn over $3 million. If you land a promotion, you'll rake in even more. As unlikely as this scenario may be (and not that you will earn less but that you will earn even more over your lifetime), my point remains: Having enough money is not the challenge.

Principle 9: It is not how much money you earn but what you do with it that matters. Had Lynn and her husband made a pledge to live by simple, sound, financial principles, they likely would have enjoyed a nice lifestyle. They were making decent money. They just didn't know—or didn't care—how to take care of it.

Imagine two identical families. Same income, same expenses—everything exactly the same. The only difference is that the Smiths are into instant gratification while the Joneses prefer delayed gratification.

The Smiths act on their desires as they come up. They buy now and agree to pay later. They carry revolving consumer debt equal to that of the average American family, which means they pay around $1,200 a year in interest on their unsecured debt.

The Joneses have no unsecured debt. If they don't have the money to pay for the things they want, they wait until they do. They do not send $1,200 a year ($100 each month) to the consumer credit industry to cover interest the way the Smiths do but instead funnel it into an investment account that earns an average 10 percent a year (historically, over time this is what we can expect to earn).

At the end of ten years, the Smiths have possessions—and $0 invested. The Joneses, on the other hand, have the same items and a tidy nest egg of $20,926.

No matter how many times I consider these facts, I am no less amazed. The fictional Smiths and Joneses live the same. They buy the exact same things; they make the exact same amount of money. They are mirror images. The only difference is the timing of their spending. The Smiths spend first and pay interest later. The Joneses manage their money first and spend later.

Three Personal Money-Management Styles

When it comes to the way people manage money, there are three basic styles.

First are those people I call revolvers. They carry credit card balances from one month to the next. They owe far more than they can pay; they spend more than they earn. They are forever juggling finances, trying to keep their heads above water.

Revolvers enjoy the idea of a cashless society. They are every consumer credit marketing department's dream customer because they fit a predictable profile and contribute to the huge profit margins of the credit card companies.

The next group is composed of those who live paycheck to paycheck and spend every dime they make. They are the daredevils. They flirt with credit cards, debit cards, and ATM cards, finding it more convenient to swipe than carry cash. These folks usually pay their credit card balances in full every month, but just barely—and often with nothing left over. Now and then it might take them two or three months to get an account back to paid status (the holidays are always a struggle), but for the most part they stay even.

The third group includes those people I lovingly refer to as DPLers. They embrace the debt-proof lifestyle. They do not live on credit, nor do they flirt with credit cards. They live according to a specific plan. What they do with their money is by design. They give, they save, they invest, they live below their means. They expect the unexpected, they are prepared, they live with confidence because they can smile at the future.

I love word pictures—visual images created with words alone. For me, a word picture is an incredibly powerful tool that turns an abstract thought into a clear concept, complete with shape and dimension.

Let me paint three word pictures to illustrate these three money-management styles.

Debt-Ridden Dexter

You probably tried walking up the down escalator when you were a kid. It can be fun—for a while. Then it becomes a challenge. That's exactly what Dexter is doing. He's a full-grown man attempting to reach the next floor but doing it completely the wrong way.

When he first started this crazy way of getting ahead, he could keep in sync with the speed of the escalator. It would move one step down; Dexter would take one step up. Down, up. Down, up.

But now he's trying to do this up-the-down-escalator action while carrying baggage—heavy debt and lots of it. He has two gigantic suitcases, one in each hand, a bulging briefcase jammed under one arm, and another very large box under the other arm. He has a heavy bag slung over one shoulder that is making things even more difficult. He can't see his feet for all the gear, most of which he keeps dropping. In his attempts to recover, he finds himself back at the bottom, hat askew, shirt torn, and shoes flying. Finally, he gets everything back under control and begins the challenging climb all over again.

Debt-Proof Living

It is frustrating to watch him. Can't this guy see what he's doing wrong? It is obvious to the spectators what changes he needs to make to get where he needs to go, but he's so wrapped up in his predicament that he hasn't the time or the inclination to listen. He is determined to do this his way.

Perspiration pours from him when he attempts to take the moving stairs three at a time. Lenders, disguised as concerned onlookers, offer a helping hand. He always reaches out to accept their "help," and it does relieve his burden—but only temporarily. They look as if they are helping to carry his heavy load, but the truth is that they are putting more weight in poor Dexter's bags, literally behind his back.

He can forget about making any progress. Actually, he's forever losing momentum. Remaining upright becomes his impossible dream. He's an exhausted, beat-up, pitiful sight. Even the slightest misstep sends him crashing to the bottom.

Dexter is debt-ridden, and he is not enjoying life as he might if he didn't have all this heavy baggage. Sadly, he will soon find himself defeated, flat on his back in the basement.

Paycheck-to-Paycheck Penelope

Penny is walking too, but instead of going the wrong way on an incline, she is on a treadmill. Things are different for her. Unlike Dexter, she has no heavy baggage, just her purse and a small bag. She stands upright, maintains a perfectly timed stride, and appears to be doing a really great job at walking. It looks as if she is going somewhere, but of course she is not making progress. She is expending all kinds of energy but is getting nowhere. Because it takes so much effort for her to stay in exactly the same place, one wonders how long she'll be able to keep it up.

Penny spends what she earns. Month after month she keeps up. She faithfully pays her credit card balances, makes the rent on time, even drives an above-average leased automobile. So what if

31

she doesn't save and has nothing in reserve, she reasons. At least she has no debt.

From time to time, Penny slips up for any number of reasons. It usually takes her three months to pay the holiday bills. When something unexpected hits, like car repairs or a new roof, of course she has no choice but to spread the payments over time. That's when she loses her rhythm and nearly falls off the edge. But she has those handrails, and she hangs on. Her situation isn't critical. She recovers quickly and then does double time to get back to that old position—back in sync, knowing she can't take a rest. She can't slow down or change a thing.

Penny gets a raise now and then, and that allows her to increase her speed slightly. Sometimes she even runs awhile. But then, because of higher prices, an added expense, or something unexpected, she settles back into her rut. She lives paycheck to paycheck, spending all she earns. Nothing is left over. She's always walking but never progressing.

Debt-Proof Peter

Look at Peter. He's walking at a brisk pace, sport jacket flung over one shoulder, head held high, smiling at everyone he sees. Not far ahead is a beautiful thing: a moving sidewalk—one of those people-sized conveyor belts.

He steps onto the moving sidewalk. Without changing his brisk pace and normal stride, he's almost flying. The air is rushing through his hair. He even feels taller.

Peter's regular steps on the moving sidewalk become the equivalent of three or more of his unaided strides. How cool is that? Without increased effort on his part, he is propelled to his destination—and in record time.

If he chooses to slow down, or even stop for a rest, that's okay. He just moves to the right so others can pass on the left. He doesn't lose momentum. He doesn't slip back or lose ground. Even though he stops walking, he continues to enjoy a pleasant ride. He has a choice: to walk briskly or to slow down and enjoy the journey. Either way, he still makes progress toward his destination.

Peter is a perfect picture of someone living a debt-proof life. He finds meaning in the journey, not the destination. Because he carries no debt—instead putting the money he isn't sending to creditors to work for his future—his money works for him and produces offspring (earned interest and appreciation) that also work for him. His momentum is turbocharged, without increased effort on his part or the need for additional energy. He doesn't stumble and fall, and he's not obsessed with money. He's enjoying life.

What's Your Style?

How you travel through life is completely your decision. You can choose to go the wrong way on a one-way escalator, carrying such a heavy load that you cannot even see where you are going; you can get stuck on a treadmill, living paycheck to paycheck; or you can choose to travel on a moving sidewalk that will take you where you want to go.

I'm pleading with you to decide right now to build a strong financial foundation into which you can drill deeply and drop the pilings for your life. Learn the principles so well that you can re-peat them in your sleep. Hang on to them for dear life when your emotions go wild, when temptations overwhelm. Depend on them when you want to quit and go to that place that exists only in your imagination—where money is no object and you can spend with reckless abandon.

I can promise that the foundation built on debt-proof living principles will stand up under all kinds of circumstances. When financial challenges come—and they will—your foundation will hold and you will make it through.

Debt-proof living is not a righteous call to deprivation. It is not defined by austerity, poverty, guilt, and fear. It is not about extremes, bizarre behavior, misery, hoarding, or finding a way to recycle dryer lint.

Debt-proof living is a lifestyle in which you spend less than you earn; you give, save, and invest confidently and consistently; your financial decisions are purposeful; you turn away from compulsive behavior; you shun unsecured debt; you borrow cautiously; you anticipate the unexpected; you scrutinize your purchases; and you reach for your goals by following a specific plan.

Debt-proof living is about generosity, gratitude, and obedience. It is about sound choices and effective decisions. To debt-proof your life means to know exactly what to do with your money and to have the freedom to earn and spend it when and how you choose. Debt-proof living is a way of life—a financially disciplined lifestyle that produces peace and joy.

Debt-proof living is your invitation to a rich and abundant life.

2

Two Kinds of Debt

Intelligent Borrowing, Toxic Debt

The only thing worse than investing in things that depreciate
is paying interest on things that depreciate.

Blaine Harris,
The Four Laws of Debt-Free Prosperity

Not all debts are created equal, nor is every type of loan hazardous
to your wealth. There is a world of difference between a home
mortgage and a revolving credit card balance. Both are liabilities
for which you, the borrower, are legally obligated to the lender. The
first I call intelligent borrowing; the latter is toxic debt.

Those who are living debt-free and are debt-proofing their lives
would sooner poke toothpicks under their fingernails than live in
the grip of toxic debt. If they incur debt of any kind, it is only
through intelligent borrowing.

Intelligent Borrowing

Intelligent borrowing means that some level of safety and limited risk for both the lender and the borrower are built into the transaction. Here is what intelligent borrowing looks like:

1. The borrower has a safety valve—a legally and morally sound way to get out of the obligation at any time.
2. The debt is secured. The lender holds something that is at least as valuable as the amount of the loan. This is called collateral. Think of it as a security deposit for the lender.
3. The loan is for something that has a reasonable life expectancy of more than three years as opposed to something that will be obsolete before the bill arrives.
4. The loan is for something that will increase in value, unlike a great new outfit or a couple of movie tickets and dinner at a fancy restaurant.
5. The interest rate is reasonable. An interest rate with double digits would generally be considered unreasonable.

The best example of intelligent borrowing is a real estate loan, often referred to as a home mortgage. Let's see how a home mortgage measures up to each of these five characteristics of intelligent borrowing.

Is there a safety valve or escape route? Yes, there is a way of escape for both the borrower and the lender. If you, the borrower, find you can't handle the payments or you want out for any other reason, you can sell the house and pay the lender from the proceeds of the sale. Because the loan becomes an asset for the lender, he can sell his position as well.

Is the debt collateralized? Yes. With a mortgage, the real estate is the collateral—the lender's security. The lender has a legal lien on the property until the mortgage is paid in full, and that gives him a legal position in the transaction. If you as the borrower do not hold up your end of the bargain to which you agreed, the lender can take the property as payment for the outstanding loan.

Does the purchase have a reasonable life expectancy of more than three years? Yes, of course. This is true not only for the structure itself but also for the land on which it sits. Buying a home is a long-term investment.

Will the home increase in value over time? Yes. Real estate is always considered an appreciating asset, even though specific values may decline during economic cycles. As a general rule, real estate gains in value over time.

Is the interest rate relatively reasonable? Yes. In nearly all situations, mortgage rates are considerably lower than other types of consumer loans, usually by as much as two-thirds.

Toxic Debt

Take every aspect of the intelligent borrowing scenario above and think of the opposite. Now you understand toxic debt.

This is the kind of debt you agree to, often impulsively, when your desire is in high gear and your brain is in neutral. It is so easy to get into—much too easy.

A person with a credit card and an available credit limit can take out very expensive loans on a whim and at nearly every place, including the internet. You simply make your decision, swipe the magic plastic, sign your name, and presto! You've made a commitment to toxic debt. Painless? It is in the beginning. But not for long, my friend, not for long.

Let's say you use your credit card to acquire the very latest notebook computer complete with LED-backlit retina display, a 2.8GHz quad-core processor, high performance graphics, 8 gigs of ram, a 500 GB hard drive and—the best part—a free printer. It's on sale (which to many of us is a clear sign of providential entitlement), and you want it right now. You can think of so many ways this computer will simplify your life. You even justify that it will help you save money (not sure of the logic there, but I do understand the thinking). Why should your pathetic lack of cash prevent you from making this really good deal? (Remember the free printer.) You have just enough credit left on your account to cover it.

As you haul that baby to the car, the last thing on your mind is how you will pay for it. You didn't consider for one second how this new debt will affect your current payment structure. It can't be that bad, you reason, because you got approved. And you got a free printer!

Let's see how this purchase measures up against the criteria for intelligent borrowing.

Does the borrower have a way out at any time? No. If you don't pay as agreed, the credit card company won't come after the computer—they'll come after you. Unless you can sell the computer for what you paid for it (fat chance), you have no way out.

Is the debt collateralized? No. The credit card company is holding nothing of value to fulfill the debt if you are unable to pay. But they've got a tight grip on you. They don't want that computer or anything else you buy with a credit card, for that matter. This loan is unsecured.

Does this purchase have a life expectancy of at least three years? No matter how you look at it, a three-year-old computer is not exactly cutting-edge technology. By its third birthday it has little monetary value, even though it may still compute. In fact, the features I listed above are already obsolete. Think about that for a minute.

Will the purchase appreciate in value? From the minute you walk out of the store, a computer is in the fast lane to obsolescence. It's depreciating with every tap on the touchscreen or click of the mouse.

Is the interest rate reasonable? No. As of this writing, the average credit card annual interest rate is 16.82 percent,[1] while a thirty-year fixed-rate mortgage is 3.72 percent per year.[2]

The computer purchase fails the intelligent borrowing test miserably by getting a no response to all five questions. Paying for a computer over time cannot qualify as intelligent borrowing. It is toxic debt.

Anatomy of a Toxic Debt

And it gets worse. Let's say this computer deal we're analyzing has a price tag of $3,200. The credit card terms are typical: 16.82 percent interest with minimum monthly payments of 4 percent of the outstanding balance. I just plugged those figures into my minimum payment credit card interest calculator at DebtProofLiving .com and—hold on to your wireless mouse—it will take eighteen years to pay the total price tag of $4,918, including the $1,718 in interest. Did you get that? Eighteen years to pay for a computer that will be functionally obsolete in three years or sooner. There's no other way to characterize such a transaction than pretty stupid.

What will make things even worse is if, after two or three years, you decide to upgrade to a new computer even though you still have thirteen years to pay on the first one. Nevertheless, if the credit is available, it is quite easy to add another purchase (like a new computer) to the growing load of debt.

In no time at all, the forever revolving credit card balance is not seen for what it really is (a very high-priced loan on a lot of stuff you might not even own anymore) but rather as a normal part of life—like the rent, the phone bill, and the cost of food. In fact, I could show you high school personal finance curriculum that suggests keeping consumer debt at a manageable level, not to exceed 20 percent of income. I find that somewhat outrageous.

More than Toxic

While the computer example is remarkably illogical, other kinds of toxic debt make the computer scenario appear somewhat reasonable. Turning restaurant meals, groceries, utility bills, movie tickets, vacations, gifts, gasoline, and school clothes into debt and then choosing to pay for them with minimum monthly payments over many years and at rates that effectively double the original costs bring new meaning to the term *toxic*.

Spending money you don't have yet to pay for things you don't have anymore is anything but intelligent. Nevertheless, that is exactly what millions of people in this country do every day, every month, year after year after year.

Semi-Intelligent, Semi-Toxic

There are times when debt cannot be so easily delineated between intelligent and toxic. Sometimes it starts out intelligently and then turns toxic. The following are examples.

Home Equity Loans

As you know, a home mortgage qualifies as intelligent borrowing because it limits risk for both the borrower and the lender and is fully collateralized—at least it's supposed to be that way. The homeowner can borrow only up to a certain limit, so the lender has reasonable assurance that the property's current market value is more than the outstanding loan.

A home equity loan is typically a second mortgage that allows the homeowner access to the equity in the home (that margin between what is owed and what the property is worth). Equity is the borrower's asset—and a precious asset at that. Home equity loans come in two flavors.

The first is a home equity loan (HEL)—a straight loan. When the paperwork is signed, the lender hands you a check for the full amount of the loan, minus costs and fees, if any.

The other type is a home equity line of credit (HELOC), which opens a large line of credit for you, for which you pledge your equity as the collateral. You can borrow against it whenever you want. In fact, the lender will be more than happy to give you access to your HELOC with a debit card that you can carry with you at all times to pay for anything. It's like an ATM in your pocket.

Technically, both a HEL and a HELOC are secured debts because of the collateral feature. And the borrower's safety valve remains because the home can be sold to satisfy the mortgage and the other loans against it. But it can be very risky—and that is what can push this type of debt into toxic territory. There are five ways the stupid factor can sneak into an otherwise intelligent mortgage situation:

1. If you borrow against your equity to clean up your credit card debt and then max out your credit cards all over again, you are left with twice the debt—that of the equity line and the credit cards. Not smart.

2. Some people treat a home equity loan as a permanent debt to be paid off when the house is sold. They would probably feel a greater urgency to pay off the debt if it was in the form of credit card balances.

3. The convenience of having your home's equity available at your fingertips can be a formidable temptation. When money is readily available, you are more likely to fritter it away on something like a family vacation instead of saving it, as you might without the easy access.

4. If you are unable to keep current on both of your mortgages, either of the lenders can foreclose.

5. Sometimes the home equity loan and the first mortgage together exceed the market value of the property. But some lenders will still offer to finance not only the full value of the home but also more than the property is worth. You read that right. Even with all the lessons learned in the subprime debacle of the late 2000s, plenty of subprime loans are still available. These 125 percent loans put the borrower in a tenuous position—the monthly payments are severe, but selling the property ceases to be a way out because more is owed than it would bring at sale.

Even taking into consideration the fact that the interest on the home equity loan may be deducted from your taxable income, the risks involved with this potentially toxic debt can be weighty.

The equity in your home is an appreciating asset, for many people their only appreciating asset. If you leave it alone, it will grow as the property becomes more valuable and as you pay down the mortgage. That contributes to the intelligence factor of your home's mortgage. To muddy those waters with a HEL opens the door to toxic debt.

Automobile Loans

A car loan can contain elements of intelligent borrowing provided you make a large down payment and select a model that retains a high resale value. An automobile loan is a secured debt; if you get into some kind of trouble, you can sell the car to repay the debt. Cars do not appreciate, however, so not all of the intelligent borrowing criteria apply.

A car loan can slide over to the toxic debt area if you put little or nothing down and stretch the payments past three years. It won't take long for you to be "upside down" in the loan, meaning you owe more than the car is worth.

Student Loans

If ever there was a gray area in this matter of intelligent borrowing versus toxic debt, it has to be the troublesome student loan.

Some argue that a student loan qualifies as intelligent borrowing because the resultant education will appreciate over time and will more than pay for itself in future income. Nevertheless, that argument makes some bold assumptions: first, that you will actually finish school; second, that you will be well suited for the field in which you are getting your degree; and third, that the field will welcome you. I find it just short of amazing that 85 percent of college graduates do not end up working in their major field of study. (But then I recall the decisions I made at that tender age, and I understand fully. I majored in music.)

Whether student loans fall into the category of semi-intelligent or semi-stupid has a lot to do with one's individual circumstances.

Recognizing the Difference

It is not difficult to recognize the difference between intelligent borrowing and toxic debt:

- Intelligent borrowing requires plenty of time to complete applications and receive approval. It makes you think. You can create toxic debt in your sleep.
- You are not likely to get in over your head with intelligent borrowing because you are qualified based on your debt-to-income ratio. Toxic debt can dump you into the deep end of the ocean before next Tuesday.
- Intelligent borrowing requires a lot of research and thinking. The last thing toxic debt wants is for you to analyze anything—just sign here!

As a person desiring to debt-proof your life, your mission is to rid your life and your future of all toxic debt, to borrow money only when it cannot be avoided, and then to do so as intelligently as possible.

The trouble with debt can be likened to the proverbial frog in the pot of boiling water. If you try to pop him in once the water is boiling, he'll jump out. But if you start him out in cold water and slowly raise the temperature, he'll just sit there and cook to death.

People are like that frog when it comes to toxic debt. We wouldn't jump into the boiling water by purchasing something really big and expensive, like a car or a boat, with a credit card. But months and years of consistently making smaller purchases while paying only the minimum payment each month allows the temperature to rise ever so slowly. Before we know it, we've reached the boiling point.

Toxic debt doesn't usually start out that way. In the beginning, it is simply a matter of convenience. You pay the entire balance during the grace period. Then one month the balance is a little too large, so you pay half and plan to pay the balance the next month. But then something comes up, and it appears to make sense to let the balance roll over to the next month. Soon you've got a balance too large to pay in full in a single month, and you're on your way. The water started boiling, and you were completely unaware.

Why Is Toxic Debt Such a Problem?

Debt promotes discontentment. When you're buying things with money you don't have, you are not content with your income. You can't be patient. You can't wait. You have to have it right now! But when you acquire things too easily without pride of ownership, it is easy for you to become dissatisfied quickly.

Debt makes arrogant presumptions about the future. By agreeing to have things now and becoming legally obligated to pay for them later, you make bold presumptions about what the future will hold in terms of money, ability, and health.

What makes you believe that although you don't have the money now you will have it later? But worse, you also promise that you will be willing to turn over money you don't have yet to pay for things you may not have anymore. What makes you think you will be all that thrilled about spending money you've not yet earned for stuff you probably won't even remember? That's an arrogant attitude and an irresponsible presumption about the future.

Debt requires you to transfer your future wealth to your creditors. If given the choice between sending monthly checks to the wealthy credit card industry or sending those same checks to build your own future, would you really choose the former? When you agree to toxic debt, that is exactly what you've done. You've made your choice, and there is no way out but to make full repayment, no matter how difficult or unreasonable.

Debt limits your options—and heavy loads of debt eliminate them altogether. Debt keeps people tied to jobs and careers they hate. It forces moms who would rather be home with their kids to work outside the home. It can even give Mr. Right second thoughts about taking on a prospective bride because of her heavy, debt-ridden baggage.

Debt steals your freedom and makes you a slave. When you are under a load of debt, you are in bondage. You have no way out but to work off your sentence. King Solomon, said to be the wisest man ever to have lived, summed it up this way: "The rich rule over the poor, and the borrower is slave to the lender" (Prov. 22:7).

From here on out, I am going to omit the word *toxic* before the word *debt*. I'm sure I've made my point by now. Just understand that whenever you read *debt* in this book, it refers to toxic debt. Intelligent borrowing will be referred to as such and should not be construed to mean the same thing as debt.

3

Caught in the Debt Trap

Red Flags and Warning Signs

Debt, n. An ingenious substitute for the chain and whip of the slavedriver.

Ambrose Bierce, journalist

Opossums are plentiful where I live in California. Those that hang around our yard have developed quite an attitude about their private little reserve. They are fearless and consider our property as much theirs as ours.

The only reasonable way to deal with these somewhat less-than-attractive marsupials is to trap and then relocate them to uninhabited areas. It is not difficult to trap an opossum if you have attractive bait. All you do is stick some opossum delicacy, like fruit (even cat food will do), inside the trap and set it out after dark. The trap's clever one-way entrance makes crawling into it nearly effortless for the opossum. Once he's in—slam! He's caught, with no way out.

Debt is a lot like an opossum trap. It is attractive, easily accessible, and the bait can be irresistible.

If you've ever been—or are now—in the debt trap, you know what a horribly confining and stressful place it can be. That's why you need to know how to gnaw your way out. You also need to learn to recognize the trap so you never get caught in it again.

Debt Traps

Some debt traps are not as obvious as others. Here are the most common debt traps:

- credit card accounts
- installment plans
- overdraft protection plans
- past-due taxes
- student loans
- medical bills
- dental bills
- personal loans

Credit cards are by far the most common of all the debt traps. Currently, there are billions of active accounts in this country, close to 70 percent of which carry a revolving balance month after month,[1] year after year. What's more, hundreds of companies are doing their level best to see the numbers increase.

One way these companies lure unsuspecting consumers into debt is through those rascally preapproved applications. Billions are sent through the mail every year. These solicitations are often quite beautiful, with lavish use of color, photography, and foil stamping on high-quality paper stock. There was a time when I got so many preapproved credit card applications that I toyed with the idea of wallpapering my guest powder room with them to make my own whimsical statement.

To further my research on the matter of consumer credit—but, more importantly, to give myself an occasional humor break—I read the fine print. This is not easy because nowadays it seems the really important information is graphically designed to be illegible.

These appeals always begin with a cordial, often gushy, letter telling me how wonderful I am and why I deserve only the very best that life has to offer. There is always some kind of acceptance form with urgency written all over it pressing me to act now! Then comes the preaddressed, postage-paid return envelope.

I have gone over every square millimeter of hundreds of these solicitations and have yet to find a single word that honestly describes what these companies are selling—debt. It is simply not there. So what's the deal? Why are they so afraid to call it like it is, to come clean and say that carrying a balance from month to month can be hazardous to your wealth? Beware the debt trap!

For fun, I looked up the word *debt* in my trusty Roget's Thesaurus (you might wonder about a person who thinks it is fun to read a thesaurus, but go with me on this). Mine is not your ordinary classroom variety but the five-inch-thick, fifteen-hundred-page, forty-nine-pound, thumb-indexed version. Here's what it says:

> **Debt.** Obligation, encumbrance, in the red, pound of flesh, arrears, inability to pay, bilked, bound, beholden, up to one's ears, over one's head, mortgaged to the hilt, in the poverty trap, unable to keep the wolf from the door, hard up, beaten down, financially embarrassed, strapped, stripped, fleeced, busted.

Instead of making any reference to debt, credit card solicitations contain flattering and manipulative words such as congratulations, easy, instant, preferred, deserve, prequalified status, spending limit, cash advance, buying power, do with as you please, accepted in a zillion places, convenience, reward, make life easier, and my favorite—you stand out in a crowd!

Warning Signs

While I suppose it is possible, it is not common for a person to wind up in the debt trap overnight. It is a process, a series of events and choices that brings one to that dismal place.

How can you know if you are headed in that direction? There are definite warning signs—red flags I wish I'd heeded back when I was moving at breakneck speed into debt's pit of despair.

Here are the danger signs that indicate you may be heading down the wrong path, ready to enter the debt trap.

You are living on credit. How can you tell if you are living on credit? Take this test:

- If you regularly pay for things with credit because you don't have enough money, you are living on credit.
- If the balance you carry from month to month is going up, you are living on credit.
- If you are applying for new credit cards, you are living on credit.
- If you ever pay one credit card bill with another credit card, you are living on credit.
- If, when you think of not having credit cards, you break into a cold sweat and fear you would never survive, you are living on credit.

You pay your bills late. What's paying your bills late? you might ask. Well, if you have to ask that question, I would suspect you are indeed a late payer. But just to be on the safe side, here is a checklist:

- You write out your bills but don't mail them because you don't have enough money in the bank to cover them.
- You count on next month's paycheck to pay for this month's bills.
- You pay half of your bills this month and half the next.

- You pay late fees willingly because you think of them as the price you must pay for your pitiful financial situation.
- You think anything within thirty days late is on time.
- You would never consider paying a bill before the final due date even if you have the money because you might need it for something else.

You are not a giver. As you will learn in coming chapters, generosity is one of the tenets of debt-proof living. It is also one of the "magic bullets" that will reverse the damage of debt and help to get you out.

One might think this matter of giving is fairly straightforward: either you are a giver or you are not. But, here again, many of us like to think in gray rather than in black-and-white terms. Here are the ways to tell you are not a giver:

- You like the idea of giving money to your church or a charity and will do so as soon as you have more than enough to cover your necessary expenses.
- You reason that you cannot possibly give what you don't have.
- You argue that because you give so much of your time—and since time is money—you are, therefore, a giver.
- You call yourself a giver-in-kind because you regularly dump loads of stuff at the thrift store drop-off station.
- You consider payment of your kids' tuition to private school as giving.

You are not a saver. Consistently and purposely saving is also part of the debt-proof living get-out-of-debt plan. It's the other "magic bullet" (there are a total of two, so now you know both of them).

- You like the idea of saving money and will do so as soon as you have more than enough to cover your necessary expenses.

- You reason that you cannot possibly save what you don't have. Once you cover your necessary expenses, you will save a lot.
- Your home is gaining value every year, so that counts as saving as far as you are concerned.
- You think of your available credit as your savings because it will be there in case you run into an emergency.

You dream of getting rich quickly and living an extravagant lifestyle. When your mind is focused on winning the lottery or falling into a get-rich-quick opportunity, you become a magnet for dissatisfaction. Your attitude becomes fertile ground for debt because easy credit tempts you to have the extravagant lifestyle now before your ship comes in or before that great get-rich-quick opportunity taps you on the shoulder.

You worry about money. When your mind is filled with worry about money, you become an easy target for debt because it masquerades as a reasonable solution. The following warning signs signal that your worrying is drawing you into the debt trap:

- You find yourself thinking about money.
- You are unable to sleep.
- You become obsessive.
- You are fearful when the phone rings.
- You think up ways to hide purchases or bills from your spouse.

You overspend your checking account. If you are living so close to the edge that you spend more money than you have in your checking account, you are flirting with the debt trap. If you fall back on the overdraft protection plan that is connected to your checking account, you may not feel you are actually bouncing checks, but that is exactly what you are doing. You are taking a loan to cover what you do not have. Your financial institution is charging you some whopping big fees and interest, and you are repaying them a little bit at a time. If you have done this more than twice in the past twelve months (I'll cut you a little slack for simply being human), that is a serious indication that you are about to be snapped into the jaws of the debt trap.

Do you recognize any of these warning signs in your life? If so, don't panic. Just know that you need to make some changes. It's time to recognize the red flags, sirens, and flashing lights that signal you may be headed for trouble.

How to Get Out of the Debt Trap

If you've gone past all the warning signs and the trapdoor has slammed behind you, now is the time to start gnawing your way out. Don't think of your situation as impossible. It is not! I got out, and I've helped thousands of others get out as well. Take a deep breath and start with step 1.

1. *Get serious.* Decide right now that you are going to do whatever it takes to get out of debt and stay out of debt forever. Make a commitment. Write it down and date it so you can refer to it often. Don't worry if you are afraid or don't think you know what to do. Remember, it is easier to act your way into a feeling than to feel your way into an action. God will give you just the amount of light you need for the step you are on. I will help you get going and be right here with you all the way.

2. *Become a giver.* If you are in the fast lane to the debt trap or have already arrived, you should see that as a pretty good indication that your method of money management could use an overhaul. If what you're doing isn't working, you might as well consider an alternative approach. In chapter 4, you will learn why giving is such an important part of debt-proof living.

3. *Start saving.* You cannot allow yourself to spend it all. You must start saving something for yourself. Even if you are deeply in debt, you need to give and save. These two activities, both discussed in chapter 4, will enable you to get out of the debt trap. When you

give and when you save, you find contentment. That impulsive thing going on inside of you that never seems to find satisfaction is quieted. When you are satisfied, you won't spend so wildly. Your mind will clear so you can think before you buy.

4. *Start tracking.* One of the reasons you've landed in the debt trap is that you've allowed money to leak from your life. I know, because I've been there myself. I get nauseous when I recall how much money flowed through my hands year after year after year. Remember, it's not that you don't have enough money. The problem is that you don't know how to manage what you do have. That's what sends you in constant search of new sources of credit. Let me tell you again: More will never be enough until you learn to manage what you already have.

Tracking, as you will discover in chapter 5, simply means counting. It means keeping track of where your money goes. There's not a successful business in the world that doesn't keep track of the outgo and the income. They know where every penny goes—and so should you.

5. *Know what you owe.* If you are in the debt trap, you probably don't know exactly what you owe—exactly the extent of your debt. Therefore, if you want out, you have to make a list of your debts. All of them. I call it facing the music. While it may be difficult to do this, you must take this big step in order to get a handle on where you are.

6. *Design a plan.* In the same way you would never dream of building a house without a detailed set of plans, you should not even dream of getting out of your debt mess without a plan—a written plan that is suitable for refrigerator posting. You need to know exactly how long your payoff plan will take, right down to the year and the month. You need a plan for how you will manage your money while you're getting out of debt. You need a plan for where you will go once you are debt-free, how you will begin to invest. You need a simple plan that shows where you are, where you're going, and how you're going to get there! A plan brings a dream to life. Good planning and hard work lead to prosperity.

7. *Know what you own.* As you work your way out of the debt trap, it is very important to know what you own—not only the contents of your closets, drawers, and home but also your financial assets. Do you have insurance? Where are the policies? How about the savings bonds you received as a kid or your family heritage documents, such as birth certificates and military records? Straightening out your records will give you a sense of where you are. This new awareness, explained more in chapter 12, will bring order to your life and aid you tremendously.

8. *Have a sale.* Once you know what you own, you'll be in a good position to decide what you really need. Excluding family heirlooms and sentimental possessions, consider liquidating what you haven't used in the past year. If you do not find something useful or it does not bring beauty to your life, get rid of it. Organize a garage sale. Run ads in the local classifieds for items with a price tag of thirty dollars or more. Dejunk, unclutter, simplify. You will experience calm and freshness in your life—and a stash of cash will jumpstart your get-out-of-debt plan.

9. *Incur no new debt.* Make a commitment that from this day forward you will incur no new debt. Let me warn you. At first it will feel as if you are swimming upstream against class 6 rapids because credit is so available, so seductive. Depending on your situation, you and your credit cards may already be enmeshed. You may have established quite a dependence on them, and that is something I fully understand. Still, having said all that, let me say again: You need to decide today—no new debt.

10. *Look for the solution.* You are a unique individual with tremendous abilities and talents, some you might not even be aware of. As you demonstrate your commitment to getting out of debt and living below your means, opportunities are going to come your way. Perhaps the solution to your debt problem is right in front of your eyes.

While working our way out of a huge debt mess, I got the idea of publishing a subscription newsletter as a means of raising the rest of the money we needed to complete our plan. Clearly, that wasn't an idea I could have come up with on my own. I'd lived for forty-five years and had never once dreamed of or aspired to becoming a writer. I believe now that God placed in me that desire and the ability to do things beyond my perceived limitations. But it didn't happen until I stepped out in faith and seized the opportunity.

I made a commitment to repay all the debt, to change my behavior, and to begin living below our means many years before I found the ultimate solution. I made a solemn promise to God that I would do whatever was necessary to repay all of the six-figure load of unsecured debt I had amassed.

11. *Persevere.* Think of getting out of the debt trap as a journey. Some days the path will be rocky and steep. Other times it will seem much easier. Know that this is going to take perseverance. You cannot give up! Find someone who will be your encourager. Grab on to your plan and God's promises, and don't ever let go!

4

A Plan to Debt-Proof Your Life

The Only Plan You Will Ever Need

We make our decisions, and then our decisions turn around
and make us.

F. W. Boreham,
Mushrooms on the Moor

Without a plan to achieve it, a goal is only a dream. If your
goal to achieve financial freedom is not attached to a specific
plan, I can safely say you will never reach financial freedom because you will not know how to start, what to do, or when you've
reached your goal.

A dream showcases the end result but completely skips the details. A plan, on the other hand, defines the goal, lays out the steps
to reach the goal, and expresses the goal in terms that are measurable. A plan eliminates confusion because you have the steps right
there in black and white.

For example, in the language of dreams, your desire to improve your health might be expressed as "I want to get into shape." In the language of achievable goals, you would first define what it means to get into shape and then outline the steps required to reach that goal. Such a statement might be "I intend to run two miles a day for the next six weeks so I will be in condition to participate in a 5K race six weeks from Saturday." Now your desire is no longer a dream because it is clearly defined and you have outlined the steps required to achieve it. The progress and outcome are measurable. Getting into shape has become a goal attached to a plan.

Maybe you had the desire to "get control of your finances" or "get out of debt" long before you picked up this book. Well, have you done it? If not, the problem might be that you never had a realistic plan. All you had was a dream.

Let's take that desire and develop it into a goal.

> I intend to achieve financial freedom and win over debt for a lifetime by consistently giving, saving, and never spending more money than I earn. I will know I've reached my goal when I have no unsecured debt; I have a $10,000 Contingency Fund; my Freedom Account is funded one year in advance; and I am consistently giving away 10 percent, saving 10 percent, and living on 80 percent of my income.

Don't worry if some of these terms mean nothing to you. They will soon enough. Just stick with me.

Notice that the goal is clearly defined: to achieve financial freedom and win over debt for a lifetime. The steps to reach the goal are specific: by consistently giving, saving, and never spending more money than I earn. And there is a statement that defines how to recognize that you have reached your goal: I have no unsecured debt; I have a $10,000 Contingency Fund; my Freedom Account is funded one year in advance; and I am giving away 10 percent, saving 10 percent, and living on 80 percent of my income.

Your dream of getting control of your finances has become a goal because it has three elements:

1. The goal is clearly defined.
2. The steps to reach the goal are clearly stated.
3. The goal has a measurable outcome.

Years ago I read something that stuck in my mind: You wouldn't dream of eating an entire salami in one sitting. But if you eat just one slice a day, in time you will eat the entire thing.

You must think of your goal of reaching financial freedom as the salami of a lifetime. You're going to get the job done one "slice" at a time.

The Plan

The debt-proof living plan is a proven money-management system that is simple to understand and to implement. It will work at your current income level and financial situation and for the rest of your life. And best of all, it is the only money-management system you will ever need. The plan consists of these five elements, which we will discuss in this and the next few chapters:

1. 10-10-80 formula
2. Spending Plan
3. Contingency Fund
4. Rapid Debt-Repayment Plan (RDRP)
5. Freedom Account

The 10-10-80 Formula

I barely squeaked through college chemistry and only because I could memorize formulas. I did not understand what I memorized. What I learned from the experience is that it doesn't always matter if you understand the details. If you get the formula right, you can count on the results.

Fortunately, the debt-proof living formula is much simpler and infinitely easier to understand than anything having to do with chemistry. I am concerned, however, that at first glance you might see the formula as an impossible undertaking. But if you use it faithfully, this formula will allow you to obtain something so valuable: You will access financial freedom. If you make a commitment to apply this formula to the management of your money, it will forever change your life.

Here's how the formula works. For every dollar that flows into your life, you give away 10 percent, save 10 percent, and live on 80 percent. For every dollar you receive, ten cents is to give away, ten cents is yours to save for the future, and eighty cents is for creating the most abundant life possible.

I know what you're thinking. Only if I win the lottery! (You are so funny.) I understand your reaction. I know 10-10-80 is radical; it's unconventional and just short of un-American. But it works.

I know something about being in terrible—even worse-than-terrible—financial trouble. For more years than I like to admit, I spent not just 100 percent of every dollar I could get my hands on but far more. I used the dollar as a down payment for something I could not afford. Of course, the only way I could do that was to spend money that didn't belong to me.

I thought I had a pretty good thing going. I didn't give (Are you kidding? We didn't have enough for ourselves, let alone anything left to give away). I didn't save (ditto!), and I could spend lots more than we made. To accomplish this, I tried every form of juggling, manipulation, trick, tactic, scheme, and loophole in the book. My method was the fast track to a horrible financial pit of despair. While it sounds like quite a feat to live well on someone else's money, it's anything but glamorous. I am here to report that without a doubt there's only one form of money management that results in joy, peace of mind, contentment, and financial ease: 10-10-80.

I do not know why this formula works. I have some clues, but when it comes right down to it, I just accept it on faith. I believe it has much to do with balance. When I give to others first and then care enough about myself, my family, and my future to say that some money is ours to keep, my insatiable desires are "hushed up." Giving and saving first allow me to see things differently. I am more satisfied with what I have. I have more patience to wait until I have saved the money for a desired purchase. I am less prone to act impulsively.

Giving and saving are the "magic bullets" I mentioned early on. They slay the two monsters all of us deal with because of the society in which we live and the fact that we are flawed humans. These financial monsters are greed and fear.

Greed. The antidote for wanting everything you see from those cute shoes in the Nordstrom ad to an SUV just like your neighbors' is gratitude. Giving is the tangible expression of gratitude. I do not believe it is possible to feel both greed and gratitude at the same moment. If you are truly grateful for all you have, no matter what that is, you will not struggle with greed and all the temptations it brings your way.

Fear. If you have no money in the bank and you struggle just to get from one paycheck to the next, you are likely filled with fear: fear of running out of money, fear of not getting the power bill paid in time, fear of eviction, fear of phone calls from creditors, fear of your spouse discovering what you've been hiding. Fear keeps you awake at night and prompts you to act in inappropriate ways with money. The antidote for financial fear is to consistently pay yourself. Saving 10 percent of your income consistently, no matter what, quells a lot of fear.

The gratification I used to receive from outrageous spending I now find when I give and when I save. It is, however, a little bit different. The rush I got from spending lasted about as long as it took me to get to the car—and it was quickly replaced by anxiety, guilt, and fear. But the gratification I receive from giving and saving goes on and on and on. Each time I give some of my money away and save some for the future, I make more than a deposit in the bank—I make a deposit in my emotional and eternal bank. That produces something satisfying that words cannot adequately describe.

Give Away 10 Percent

I'm fully prepared for your arguments as to why giving away your money—any percentage at all—is not something you would even consider. I understand. I've heard every reason you could possibly imagine. I remember how many years I felt the same way. I intended to become a giver someday, and when that day came, I would do it flamboyantly. I would give thousands of dollars at a time, not paltry sums. I had big plans, and I was going to do it my way someday. So go ahead. Make your list of all the reasons you absolutely cannot give away any of your income.

Now I will counter by saying that nothing you've listed holds water. Feel the way you will, but nothing you can say will change the fact that if you fail to open your life to the power of giving, you will never find the financial freedom and success you long to achieve and for which you were created to enjoy.

This is what giving does for me (and will do for you). Giving proves the condition of my heart. The act of giving is an expression of gratitude. It is a tangible way I can say thank you for everything I have and for every way I have been blessed. Without gratitude operating in my life, more is never enough, and nothing brings genuine satisfaction.

Giving connects me to the world. We live in a materialistic society. Because we have so much, it is easy to become complacent, perhaps even spoiled with feelings of entitlement. Giving keeps me from being self-centered. It opens my eyes to the big picture—to the needs of others. It allows me to see the world through eyes of compassion. I see how vast the need, how short the time, and how unimportant my stuff is by comparison. When I connect to the world, I allow my heart to be broken. It is in that brokenness that my pride and arrogance can be washed away. Then I become content with what I have, and that makes me more useful.

Giving connects me with God. Giving opens my eyes to who I am. When I take a step of faith and give back to God the first and the best part of my income, I make statements of affirmation about my past, my present, and my future:

My past: I am grateful for everything in my life that brought me to this place.

My present: God is number one in my life.

My future: I trust God to meet my needs.

Giving teaches me that I have more than enough. When I give, I tell myself I am beyond scarcity. I affirm that someone greater than myself is in control, that I have what I need, and that I am grateful. Giving reminds me that I am only the caretaker of the resources I've been given to manage. I am a steward, and I am responsible for the decisions I make.

Since I made the decision back in 1982 to become a purposeful giver, I have paid back more than $100,000 in unsecured debt. I have found unbelievable fulfillment in a career I never could have imagined, using talents I did not know I had. I've had the privilege of leading thousands of people out of debt. Has giving changed and blessed my life? You be the judge.

How to Give

How do I give? may seem like an elementary question, but it is one I get quite often.

First, let me clarify that I am talking about giving away 10 percent of your net income—your money! I often receive letters from people telling me they give their time and their skills but not their money because they cannot afford it. I can only assume they are trying to convince me that the first two are substitutes for the last. I agree that we should be good stewards of everything, not only our money, but you will be missing the boat if you do not include your money—something that is very precious. It takes faith and courage to give away what is precious. That's what makes giving meaningful and so powerful.

One of the easiest ways to get started with consistent giving is to treat it like a regular bill. Decide the exact amount you are going to give right off the top of the money you receive. Make up envelopes and payment coupons and put them in the front of your bills-to-be-paid folder. Then when you do your regular bill paying, make giving your first payment.

If you have never been a giver, facing the 10 percent hurdle might be daunting, to say the least. Please don't let the number appear so large that you convince yourself to give nothing. If you don't have the faith to start with 10 percent, start some other place, like 2 percent. Then move to 3 percent, then 4 percent. Soon you'll be at 10 percent. Remember, more than anything else, God is concerned about the condition of your heart.

WHERE TO GIVE

As you begin to consider all the needs around you, I have a feeling something or someone is going to come to mind. What are the issues about which you are passionate? What is your source of inspiration? Do you attend a church where your soul is fed? That would be a good place to start. Think about your own community. What needs have you heard about that tugged at one of your heartstrings? That tugging just might be God's prodding. Where you give is a personal decision and one I believe you will make easily once you start thinking about it.

Once you've made your decision about where to give, do it with no strings attached. Just give the money away. Write the check or deliver the cash. Giving in its purest form is done with a heart that says, "I wish it were more, and I expect nothing in return."

Save 10 Percent

The "pay yourself first" concept is not new (I'd be surprised if you've never heard it before). But I'll never forget the first time I really understood what it meant. I read about it in a fascinating little book called *The Richest Man in Babylon* by George Clason.

Say to yourself, "A part of all I earn is mine to keep." Say it in the morning when you first arise. Say it at noon. Say it at night. Say it each hour of every day.

Say it to yourself until the words stand out like letters of fire across the sky. Impress yourself with the idea. Fill yourself with the thought.

Then take whatever portion seems wise. Let it be not less than one-tenth and lay it by. Arrange your other expenditures to do this if necessary. But lay by that portion first.

Soon you will realize what a rich feeling it is to own a treasure upon which you alone have claim. As it grows it will stimulate you. A new joy of life will thrill you.

Greater efforts will come to you to earn more. For of your increased earnings, will not the same percentage be also yours to keep?[1]

During my worst years when I was spending with reckless abandon, I would have told you with all sincerity that we didn't have enough money to save any. Ironically, even though I was spending as if there were no tomorrow, I would have considered it conceited and self-serving to keep any money for myself. How could I keep any for myself when I owed lots of money to others? If that is your reaction, I want to encourage you to let it go. Not only is it okay for you to pay yourself even though you are deep in debt, you must because that is the only way you are ever going to break your cycle of debt. You have to start building your defenses so that soon you will not have to depend on credit card companies. You'll be funding your own emergencies.

Understanding that a part of all you earn is yours to keep is a reasonable way you can acknowledge your worth, prepare for the unexpected, more quickly repair the damage that debt has done in your life, and go on to build a retirement nest egg. It is simply the right thing to do.

You need to begin saving 10 percent of your net (take-home) income even if you participate in an employer-sponsored savings plan like a 401(k). The 10 percent is over and above any money you are saving now for retirement.

Live on 80 Percent

Debt-proof living depends more on your spending habits than the size of your paycheck. It may be challenging to adjust your living expenses so that, including your debt repayment and current bills, you are spending no more than 80 percent of your net income. But it will get easier with time. The dollars being sent to creditors every month will become discretionary income once you reach debt-free status. The more you practice restraint in your spending, the easier it will become because, simply put, you're going to get better at it.

If you, like the majority of your fellow Americans, live on something closer to 122 percent of your income (seeing that in print does send shivers up your spine, doesn't it?), a drastic idea like living on 80 percent might cause you to give up right now. But remember, you didn't get where you are overnight, so expecting an instantaneous reversal is unrealistic.

Nevertheless, now is the time to start. You can choose to turn around so that you are headed in the right direction. Then every step will be one of progress.

To reduce your living expenses so they fit within 80 percent of your income, you must scrutinize every expense and then find the best way to reduce it. By reducing everything a little bit, you may be able to avoid eliminating any spending categories. This is going to require creativity and discipline. And your reward for your willingness to endure temporary sacrifice will be a light at the end of your tunnel, and I promise it's not a train.

I don't know what frugality means to you. The word has taken a good bit of heat in the past few years as the buzzword for some economic extremists. As a result, many people have come to view frugality with disdain, assuming it demands a lifestyle based on dumpster diving and recycling dryer lint. Believe me. That's not it. To me, frugality means doing whatever it takes to keep your living expenses within 80 percent of your net income.

Frugality is not about stuffing everyone into the same mold so we all spend the same amount of money on things like food or housing. Frugality is about personal restraint, discipline, finding the best value, and not being wasteful. It's about making choices and understanding that if you say yes to one thing you may need to say no to something else. And that is okay, because finally you are going to be managing your money in a way that will bring you tremendous personal satisfaction.

Because I live frugally doesn't mean I don't spend money. It means I spend money thoughtfully and with a sense of discipline and purpose. As my life is blessed and my income increases, the 80 percent portion of my net income increases as well. It's a beautiful thing.

5

Where Does All the Money Go?

Tracking Is the Way to Find Out

Happiness is a place between too little and too much.

Finnish Proverb

Most people have no idea where their money goes or how they spend it. This is partly due to human nature. So don't feel like the Lone Ranger if this describes you.

We trick ourselves by expressing our income in grandiose gross annual terms while talking about our expenses as daily incidentals. For example, let's look at Sharon, who spends $4 a day on lattes[1] and has an annual salary of $50,000. Why not spend $4 a day on lattes, she reasons. Anyone who makes $50,000 a year can certainly afford a lousy $4 latte every morning as a reward for her hard work! It does seem rather insignificant when she puts it that way.

But the truth is that she takes home something close to $3,000 (after taxes) a month and spends $120 of it on lattes. My point is this: $4 out of $50,000 (.008 percent) is a lot different from $120 out of $3,000 (4 percent). We think of our income and expenses in unrealistic terms.

Do you know what happens to every penny of your paycheck? You know where the big amounts go, like the mortgage payment or maybe the utilities. But what about the $200 ATM withdrawals you often make? Where does that money go? How much are you spending on groceries and other food to feed your family? How much do you spend in a month on something as benign as new apps for your phone? Or, speaking of phones, what is that data plan costing you each month? Gasoline? Auto maintenance? Movie tickets? Video games? Fast food? Clothing? Gifts?

If your employer made a new rule that your paycheck next month would be equal to only the amount of this month's check you could document with a list and receipts, how close would you come to getting a full paycheck next month? I think you would be motivated to find out where all the money goes!

I believe I can safely say that money is leaking out of your life. It might be only a dollar here and fifty cents there, but it is happening day in and day out. Like a dripping faucet, it doesn't seem like much when it is only one drop at a time, but stick a bucket under there and look again in the morning. You will be amazed at how that tiny leak can accumulate into something significant.

You will never reduce your expenses effectively and consistently until you find out where your money goes. Only then will you be able to take the steps necessary to get your spending in line with 80 percent of your net income.

In this chapter, you are going to learn how to create a monthly Spending Record. This is necessary in order to create a monthly Spending Plan in chapter 9. I will refer to your Spending Plan quite often in this chapter in preparation for what will come.

Oh, Please . . . Anything but a Budget!

For me, the word *budget* is like fingernails on a chalkboard. It screeches confinement, deprivation. Like a straitjacket. Or worse, a diet! (Am I the only one here with budget issues?)

A plan, on the other hand, is a detailed strategy designed to help you accomplish a specific goal. Psychologically, there's a huge difference between a budget and a plan. Budgets confine, plans liberate. Budgets are fixed, plans are flexible. Budgets are absolute, plans are guidelines.

If a budget were an article of clothing, it would be ready-made, off-the-rack, with the dreaded one-size-fits-all label. But as a Spending Plan, it would be a custom outfit with exact measurements from the hands of an expert tailor.

In the same way an architect "builds" a house on paper long before the actual construction begins, you need to design a Spending Plan on paper for how you plan to distribute your income. A Spending Plan directs spendable income the way a conductor directs an orchestra. And you are the composer. You are going to write the score.

If you've ever attempted to create a budget in the past (who hasn't?), you probably took out a sheet of paper, wrote down your expenses, and ran a total. Then you jotted down your income, deducted your expenses, and remarked while scratching your head, "So what's the problem?" For most people, the situation looks great on paper. But usually that information is nowhere close to reality.

Perhaps you've met with a counselor or taken a class on money management so you could get on a budget. You sliced the pie charts and tried to cram yourself into the bar graphs and rigid framework that had "Budget" plastered across the top. Like getting into a new pair of jeans two sizes too small, with a lot of struggle and the equivalent of starving yourself, you finally got that budget on, but you couldn't move. You tried to "wear" it for a while but gave up because it just didn't fit. It was impossible.

So much for budgets.

Maybe it's semantics, but for whatever reason, my experience is that budgets just don't work. So let's forget the b-word. Instead, I am going to teach you how to create your own custom Spending Plan—a system that will fit you and your situation perfectly. But more than that, it will remain flexible and fluid so it can move and grow in the same ways you will change and develop in the future.

Think of developing your Spending Plan as a five-chapter process. In this chapter, you will learn how to establish your spending baseline with a Spending Record. In chapters 6, 7, and 8, you will develop the infrastructure of your Spending Plan with a Contingency Fund, a Rapid Debt-Repayment Plan, and a Freedom Account. Think of these elements, beginning with the Spending Record, as necessary components of the Spending Plan you will put together in chapter 9.

Your Spending Plan will be a one- or two-page document more user-friendly than you ever dreamed possible. You will come to think of it as your crib notes because it will hold all the secrets for how you are going to manage your money to get out of debt, live financially prepared even for the unexpected, and be on your way to financial freedom.

The Spending Record

The first thing you need to get started is an accurate record of your spending. To begin, you are going to create a monthly Spending Record. There are two critical pieces of information you need to prepare this:

1. your average monthly net income
2. a detailed record of where that income goes

If you don't have this information readily available, join the crowd. Most people do not know their average monthly net income, nor do they know with certainty where all their money goes. In fact, most of us would just as soon not have to deal with this information.

The time and commitment required to do this will be worth the effort, so let your fears go and let's move ahead. Do you recall the "article of clothing" analogy a few paragraphs above? Your Spending Record is the "fine fabric" from which your Spending Plan eventually will be created. This information is absolutely critical to the process.

Monthly Income

Your first order of business is to determine your total average monthly net income. This is what you actually bring home once all the deductions (whether mandated by law or chosen by you, as in the case of a retirement plan) have been made. Your net income is what you can count on every month.

Regardless of your payroll schedule or the frequency with which you receive other sources of income, you need to come up with your average monthly income. Note: If you are self-employed, don't assume this does not apply to you. As an employee of yourself, you need to put yourself on a strict salary so you can afford to pay yourself during both good months and those that are lean. Now use that salary to proceed. (See chapter 12, "The Irregular Income Challenge," in my book *Debt-Proof Your Marriage* for a detailed plan for dealing with the thrill and agony of self-employment.)

Here's a quick formula to determine your average monthly income if you receive it other than once a month:

To Determine Your Average Monthly Income	
paid weekly	multiply your weekly net income by 4.333
paid biweekly	multiply your biweekly net income by 2.167
paid semimonthly	multiply your semimonthly net income by 2
paid quarterly	divide your quarterly net income by 3

Determining your average monthly income can get a little tricky depending on whether you have more than one income in your household, how often you are paid, and if you have additional sources of income you can count on. If you and your spouse have more than one income and you are paid on different schedules, calculate them separately to come up with the monthly figures and then add those numbers together to come up with one figure. When you get that number, take a moment to be either shocked or delighted, but keep your response as nonemotional as possible.

Once you determine your total average monthly income, write it down. Concentrate on it. Begin now to replace your prior idea of your annual gross figure with this more realistic monthly figure.

Where Does It Go?

Determining your average monthly income is a cinch compared to your next task. Discovering what happens to your average monthly income will be a challenge. I'm not going to sugarcoat this step. It will be tedious at times, emotionally threatening, and basically a pain in the neck. But I know you are up to the task. I have more faith in you than you could possibly imagine. I base my confidence on the fact that you've come this far in the book and appear to have every intention of going the distance.

The goal of this step is to account for the money that comes into your life—all of it. I know that sounds radical and nothing close to the way you may define "financial freedom." That's because we have a way of equating financial freedom with not having to think about the money we spend. This is an unrealistic expectation.

The truth is that not thinking about where the money goes is the fast lane to financial doom. Anyone who enjoys financial freedom will tell you that the only way to achieve it is to know what happens to every dollar and be very reluctant to see it go bye-bye. Financial bondage is the result of spending without limitation. Submitting to reasonable boundaries and limitations is the key to freedom—freedom from both want and worry.

If there was a way for you to reconstruct your spending over the past few months so you could see where all your money goes, that's what I would ask you to do. But if you haven't been tracking your spending, that would be impossible. Sure, you can come up with the big amounts such as mortgage payments and other items for which you have a paper trail of canceled checks and account statements. But as big and important as those expenses are, they alone do not give an accurate account of what happened to your money.

The only way to find out is to begin tracking.

The Daily Spending Record

Right now you are in a financial fog. You have no idea where all your money goes. You're going to lift this fog by creating a Spending Record (not to be confused with a Spending Plan). For the next thirty days, you are going to write down every single expenditure you make, no matter how small or seemingly insignificant. The goal is to see in black and white where every bit of your monthly income goes. To the penny. Every dime. This is the only way to get a realistic picture of your current spending situation and habits. The more detailed and specific you can be, the more prepared you will be when you move to the next step.

While you can start doing this at any time, you need to make sure you track for at least one calendar month. You can simplify things if you think of every month as the same regardless of the total number of days in the month, like this. Days 1–7 are always week 1. Days 8–14 are always week 2. Days 15–21 are always week 3. Days 22 to the end of the month are always week 4. You can see that week 4 will have anywhere from six to nine days depending on which month it is, but that's okay. Always treat every month the same.

The debt-proof method also deals with your income on a monthly basis, even though it is quite possible you receive your income on some other schedule. I have found that biweekly (or semimonthly) seems to be the more common way people are paid. However, for most of us, our expenses are billed and paid monthly (i.e., rent, mortgage payments, credit card payments, utilities, and so on). I could have chosen for you to work on average weekly net income figures and weekly expenses, but I've determined that would be more difficult. Choosing a monthly time frame makes the most sense. Of course, you can make your own adjustments later after you become more familiar with the process. For now, however, we will use monthly figures for both income and expenses.

You are not making changes in your spending habits yet. This tracking exercise takes a snapshot of your spending habits and shows exactly where all your money goes.

You may be thinking, "I hate this!" Boy, can I identify. It may feel for you as it did for me, like being called to the principal's office or getting a letter and seeing IRS in the top corner. Believe me, I know how this feels, and at first it feels horrible. But I also know it's not going to be as bad as you may be thinking. It's like going to the doctor or the dentist. The anticipation is worse than the reality. What you are going to learn is simply where the money goes. Your Spending Record is about research and observation. And it couldn't be simpler. Really. You're going to be amazed.

Getting Started

You (and your spouse, if you're married) need a notebook, index cards, or (my favorite) business cards that are blank on one side. You probably have something like this already. Use what you have; don't run out and spend money on supplies. The point is to come up with a way you can conveniently and discreetly record your spending.

Each day, you (if you have a partner, both of you need to do this) will start out with a fresh page or card. Put the date at the top. Throughout the day as you spend cash, swipe plastic, or write a check, jot down two details of that transaction: What for? and How much? That's it. If it's for coffee that costs $1.50, record: Coffee: $1.50. When you buy gas, write down: Gas: $222.59 (Ha-ha. You can see I live in California, where gasoline prices are insane!). Regardless of the method of payment, write it down. One page or card per day, every day. No days off, no endless details, and no daily totals. Just two-part entries.

If you have automatic payments deducted from your bank account, be careful to include these on the days the money leaves your account. You may need to make a few phone calls or log on to your bank's website to see exactly which payments you have authorized and when they are deducted from your account.

(Note: Recording your spending in the manner outlined above will not take the place of recording your checks and ATM activities in your checkbook register. Your Spending Record is in addition to, not instead of, the way you've been managing your bank accounts in the past.)

Designate a place (a drawer works well) for your daily records. This should be a convenient place where both of you can deposit your daily Spending Records at the end of each day.

Let me predict some things that are going to happen, if not in this first week for sure in the weeks that follow.

The first two or three days of recording your expenses will be awkward at best, challenging at worst. You may feel like you've regressed to childhood and are under the authority of a stern parent.

You'll look for shortcuts, like not writing down purchases at the time you make them but intending to write them down later when you get home. That's a shortcut that will sabotage the effort. Trust me, you won't do it. Not out of rebellion so much as out of forgetfulness.

How do I know this? Because I've been exactly where you are, remember? We are a lot alike, I'm sure of it. Believe me when I say you need to record each transaction as it happens—as you stand at the checkout, before you put away your wallet or purse, before you walk back to your car. You need to take five seconds to write it down at the very moment the money leaves your possession. This is why I don't suggest a three-inch-thick three-ring binder for keeping track of your spending. Anything the size of Nebraska is too cumbersome and embarrassing to haul around. Keep it simple and you'll improve your chances of sticking with the program.

You will be tempted to cheat. At first you'll cheat by omission—simply forgetting to record transactions. But you will consider more serious transgressions too, as in, "I shouldn't have to write down how I spend my own money." Wrong. You must record every expenditure regardless of the source. You will be tempted not to record embarrassing or "personal" expenses like three runs to McDonald's or enough lattes to float a small ship. You'll want to hide those eBay auction items you won that you pay for through online services like PayPal. Or any number of other things only you know about. Cheating in any of these ways will only delay your progress.

If you are doing this as a couple, you are going to be more interested in your partner's daily records than your own. You will be tempted not only to review but also to comment on, criticize, and question what your spouse has recorded. Do not do this. There will be a review time soon enough. For now, don't question, don't nag. Just keep recording.

After a few days, something amazing is going to happen. You will begin to wake from your "spending coma" to see all the ways money leaks from your life. That might feel great or somewhat painful. And don't be surprised if you change your mind about buying something because it's too much trouble to write it down or too embarrassing to own up to it in writing. While I don't want you to change your spending patterns in anticipation of creating your Spending Record (we're looking for a realistic picture of your money situation), rethinking and refocusing in this way is excellent. You should see it as the first sign of progress.

First Week Review

At the end of week 1 (seven full days of recording), take your daily records and merge them into a week 1 Spending Record by combining like expenses. For example, if you went to the grocery store seven times and your spouse went once (Ha-ha . . . it's a joke, but then again I must admit that I used to go to the store nearly every day), add those eight amounts together to come up with one figure for groceries. If you have entries for payments to two credit card companies, combine them under one category such as "credit card payments."

Continue to combine your spending entries into categories until each entry has made it from the daily Spending Records to the week 1 Spending Record. Depending on the week, this could be quite simple or quite complicated. That's okay. Just take it one step at a time, avoiding the temptation to combine many things into that famous catchall category "miscellaneous." You want to be as detailed as practical while keeping it simple. Once everything is on one sheet of paper, calculate a spending total for week 1. Put this away in the drawer. For now, don't stop to evaluate it or even discuss it with your spouse.

Continue with your daily Spending Record, and at the end of day 14, create your week 2 Spending Record. Continue in the same manner for week 3 and week 4.

The Monthly Spending Record

Once you have four weekly records, you have the ingredients for your first complete monthly Spending Record. You are not going to merge the weekly records but rather list them side by side according to categories. You may need to combine categories at this point in the event you got too detailed back in the earlier weeks.

After you create totals for individual categories that reflect the amount spent in a month, you must face the big question: How does your spending compare to your average monthly income? I will not be terribly surprised if spending exceeds income. The only way that can happen is if you are putting some of your spending on credit cards, an activity you've been programmed to do.

You should find your first monthly Spending Record quite revealing, although it is not an altogether accurate picture. Undoubtedly, you have expenses that don't show up here because they do not occur regularly each month in the same way your mortgage payment and telephone bill do—expenses like vacation and Christmas. Or how about clothing? That's not a fixed amount every month in the same way your car payment is.

You have many irregular, unexpected, and intermittent expenses. It's possible you had a big, unexpected expense during this first month of recording that made this month appear to be unusually expensive. A single monthly Spending Record is a wonderful first step, but there is no way it will give you a true overall picture.

In the chapters that follow, we're going to take care of this problem. There is a way to make every month more realistic.

Money Leaks

As you study your first monthly Spending Record, look for leaks— places where money is pouring out of your life. The first place, not surprisingly, is probably in the area of food. This is why I suggest you break down food into several categories such as groceries, fast food, school/business lunches, and restaurant dining. I've seen Spending Records where fast food represented more than a leak— hemorrhage would be a better characterization.

Your assignment for now is to identify all the places where money is leaking and to come up with a way you can plug those leaks in the coming month. As you look at the totals for various categories, mark those that can be reduced significantly. In the same way that all of those small expenditures add up, reducing lots of areas by a small amount will also add up to something significant.

Remember, your Spending Record is just one piece of the puzzle. If you were to move forward into next month assuming your expenses will be the same as the month you just tracked, you will be setting yourself up for a disaster. That's because you don't have all the pieces to the puzzle!

In chapters 6, 7, and 8, we're going to develop the other important puzzle pieces. Then in chapter 9, using all the pieces, you'll be ready to put together the complete puzzle of your first Spending Plan—your own unique debt-proof living blueprint.

6

Step Away from the Edge

The Contingency Fund

There is no new suit of clothes, no vacation, no new car that can offset the pain of being truly worried about running out of money.

Ben Stein

The edge is a miserable place to live. People who exist from paycheck to paycheck know this. They spend all they have. And when something unexpected happens, they must run to the credit cards, the finance company, or worse, the bankruptcy court.

The antidote to living on the edge is simple. Move away! It starts with a single step away from the edge. Follow that with another and another until you have created enough space between where you live and the edge so that you can relax—and sleep at night.

I know you are anxious to get to the "good stuff" in the next chapter—the part where you are going to get out of debt (yes, you are!). But there is a very good reason why you need to read this chapter first. If you start focusing on how you are going to get out of debt rapidly, you may decide to speed up that process. In fact, it will not surprise me if you get so excited that you decide you are going to complete your debt-free plan in half the time. But wait! That may not be such a great idea.

Let's say you devote every dollar you can find to get out of debt fast—to the point that you refuse to save even a nickel. I suppose it makes sense on some level that if you are in debt you shouldn't keep anything for yourself until your creditor is repaid. But that is very foolish!

What will you do if something big happens while you are re-paying that debt at lightning speed? If you have no savings, no Contingency Fund, nothing put away in case of an emergency, what will you do when you get laid off or your car dies? You'll be right back where you were before you picked up this book, running to credit cards for a bailout.

You need to decide right now that you are going to get out of debt the right way, the sane way, and the prudent way. And that, my friend, means you must start saving money—even if it is just a small amount to start, even if you are deeply in debt, even if you are so anxious to get out of debt that you can think of nothing else. We are going to get to that in just a few more pages, but first you need to meet your new best friend.

The Contingency Fund

What puts distance between you and the edge is called a Contingency Fund. It is a tangible hedge of protection. It is a pool of money available to you at all times on which you can get your hands in a short period of time. Your Contingency Fund will be stored in a safe place that pays at least enough interest to stay ahead of inflation.

A Contingency Fund has nothing to do with your retirement savings or investments. It is not the money you put aside to pay for unexpected, irregular, and intermittent expenses—expenses that do not occur on a monthly basis and have a way of catching us off guard (we'll talk about how to handle these expenses in chapter 8). A Contingency Fund is not for discretionary spending. It is money set aside for major catastrophes, when your only other recourse is to run for credit. It will be there if you lose your job or if your safety or health is at risk.

Financial experts typically suggest that a family needs the equivalent of three to six months' living expenses in reserve. I find that recommendation somewhat nebulous. How much money is that? We need a dollar figure.

I have no idea how much money you would need to survive for three months without a paycheck. You would have to pay your basic bills and keep food on the table, gas in the car, medicine in the cabinet, and so on. You would likely go on quite a spending diet while hopefully receiving some amount of unemployment benefit. So you can see there are many unknowns.

For our purposes here, let's set an arbitrary figure of $10,000 for the average family. It's a nice round figure. But please keep in mind that you could need much more, or possibly less. If your monthly expenses are high, you should adjust the amount to cover what you would need to live for a full three months without any income.

Think of your Contingency Fund as your personal debt insurance. Its short-term purpose is to give you an alternative to using credit to cover emergencies such as medical bills for which you are not otherwise prepared.

Eventually, your Contingency Fund will become your second line of defense against debt (see chapter 8 for the Freedom Account—your first line of defense). Once your Freedom Account is in place, the Contingency Fund has one primary purpose: to be the bridge you will need in the event you and your income temporarily part company. It is difficult enough to get out of debt, but if you are continually adding new debt, it becomes nearly impossible.

Creating Your Contingency Fund

If you have no savings at this time, you may have already concluded there is no way you will ever be able to save $10,000. I understand. But remember the salami. You cannot save $10,000 at one time, but you can start with $1.

The second "10" in the 10-10-80 formula is the money with which you will begin building your Contingency Fund. Ten percent of everything you receive from now on goes straight into that. I am not kidding when I say you can start with $1. There is even a bank I will tell you about in a bit that will allow you to open a savings account with $1. So no excuses, okay?

The goal is to accumulate and then maintain a $10,000 Contingency Fund as your normal way of life. If you find it necessary to withdraw money from your fund, it should be replaced as quickly as possible—becoming your top savings priority until it is restored to a full $10,000.

Maintaining Your Contingency Fund

You will be tempted to start seeing your Contingency Fund as a long-term investment. Avoid doing that, because this isn't an investment. It is money that is available to you in an emergency. It is insurance that will keep you afloat. When looking for a place to park your Contingency Fund, you need to be concerned about safety, availability, and growth—in that order.

- *Safety*. Your Contingency Fund must be in an account where the principal is not at risk. This is why your Contingency Fund should not be invested in the stock market.

- *Availability*. Because of the nature of emergencies, this fund needs to be liquid—meaning you could get your hands on at least part of it within twenty-four to forty-eight hours.
- *Growth*. You will be maintaining your Contingency Fund for many years. As a good steward, you want to expose it to the best compounding interest available, with no fees if possible, while still meeting the safety and availability requirements.

Whether you have no savings now or have a great start on accumulating at least $10,000, you'll want to start thinking about where to keep your Contingency Fund.

CREDIT UNIONS AND BANK ACCOUNTS

Banks are for-profit corporations, while credit unions are non-profit organizations that exist for the benefit of their members. When a credit union generates a surplus, it is paid out to account holders in the form of either a small dividend or a rebate of loan interest at the end of the fiscal year. Typically, credit union fees are lower, while their interest rates are a bit higher. To find a credit union you can join, go to CreditUnion.coop and click on "Locate a Credit Union."

When you walk into a bank or credit union to open an account for your Contingency Fund, you'll be given a choice depending on your opening deposit that may include the following:

Bank money market accounts. Don't confuse these with money market funds that are offered by mutual fund companies. Bank money market accounts carry the same federal insurance provision as other bank deposits, but they typically pay lower interest than a money market fund.

Certificates of deposit. These are similar to a passbook savings account in that you deposit the money and are paid a set rate of interest. The difference is that, in exchange for your promise to leave the money for a set period of time (90 days,

180 days, 1 year, etc.), you are guaranteed a higher rate of interest. If you must withdraw early, there is a penalty that will apply to the interest portion only. The penalty will never touch your principal. If you take a short-term CD, you will receive slightly less interest.

ONLINE SAVINGS BANKS

These are not like regular banks that you walk into. They are online and operate via the internet. Once you open your online savings account, it is linked to your current checking account, no matter where you have that account.

You can open an online savings account either online or by mail, and you can set up automatic deposits and have access to your account 24/7. These online savings banks do not have the overhead and operational costs of other banks and pass the savings to their customers in the form of no fees, no minimums, and excellent interest rates. And they have no required minimum balances. You can open an account with just $1.

At this writing, interest rates are abysmally low no matter where you park your Contingency Fund. However, online banks offer rates that are higher than the rates you will find at the typical walk-in bank or credit union. Here are a few options for an online savings bank:

Sallie Mae Bank. The savings rate is 0.90 percent APY, with no fees and no minimum. Salliemae.com/banking is FDIC insured.

Smarty Pig. The savings rate at this very fun, FDIC-insured online savings bank is 1.00 percent APY, with no fees and no minimums. See SmartyPig.com.

Wesleyan Investment Foundation. The savings rate here is 1.00 percent APR for a total principal up to $4,999, 1.50 percent for balances $5,000–$34,999, and 2.00 percent APR on balances $35,000 and up. This investment foundation is not FDIC insured, but there are no fees on savings accounts. See WIFOnline.com.

Ally Bank. Savings accounts here have no fees or service charges and currently pay 0.85 percent APY. See Ally.com.

ALTERNATIVE PARKING PLACES

While the following options are not quite as convenient to access as the accounts I've mentioned above, I would be remiss if I did not include them.

Treasury bills. The minimum investment required is $1,000. Government securities are sold at auction, and there is a process you will need to learn to become an active participant. The benefit of having your Contingency Fund in Treasury bills is that you will not be tempted to spend your money mindlessly because of the additional effort it takes to cash them in.

Money market funds. A money market fund (not to be confused with a money market *account* at a bank) is a large pool of money managed by professionals and invested in safe and stable securities, including commercial paper (short-term IOUs of large US corporations), Treasury bills, and large bank CDs. Money market funds are a very attractive place to grow a Contingency Fund because of:

- *Safety*. Even though not guaranteed by the federal government, this type of account is regulated by the Securities Exchange Commission.

- *Liquidity*. Deposits are not tied to any time frames, which means your funds are available at any time and in any amount. You can take out only the amount you need.

- *Higher rates of interest*. The return on money market funds is typically 1 to 1.5 percentage points higher than on bank or credit union accounts.

- *Check-writing privileges*. This feature allows you access to the funds in your account without having to go through phone calls and wire transfers. But you cannot think of this as a checking account, and that's good. Money market funds have restrictions against writing checks for small amounts, say less than $200. Typically, there are no fees imposed or restrictions on the number of checks you can write in a month.

If your funds are parked in a money market fund, you don't have to worry about maturity dates, the possibility of early withdrawal penalties, or getting in before the auction closes. The interest effective yield (interest rate) moves with the general state of the economy.

While most money market funds require a minimum deposit of at least $2,500, some waive that requirement if you authorize automatic deposits of at least $50 a month. Be certain to inquire about such a provision.

There are literally hundreds of money market funds from which to choose if you decide this is a good place for your Contingency Fund. Before opening any account, you need to call for and read a prospectus so you fully understand the rules and risks involved. With the prospectus you will receive an application that looks daunting but is actually quite simple to complete. If you have any questions, you should call the toll-free customer service number.

Automatic Deposit Authorization

I am a big proponent of automatic deposits, especially when it comes to building a Contingency Fund.

With my busy lifestyle and my tendency to put things off, I know I would forget or find some reason to skip my savings deposits from time to time. Authorizing my bank or investment account manager to reach into my checking account on a specified day every month to take out the amount I authorize is one way I simplify my life. In a way, it's like delegating work to someone else so I can be free to do what I do best. I think of it as hiring a staff person to handle the savings and depositing that I've committed to do.

If you have any tendencies toward procrastination and feel better when things are taken care of for you, I suggest you think seriously about arranging for automatic deposits into your Contingency Fund. Even more important than knowing you won't have to remember to make the deposit is that if the money is gone before you see it, you won't miss it. I've proven this for myself and have had it confirmed over and over again by people who have tried it.

In the beginning, you might feel the pinch of having your savings automatically deducted from your regular checking account and deposited into your savings vehicle. But before you know it, this will become ordinary. You won't miss the money, and you won't have to worry about remembering to make the transfer of funds. Some larger employers offer such a service as a payroll deduction plan. You simply fill out an authorization form with the specific account numbers, and your pay stub indicates that the money has been deposited automatically. Of course, you can change your automatic deposit authorization at any time. You can increase the amount, change the date, or even change your mind. You're the boss, and that is a wonderful feeling!

Once You Reach Your Goal

The day will come—and sooner than you think—when your Contingency Fund reaches the goal you have set. So, you may be asking, can I stop saving money then? No, never! Always and forever you must pay yourself 10 percent.

Think back a moment to the debt-proof living formula: 10-10-80. I told you this is a formula you should follow for the rest of your life for managing your money. But you are right. You will not contribute to your Contingency Fund indefinitely. That would be foolish, because as I said before, it is not an investment account. It is an industrial-strength emergency fund. But let me back up just a bit to allow you to see a bigger picture.

The debt-proof living plan is divided into four savings levels. You will learn more about this in chapter 9, but I will tell you this much now. Savings level 1 is where you create and build your Contingency Fund to the goal you have predetermined for your specific situation—enough to live on for six months without a paycheck or at least $10,000.

Using Your Contingency Fund

As with any kind of emergency preparedness, like a first-aid kit or emergency food and water in case of an earthquake or hurricane, you don't look forward to needing it. But if an emergency happens, you are thankful to be prepared. The same is true for your Contingency Fund. Once you have saved and put away the cash, you will not find it easy to dip into it. That's good. Remember, this fund is not to tide you over until next payday or to buy a new sofa. Your Contingency Fund is for life's big financial challenges: unemployment or other financial surprises that could throw you off course such as a medical emergency.

If you hit a rough spot in the road of life and are compelled to draw from your Contingency Fund, it is important that you think of it as giving yourself a loan and that you pay it back as quickly as possible to get your Contingency Fund back to fully funded status. How? The same way you built it: by sending 10 percent of your net take-home pay straight to your Contingency Fund.

Do you see what is happening here? Instead of looking to credit cards, parents, or some other source of lending when you face an emergency, you become your own bank. Your Contingency Fund and money-management skills allow you to fund your own emergencies without any need to apply, plead, or pay fees or interest—to say nothing of the stress a financial emergency can create.

This Is a Must

No matter your situation—even if you are up to your eyeballs in credit card debt—you must have a Contingency Fund.

Your attitude about your Contingency Fund will either make or break it. If you see it as a pool of money to be used at will for anything that suits your fancy at the moment, you have completely missed the purpose of a Contingency Fund.

A Contingency Fund creates margin and allows you to step away from the edge. Money in the bank changes everything.

7

Break Out of the Debt Trap

The Rapid Debt-Repayment Plan

No investment is as secure as a repaid debt.

Austin Pryor,
The Sound Mind Investing Handbook

If your kitchen is on fire, fireproofing your home is the last thing on your mind. All you can think about is getting that fire out. But while your efforts are directed specifically at the problem at hand, you are also watching to make sure fires are not appearing in other rooms of the house as well.

The same goes for debt-proofing your life. Any debt you have is tantamount to that kitchen fire. You need to devote your efforts to getting out of it! At the same time, you must do everything in your power to make sure you don't create more debt in other areas of your life. When you get that fire out, I assure you you'll be a lot more interested in fireproofing your house. In the same way, once you are out of debt, you will be seriously concerned about debt-proofing your life.

You Need a Get-Out-of-Debt Plan

Several methods will help you get out of debt. Some concentrate on debt with the highest interest rate; others start with the smallest debt. Some plans require you to increase all your payments from the get-go, while others work with the minimum monthly payments you have presently.

If you're in debt, you have to get out by whatever means works for you. So put your mind into high gear and put together a plan—then stick with it. Commit to do whatever is necessary to complete the plan. (If you want to do yourself the biggest favor of all, commit to completing it in half the time.)

Above all, remember that a plan is only as good as your ability to stick with it. As with diets, all of them work in theory. The true test, however, is which plan you will stick with.

No matter how good a plan looks on paper, if the regimen is outlandish and impractical, you will not stick with it. When evaluating a get-out-of-debt plan, you should look for the following characteristics:

- It is specific.
- It is easy to prepare.
- It is simple to understand.
- It is visually pleasing and reader friendly.
- Its results can be measured.
- It has a specific finish date.
- It is self-directed.

When it comes to this kind of effort, the simpler the better. But don't sacrifice quality on the altar of simplicity.

The Rapid Debt-Repayment Plan

Surprise! I have developed a plan that fits the above criteria. It's a simple plan, and it's effective because it works. I call it the Rapid Debt-Repayment Plan, or RDRP.

This plan is specifically designed for unsecured debt—not your mortgage, home equity loans, or auto loans. The plan itself would not know the difference between a secured and an unsecured debt, so if you were to include, for example, a home equity loan with your unsecured debts, the RDRP could put the home equity loan ahead of a large, high-interest credit card debt, and that would be counterproductive. Remember, one of the tenets of debt-proof living is that unsecured debt is the first thing that has to go. Secured debts are targeted for repayment at a point later in the plan.

The RDRP is simple because it has five simple rules. If you adhere closely to all five rules, you will get out of debt in record time. Just imagine how your life will change when you are completely free of your unsecured debts. That can happen more quickly than you might have dared to dream. And more than that, if you stick with it, it *will* happen!

Rule 1: No new debt. That's simple. You have to stop using the credit cards or adding any new unsecured debt. Now. If you don't stop adding to the problem, you'll be like the homeowner with the kitchen fire—except instead of putting out the blaze that's ready to destroy the entire structure, you'll be pouring gasoline on it. The fire might be manageable for a while, but you'll be on your way to a full-on raging inferno. The rule is simple: no new debt.

Rule 2: Pay the same amount every month. Make a list of the minimum payments you are required to make on all your unsecured debts this month. Include your credit card accounts, store charge cards, installment loans, student loans, and personal loans. Include any medical and dental payments—every unsecured debt for which you are currently responsible. Add them together. Look at that number. It is very important. Think of it as one single debt payment rather than a bunch of payments, some of which vary from month to month.

Pay that same amount every month until you reach $0, even if your statement arrives in the future and you notice that your required payment has dropped. Do not pay attention to that. And since you will not be adding any new purchases, the required payments won't go up.

You may have heard and even come to believe a myth about paying off credit card and other kinds of debt. It goes like this: You will never get out of debt if you do not pay more than the minimum required payment every month. I want to assure you that you can and you will get out of debt even if you cannot pay one penny more than the amounts you are required to pay this month.

This should come as great news if all you can pay is the minimum amount. That's all that it takes for you to get out of debt. If you can pay it this month, you can pay it next month and every month thereafter.

From now on you will not pay attention to your creditors when they reduce your minimum monthly payment, which is what we call the "falling payment" method. For example, if your payment this month to your Visa credit card account is $143, under rule 2, you will always pay $143 to that credit card until you reach $0 on that debt, even though your statement may say that you need to pay only $125, $94, or whatever as the balance declines. Remember that the bank who issued your Visa card is not at all interested in you paying that debt in full. Accepting smaller payments each month is one way they attempt to keep you on the hook and in perma-debt.

Rule 3: Line up your debts according to the number of months left to pay off. To do this, answer this question for each of your debts: How many months will it take to reach $0 if I add no new purchases and I make my "fixed" payment every month? You might assume that this would put the debt with the smallest outstanding balance at the top and the largest at the bottom, but that is not necessarily the case. And this step can be a little trickier than simply dividing the current balance by the current payment because of the way interest is calculated. For now, go ahead and arrange your debts from smallest (shortest time to payoff) to largest with the small one at the top of the list. Note: I have a calculator that is going to do all the math for you, and I'll tell you about that in a bit.

Rule 4: Ignore the declining minimum monthly payments you will see on your statements. You will be tempted to watch your monthly statements closely, if for no other reason than to watch your progress. And there will be times when you may be tempted to pay the amount you see due on your statement rather than the fixed payment on your RDRP. Let me repeat: The amount you pay in the first month is the amount you are going to pay until your total debt reaches $0 regardless of a lower "amount due" appearing on your statement.

Rule 5: As one debt is paid, add its payment to the regular payment of the next debt in line. This is where the "rapid" kicks in because as one debt is paid, you'll begin sending much larger payments to the next debt in line. This is where it gets exciting. Your total monthly debt payment established in rule 2 remains the same to the victorious end. This is the secret of the RDRP and getting out of debt fast.

Meet the Greens

Let me show you how this plan works using Bob and Sally Green as our fictitious subjects. Below is a list of their unsecured debts: the name of each creditor, the current balance, the interest rate (APR), and the current minimum monthly payment.

The Greens have a lot of unsecured debt, including a signature loan with a credit union, two credit card accounts, an old personal loan from Sally's parents, as well as student debt from Bob's college days.

Here's a snapshot of the Greens' unsecured debts as of this month:

Debt	Principal	Interest Rate	Current Payment
Credit Union	$1,500.00	9.00%	$125.00
MasterCard	$3,897.00	16.90%	$115.00
Mom and Dad	$900.00	5.00%	$150.00
Sallie Mae	$16,750.00	6.80%	$109.00
Visa	$775.00	9.90%	$42.00
Total	$23,822.00		$541.00

Following are three charts representing three debt repayment scenarios for the Greens. We'll call them scenarios A, B, and C.

Scenario A

In this scenario, the Greens are following rule 1—they agree to stop adding any new debt—but do not follow rule 2. Instead, they follow the payment schedule set up by their creditors that they see on their statements each month.

Debt	Principal	Interest Rate	Current Payment	Total Interest	Months to Payoff
Credit Union	$1,500.00	9.00%	$125.00	$548.78	123
MasterCard	$3,897.00	16.90%	$115.00	$4,703.87	267
Mom and Dad	$900.00	5.00%	$150.00	$138.48	83
Sallie Mae	$16,750.00	6.80%	$109.00	$23,341.00	485
Visa	$775.00	9.90%	$42.00	$272.13	88
Total	$23,822.00		$541.00	$29,004.27	485

The Greens' monthly unsecured debt payment is $541 (rule 1.) If they add no new debt and follow their creditors' repayment schedules, they will end up repaying $23,822 in principal plus $29,004 in interest, for a total of more than $50,000. And it will take them 485 months to do it. That's more than forty years.

How can that be? The culprit is something known as "falling payments." Some creditors determine the minimum monthly payment as a percentage of the outstanding balance. This way, as you pay down the balance, the amount they require each month goes down proportionately so that the debt just goes on and on and on.

Scenario B

In scenario B, the Greens follow rules 1 and 2. They determine to add no new debt and to keep their monthly payments the same as they are right now. They will pay $541 toward their unsecured debt load every month until they are debt-free. But as one debt is paid off, the money they've been paying to that creditor each month is absorbed into some other area of their lives, not their RDRP.

Debt	Principal	Interest Rate	Current Payment	Total Interest	Months to Payoff
Credit Union	$1,500.00	9.00%	$125.00	$77.84	13
MasterCard	$3,897.00	16.90%	$115.00	$1,436.95	47
Mom and Dad	$900.00	5.00%	$150.00	$13.36	7
Sallie Mae	$16,750.00	6.80%	$109.00	$22,723.72	363
Visa	$775.00	9.90%	$42.00	$69.23	21
Total	$23,822.00		$541.00	$24,321.10	363

Because in scenario B the Greens are diligent to pay the same amount of $541 toward their RDRP regardless of the lower amounts their creditors might accept as their balances fall, the Greens do improve their situation. They pay $24,321 in interest, which saves them $4,684 over scenario A, and they cut their payback time to 363 months, just slightly longer than thirty years. But is that really that much better? Now consider scenario C.

Scenario C

Debt	Principal	Interest Rate	Current Payment	Total Interest	Months to Payoff
Mom and Dad	$900.00	5.00%	$150.00	$13.36	7
Credit Union	$1,500.00	9.00%	$125.00	$66.85	10
Visa	$775.00	9.90%	$42.00	$51.54	11

Debt	Principal	Interest Rate	Current Payment	Total Interest	Months to Payoff
MasterCard	$3,897.00	16.90%	$115.00	$735.84	19
Sallie Mae	$16,750.00	6.80%	$109.00	$3,392.54	52
Total	$23,822.00		$541.00	$4,260.14	52

In this scenario, the Greens follow all five rules, treating them as nonnegotiables. They stop incurring new unsecured debt, and they pay the same amount of $541 every month. They put their shortest payoff debt at the top of the list, and as one debt is paid off, they take its payment and redirect it to the next debt in line, thereby accelerating the payoff plan.

In scenario C, the Greens repay $23,822 in principal plus $4,260 in interest in just fifty-two months—four years and four months.

Here's a quick recap:

Scenario Comparison Summary

Payment Plan	Number of Months	Total Interest	Interest Savings
A: rule 1	485	$29,004	$0
B: rules 1, 2	363	$24,321	$4,684
C: rules 1, 2, 3, 4, 5	52	$4,260	$24,744

When we compare the different scenarios, we see that there are definite advantages to following all the RDRP rules. If the Greens faithfully commit to the debt-repayment plan laid out in scenario C, their payment schedule will look like the following.

Rapid Debt-Repayment Plan Schedule

Month #	Month Year	Mom and Dad	Credit Union	Visa	Master-Card	Sallie Mae	Total
1	Aug 2014	150.00	125.00	42.00	115.00	109.00	541.00
2	Sept 2014	150.00	125.00	42.00	115.00	109.00	541.00
3	Oct 2014	150.00	125.00	42.00	115.00	109.00	541.00
4	Nov 2014	150.00	125.00	42.00	115.00	109.00	541.00

Month #	Month Year	Mom and Dad	Credit Union	Visa	Master-Card	Sallie Mae	Total
5	Dec 2014	150.00	125.00	42.00	115.00	109.00	541.00
6	Jan 2015	150.00	125.00	42.00	115.00	109.00	541.00
7	Feb 2015	13.36	261.64	42.00	115.00	109.00	541.00
8	Mar 2015		275.00	42.00	115.00	109.00	541.00
9	Apr 2015		275.00	42.00	115.00	109.00	541.00
10	May 2015		5.21	311.79	115.00	109.00	541.00
11	June 2015			136.76	295.24	109.00	541.00
12	July 2015				432.00	109.00	541.00
13	Aug 2015				432.00	109.00	541.00
14	Sept 2015				432.00	109.00	541.00
15	Oct 2015				432.00	109.00	541.00
16	Nov 2015				432.00	109.00	541.00
17	Dec 2015				432.00	109.00	541.00
18	Jan 2016				432.00	109.00	541.00
19	Feb 2016				163.59	377.41	541.00
20	Mar 2016					541.00	541.00
21	Apr 2016					541.00	541.00
22	May 2016					541.00	541.00
23	June 2016					541.00	541.00
24	July 2016					541.00	541.00
25	Aug 2016					541.00	541.00
26	Sept 2016					541.00	541.00
27	Oct 2016					541.00	541.00
28	Nov 2016					541.00	541.00
29	Dec 2016					541.00	541.00
30	Jan 2017					541.00	541.00
31	Feb 2017					541.00	541.00
32	Mar 2017					541.00	541.00
33	Apr 2017					541.00	541.00
34	May 2017					541.00	541.00
35	June 2017					541.00	541.00
36	July 2017					541.00	541.00
37	Aug 2017					541.00	541.00

Month #	Month Year	Mom and Dad	Credit Union	Visa	Master-Card	Sallie Mae	Total
38	Sept 2017					541.00	541.00
39	Oct 2017					541.00	541.00
40	Nov 2017					541.00	541.00
41	Dec 2017					541.00	541.00
42	Jan 2018					541.00	541.00
43	Feb 2018					541.00	541.00
44	Mar 2018					541.00	541.00
45	Apr 2018					541.00	541.00
46	May 2018					541.00	541.00
47	June 2018					541.00	541.00
48	July 2018					541.00	541.00
49	Aug 2018					541.00	541.00
50	Sept 2018					541.00	541.00
51	Oct 2018					541.00	541.00
52	Nov 2018					491.14	491.14

Notice that the debts are sorted so that the loan (Mom and Dad) with the fewest number of payments is in the first position. The Greens' monthly total is still $541, the amount they commit to pay each month toward their RDRP. They also agree to no new debt. However, after the loan from Mom and Dad is paid in full, the $150 that was going there is added to the credit union payment. When the credit union loan reaches $0, both Mom and Dad's payment and the credit union payment are added to Visa's regular payment. The Visa debt reaches $0 in month 11, and MasterCard's payment jumps from $115 a month to $432 a month until it is paid. Finally, the entire $541 goes to Sallie Mae to wipe out the student loan in fairly short order. According to this schedule, Bob and Sally Green become free of all unsecured debt in November 2018. They avoid paying $24,744 in interest charges (that's money from their future paychecks they will get to keep), and they are debt-free in fifty-two months, or four years and four months.

Oh, the power of a plan. Bob and Sally can see exactly when they will be finished paying off their debts. And if they decide to accelerate their plan even more, they can simply add to the amount they pay to the first debt.

Once the Greens are debt-free in November 2018, they can immediately redirect the entire $541 to some other specific purpose—such as rapidly repaying their mortgage, contributing to an investment program, or some combination of the two.

Let's see what will happen if the Greens (both will be thirty-nine years old when they finish paying off their debt in November 2018) redirect $541 a month ($6,492 annually) into an investment vehicle that earns 8 percent growth compounded annually (this is a realistic growth rate if they invest over a long period of time) until they retire at age sixty-five.

Show Me the Money!

#	Year	Age	Annual Invested	Interest Earned	Investment Value	Cash Invested	Accumulated Earnings
1	2019	40	$6,492.00	$519.36	$7,011.36	$6,492.00	$519.36
2	2020	41	6,492.00	560.91	14,064.27	12,984.00	1,080.27
3	2021	42	6,492.00	1,125.14	21,681.41	19,476.00	2,205.41
4	2022	43	6,492.00	1,734.51	29,907.92	25,968.00	3,939.92
5	2023	44	6,492.00	2,392.63	38,792.56	32,460.00	6,332.56
6	2024	45	6,492.00	3,103.40	48,387.96	38,952.00	9,435.96
7	2025	46	6,492.00	3,871.04	58,751.00	45,444.00	13,307.00
8	2026	47	6,492.00	4,700.08	69,943.08	51,936.00	18,007.08
9	2027	48	6,492.00	5,595.45	82,030.52	58,428.00	23,602.52
10	2028	49	6,492.00	6,562.44	95,084.97	64,920.00	30,164.97
11	2029	50	6,492.00	7,606.80	109,183.76	71,412.00	37,771.76
12	2030	51	6,492.00	8,734.70	124,410.47	77,904.00	46,506.47
13	2031	52	6,492.00	9,952.84	140,855.30	84,396.00	56,459.30
14	2032	53	6,492.00	11,268.42	158,615.73	90,888.00	67,727.73
15	2033	54	6,492.00	12,689.26	177,796.98	97,380.00	80,416.98
16	2034	55	6,492.00	14,223.76	198,512.74	103,872.00	94,640.74

#	Year	Age	Annual Invested	Interest Earned	Investment Value	Cash Invested	Accumulated Earnings
17	2035	56	6,492.00	15,881.02	220,885.76	110,364.00	110,521.76
18	2036	57	6,492.00	17,670.86	245,048.62	116,856.00	128,192.62
19	2037	58	6,492.00	19,603.89	271,144.51	123,348.00	147,796.51
20	2038	59	6,492.00	21,691.56	299,328.07	129,840.00	169,488.07
21	2039	60	6,492.00	23,946.25	329,766.32	136,332.00	193,434.32
22	2040	61	6,492.00	26,381.31	362,639.63	142,824.00	219,815.63
23	2041	62	6,492.00	29,011.17	398,142.80	149,316.00	24,8826.80
24	2042	63	6,492.00	31,851.42	436,486.22	155,808.00	280,678.22
25	2043	64	6,492.00	34,918.90	477,897.12	162,300.00	315,597.12
26	2044	65	6,492.00	38,231.77	522,620.89	168,792.00	353,828.89

If the Greens invest $541 every month at a return of 8 percent compounded annually, in twenty-six years, their total investment, which includes the cash invested and their accumulated earnings, will be $522,620.89. This is representative and not a guarantee. Nor is there a ceiling on the amount of wealth these monthly contributions can grow. It is a conservative estimate.

The RDRP Calculator®

Premium members of my website DebtProofLiving.com have access to the Rapid Debt-Repayment Plan calculator and manager. Visitors to the site can see how the calculator works by clicking on the RDRP calculator demo on the home page.

The RDRP calculator prompts you to input basic data regarding your unsecured debts: current balance, interest rate, current minimum payment, and whether the payment is fixed or falling.

You may have some loans with fixed payments, in which case the payment remains the same until the balance is paid in full. Examples may be your student debt or a medical bill. Even if you pay down the balance more rapidly than required, the monthly payment will be the same next month and every month thereafter.

Credit cards, on the other hand, are typically subject to falling payments, meaning that the payment each month is a percentage (2 to 4 percent is typical) of the outstanding balance. As the balance declines or falls, so does the required monthly payment. It is critical that you check the proper method of payment for each of your unsecured debts as you input them into the RDRP calculator. Interest is calculated differently for fixed payments and for those that are subject to the falling method.

After you've input all your unsecured debts, click on "compute." You will receive three sets of results that correspond to the scenarios A, B, and C above. Following this you will find your scenario comparison summary and your specific rapid debt-repayment schedule. Cast your eyes to the bottom of this schedule and you will see the exact month and year you will celebrate your personal debt-free day!

The Question

If you haven't already asked the following question, you probably will at some point: Wouldn't it be better to line up my debts according to interest rate, with the highest interest rate debt in the first position rather than the debt with the shortest payoff time?

Theoretically, perhaps that is the way to go. And some financial experts do in fact advise that method. But keep in mind that I designed this plan with myself in mind.

When I tackle a challenging job, I need gratification as quickly as possible—and right now would not be too soon. If I approach my debt-repayment plan with the largest interest rate as the first priority, I might be working on my largest debt. It could be many years before I reach my first zero balance. That would be like going on a diet and not losing any weight for three years . . . maybe four. Who would stick with such a plan?

I have worked these plans every which way possible and still believe that the potential difference in interest is minuscule compared to the benefit of using a plan that has a high probability of taking me across the debt-free finish line.

The difference, if any, in the long run between a plan that puts the highest interest rate debt in the first position and one that puts the debt with the shortest payoff time first is going to come down to one or two months at the end. And I say if this is a plan that has every possibility of getting you to the end, that trumps everything—even one or two additional months to get debt-free. The RDRP is a plan that works because it is something you can live with. It is both economically and emotionally sound.

Optional Rule 6: Report. Over the years, many people have reported using the RDRP successfully. I know because they write to me and tell me of their progress and when they pay off that final debt. If you are carrying unsecured debt, I hope to hear from you too. Please let me know when you cross the finish line. I do care, and I will celebrate your victory.

Just recently we received a call at the DPL office. I was out at the time, but my assistant spoke with this caller who was experiencing a particularly emotional moment. She explained that she couldn't give her name or number, but she needed to speak with someone . . . anyone!

She had begun working on her RDRP several years previously when she had more than $24,000 in unsecured debt. She explained that just prior to calling she'd mailed the last check. Her RDRP was complete. She had made it. She needed to tell someone who would care. I'll never know who this dear woman was, but I am still doing mental cartwheels to celebrate her accomplishment.

Turbocharge Your RDRP

One reason the RDRP is such a great tool is that it does not require you to increase any of the payments beyond the current minimums you are making right now. If you are making your current payments, you can get out of debt. I hope that is encouraging if you, like most people, assume that you need some major financial intervention—like an unexpected inheritance or a winning lottery ticket—to help you get debt-free. Now, having said that, let me suggest ways you can speed up the process.

Increase the monthly payment. If you are able (it would be advisable to stretch yourself if at all possible), increase the amount you commit to the RDRP total monthly payment. Using the Greens' example, let's say they could come up with an additional $159 each month, increasing their $541 monthly commitment to $700. That would change Mom and Dad's payment from $150 to $309 (applying the full amount of $159 to the first debt). Here is how that move would affect their plan. Instead of being debt-free in fifty-two months, they would be debt-free in thirty-nine months, and their interest savings would increase to $25,875.

Debt	Principal	Interest Rate	Current Payment	Total Interest	Months to Payoff
Mom and Dad	$900.00	5.00%	$150.00	$7.43	3
Credit Union	$1,500.00	9.00%	$125.00	$47.16	6
Visa	$775.00	9.90%	$42.00	$37.27	7
MasterCard	$3,897.00	16.90%	$115.00	$535.97	14
Sallie Mae	$16,750.00	6.80%	$109.00	$2,501.40	39
Total	$23,822.00		$700.00	$3,129.23	39

Increase payments occasionally. The beauty of this plan is that even the smallest windfall can be applied to a specific and noble cause—getting out of debt.

Let's say you work overtime one month and see an additional $50 in your paycheck. You can direct that amount to the regular monthly payment of the first debt as a one-time boost. Then you can simply recalculate your plan.

To be perfectly honest, I have a feeling your creditors will be confused beyond belief by your odd payments, and that should keep you chuckling all the way to the bank! By law, credit card companies and others whose loans are considered "open-ended" must accept and apply any amount you send, at any time, even if it means a reduction in the amount of interest you will pay.

Ask for lower interest rates. I cannot guarantee results, but if you have a debt with a double-digit interest rate, it cannot hurt to ask for a reduction. I have heard from many people for whom this was remarkably effective.

For high interest credit card balances, start with customer service. Call the toll-free number on your statement or the back of your credit card and tell the person who takes your call that you are distressed by the high rate you are being charged. Point out to him or her that you are being offered considerably lower rates all the time and you are thinking about switching. If you've been a good customer (and you have been if you've been paying lots of interest over the years), chances are good that they might accommodate your request.

Transfer credit card balances to lower-rate cards. Okay, now that I've made the suggestion, let me quickly tell you all the reasons why this is not only risky but also potentially hazardous to your wealth. What could go wrong? Plenty. And most of it can be found in the fine print on the typical credit card application. If you choose to consider this tactic, grab a magnifying glass so you can read the ultra-fine print.

The low interest rate could be only introductory or a "teaser rate" to get you to act. Read carefully to see how quickly that 3.9 percent rate morphs into something closer to 13.9 percent or even 23.9 percent.

The low interest rate that captured your attention could be very restrictive. Does it apply to balance transfers or only to new purchases? And watch out for balance transfer fees. Some issuers charge transaction fees as high as 5 percent of the transferred amount. That is significant.

Does that new card have an annual fee? If so, there goes the benefit of switching.

What about late fees and over-limit fees? Here is where the companies are making up for what they're "losing" on that low interest rate they are offering to give away on the front end. Read all the provisions very carefully because in many instances not only will you be hit with a huge late penalty, but you can also kiss that low interest rate good-bye. And if you are late twice, watch out. The interest could zoom to 29.99 percent or more. Look for something called the "penalty rate."

Another caution: Too many credit inquiries can spell trouble for your credit report. Card hopping shows up as a suspicious activity. Say you apply for a real estate loan in the future. The lender may see any open credit lines and multiple applications as *potential* outstanding debt. Even though you may not be heavily in debt at the time, you have the *potential* to run it up overnight, and that would be considered a negative.

While transferring balances to lower-rate cards may be a beneficial tactic in a rare case, it is important to remember that these companies are in business for the money—not to make your life easier or to decrease the amount of interest you will end up paying. On the contrary, they are looking for excuses to charge you more. If you do not have perfect credit and do not maintain an impeccable payment schedule, they will take advantage of you.

Getting out of debt is unlike any other kind of recovery program I know of or have participated in. In other kinds of endeavors, such as weight loss, which I'm very familiar with, the joy is not in the recovery itself but in reaching the goal. Rapidly repaying debt, however, seems to be a different kind of recovery. The joy is in the recovery. The joy comes in sending those checks every month, in seeing the balances decline, in knowing that you're traveling in a different direction than the one that got you into the trap.

Repaying debt in a conscious and reasoned manner brought me the same kind of exhilaration that spending did. I cannot explain that in rational terms; I can only testify to you that it is true. I have had many readers confirm this in their lives as well.

For readers who are not struggling with a load of unsecured debt, let me suggest that knowing how to get out of debt rapidly is an important part of the debt-proof living process. It's something you need to know. There may come a time when an adult child, spouse, or relative needs your wisdom and encouragement to get out of debt. Perhaps you will someday find yourself in the position of counseling others in this regard. Your encouragement and effectiveness will come from your empathy and knowledge of how to lead them out of debt.

RDRP Feedback

We are just beginning our RDRP and are so excited about it. My husband has never been one to get involved when it comes to the bills (except to accumulate them), but now that I have shown him this plan, he is ready to start!—Lisa

My husband and I have finally started our RDRP. I have been literally at the point of waking up nights in a sweat because of financial worry. It has taken us a long time to take the first step of putting the plan into action, but what a freeing feeling! According to the calculations, we will be debt-free in twenty-six months. It will be a long road for us but a journey that will—and already has—taught us many lessons. Thank you for sharing your life and for the awesome calculator on your website!—Karen

Just wanted to drop you a note and say thank you for having an influence on my life. I just wrote my last credit card payment and am now debt-free except for my home. That's my next major hurdle—to be completely debt-free. I have followed your advice for two years. You have had a major impact on my life, and I am so grateful. Thank you for caring enough to share your heartaches and experiences.—Brenda

I am a sixty-three-year-old woman, retired and on a fixed income. All my adult life I have had credit cards and revolving balances. Last year I decided to develop my Rapid Debt-Repayment Plan. I made a commitment not to charge anything else and began paying down my debts—more than $5,000. In less than one year, I have completed my plan; I am debt-free for the first time and much happier for it. Indeed, this year was my turning point.—Tracy

I must tell you that I have figured my Rapid Debt-Repayment Plan using the online calculator. You showed me how to save $7,113 in interest and cut my payoff time from 118 months to 21 months using the same amount of money I always use to pay my bills. I can't begin to express how happy that has made me and how much it has inspired my husband to help me with becoming debt-free!—Dana

Today is independence day for our family. We are free of debt—only our home and one final round of truck payments remain. We have followed our RDRP to the letter for the past two years. I am so proud to be able to stand here and say it's possible and what freedom you acquire when you're finished. It's amazing how much money is suddenly coming our way to invest and save now that the bills are paid.—Linda

8

Expect the Unexpected

The Freedom Account

That which we call our necessary expenses will always grow
to equal our income unless we protest to the contrary.

George Clason,
The Richest Man in Babylon

Have you ever noticed that no matter the size of your apartment,
condominium, house, garage, drawers, closets, hard drive, hand-
bag, or briefcase it is mysteriously filled to capacity?

Our first apartment was three hundred square feet. We were
newlyweds, didn't have much, and were still in the cozy stage, so
it wasn't a problem. Three years later we were packed to the gills
and longed for a little breathing space, so we moved into a twelve-
hundred-square-foot house. Wow, so much extra room. In less time
than it took to unpack, the place quickly and quite mysteriously
filled to capacity.

A year later we moved into an eighteen-hundred-square-foot house that had a big family room addition and a two-car garage. Again, we were soon full to the rafters.

Twelve years later we moved into a home twice the size, and—you guessed it—we're full. Paring down, cleaning out, and simplifying has become an unrelenting challenge. We must be in a constant mode of "protesting to the contrary" to maintain control of our possessions and our lives.

This great mystery of life operates in the area of finances as well. It goes like this: No matter what your income, your necessary expenses will be equal to it.

Think back to your last pay increase. It's likely that before you could even enjoy the extra money it was mysteriously absorbed into this nebulous thing we call necessary expenses.

Just like the problem with stuff that fills closets, drawers, homes, and hard drives, unless you "protest to the contrary," which means work really hard to combat it, the forces that are at work constantly to ratchet up your "necessary expenses" will send you down in defeat.

Most people, without actually thinking about it, assume that their necessary expenses are those that repeat every month. But they are wrong. Not all necessary expenses are as systematically recurring as the rent, grocery bill, telephone bill, and car payment. When we assume that those are the only necessary expenses and allow them to expand to equal our incomes, everything falls apart when the unexpected and nonrecurring expenses appear out of the blue.

This is the way most of us think: The expenses I have right now—this month—are my necessary expenses. Once they're paid, if there's any money left, it's mine to spend on whatever I want. And if I have an emergency before next payday, I'll use credit. That's why we have credit cards, right? For emergencies.

Before the era of easy credit, people had no choice but to anticipate and plan for emergencies and irregular expenses—those that didn't occur every month. Whether you had a lot or only a little, you never spent all of it. Preparing for rainy days meant survival.

The advent of consumer credit perpetuated a dangerous, albeit most welcomed, message that we didn't have to worry anymore. Running out of money was no longer a possibility. Running out of cash? Sure, but that didn't mean running out of money. The consumer credit industry assured us that if we could spend money, it was the same as having money. The message was that as long as we had the umbrella of credit, we would stay dry no matter how rainy the days became. Our incomes were now freed from all cares about tomorrow. Our paychecks in their entirety were now available to make the present just as wonderful as possible.

Credit was the new wave of the future and appeared to be far superior to the past. The convenience and security of plastic made everything else seem old-fashioned. We rolled our eyes as our grandparents lectured about how things were in the old days, the importance of frugality, and not buying on credit. We thought we were modern in our thinking. Our grandparents thought we were headed for trouble.

We learned that while an emergency was once defined as a situation in which one's health or safety was in imminent danger, the new meaning included much more—a brake job on the family automobile, Junior's preschool tuition, the Christmas holidays, and anything we found on sale. We turned into a nation of spoiled consumers who overconsume and overspend because we believe that what we have is ours to spend now and the purpose of credit is to be there whenever life takes us by surprise.

During my wild spending years, I practiced anticipation, but only if it was personally beneficial. I anticipated that my husband would receive regular pay increases and bonuses. I expected and acted on it. I anticipated that the home we purchased in 1975 for $38,000 would be worth—and this was only a rough estimate—between 5 and 10 million dollars someday. I anticipated king-sized tax refunds and a future free of financial worries.

On the other hand, it didn't cross my mind that I should anticipate an urgent trip to the dentist or the cost of a new set of tires. I loved my new Cadillac, but in my wildest dreams I could not anticipate the $600 price tag tied to that first maintenance appointment or that my land yacht was no more mine than it would be in three years when the lease was up.

Not once did I anticipate the expense of clothing a family of four, but somehow I consistently managed to avoid anything close to a fashion risk. Anticipate a burned-out water heater? Get real. A trip to the emergency room to repair the damage sustained during a boy's maiden voyage on his new bike? No way.

Thanks to available credit, I began labeling all kinds of things as emergencies and felt completely justified in doing so. The provision was there in the form of available credit, so why not take full advantage of it?

All you have to do is look at the horrible amount of debt I amassed to understand how often we ran into problems we'd not anticipated. And I must admit that the credit card companies came through quite nicely.

Most people just don't make allowance every month for all the things that will happen on an occasional or unpredictable basis. The failure to anticipate has become a pervasive financial problem in this country, evidenced by the fact that in 2012 outstanding non-mortgage consumer debt hit an all-time high of $2.78 trillion,[1] up from $1.4 trillion in 1998. That is not what the government owes; that's what individuals owe as a result of impatience and failure to anticipate. And if we throw mortgage debt into the mix? The number becomes a staggering $11.16 trillion.[2]

If you are like most, your financial situation looks pretty good on paper. When you add up your necessary expenses and deduct them from your income, it looks as if you have enough. Ends should meet. On paper it might even appear that you have a surplus. Rarely does that scenario play out in real life.

Without fail, it seems, something always happens. There's never enough money to get through the month, or if there is, it is rare. If it's not a brake job, it's a busted water heater or soccer sign-ups or a million other little things that catch you by surprise. So much for any surplus you've managed to accumulate.

The diagnosis is clear. You have a case of selective amnesia. Selective amnesia is a condition that attacks your memory in the irregular, intermittent, and unexpected expenses region. You've lost your ability to anticipate those things that you should anticipate as a normal part of life, and in so doing, you've conveniently lost your memory.

Your predictable monthly bills are not the problem. Somehow the rent or mortgage and utilities get paid, and the family is fed. Some months it's tight, but you manage to get by. Once in a while there's even a bit of money left. You breathe a sigh of relief, and you automatically assume every month from now on is going to be as easy. Wow. It feels great to have the bills paid. And money left over. Finally we're getting ahead of the game. Let's put in a pool!

Next month, to your utter amazement and complete bewilderment, everything falls apart. The car breaks down, your young soccer player breaks his arm, the quarterly insurance premium is due, three family members have birthdays, the dog gets sick, and the washing machine dies. Expenses you've not planned for are screaming for money you don't have.

Selective amnesia allows us to forget that every day we are incurring expenses. We are using up and wearing out our cars, our clothes, our homes. We are clicking away at our prepaid insurance and inching ever closer to vacations, Christmas, and college educations. When these kinds of expenses come at us from out of nowhere, we collapse into a pitiful heap and bemoan the fact that once again we've been broadsided by an emergency. Another financial crisis.

And where do these financial crises send us? To the credit cards, of course. After all, we've been educated to believe that this is the purpose of a credit card. We've been suckered into believing that plastic was invented to rescue us from life's financial emergencies.

Imagine this. It's the middle of March. Spring flowers are poking their way through the ground; thoughts are turning to summer fun. You sit down with a pile of bills and your checkbook. You line them up in order of priority (past dues first, then whatever else you can work in—you know the routine). Are you thinking about next Christmas? No. It's understandable since some of those past-due bills are from last Christmas.

Let's try another scenario. It's September 16. Yesterday was the final day to mail your semiannual property tax installment. How much are you thinking today about the next installment that will be due March 15? As little as possible, I have a feeling. You are just relieved that yesterday is over and you scraped together enough credit to cover the big check you had to write.

One more. It's any day of the year. You're driving home from work, the car is running perfectly, the weather forecast is nearly too good to be true, and you're looking forward to a restful weekend. How much are you thinking about your brakes that are going to brake their very last time seven weeks from now?

At this point you might be thinking, "Sure, I can understand planning for Christmas and for property taxes, but you can't expect me to plan for totally unpredictable expenses like brake jobs." Yes, I can, and so should you.

You have to agree that every time you step your foot on that brake pedal you are using up part of your brakes' useful life. You are in fact "spending" your brakes one day at a time. Contrary to the way you choose to think on a daily basis (or not think, as the case may be), they will not last forever. And the chances that you'll be any more prepared financially to replace them seven weeks from now than you are today are not very good—perhaps worse, since you don't know what else might happen between now and then.

My point is that—and let me repeat this—we regard anything that is not urgent right now as an optional expense. Only when an unexpected, irregular, or intermittent expense brings our lives to a screeching halt does it get our full attention and become essential.

So how do you handle it when a big, unexpected car repair bill or a semiannual insurance payment comes along and at the eleventh hour you finally concede that it is not optional, that it is serious? More than likely you find justification in using the credit cards. For some people, I would enlarge that to say they feel "righteous justification" because they look at their available credit line as a providential provision to take care of the problem. I have actually had people tell me that their debts are not their fault because they had to go into debt to pay for car repairs and "other big things like that."

As a person who ran up debt rivaling the net worth of a small nation, I know about this kind of thinking because I've been there. Believe me, not all the debt I amassed went to pay for luxury cruises and shopping sprees on Rodeo Drive. In fact, none of it went for that.

We used credit to pay for property taxes and car repairs and Christmas and clothes—all perfectly essential expenses. The reason we went into debt for those things was because we didn't view them as essential every month but only as they occurred. And because our regularly occurring expenses grew to equal our income, there was nothing available for the other kinds of expenses. So we relied on credit to bridge the gap.

This problem does not affect everyone in the same way. Some people do not run for credit when the unexpected, irregular, and intermittent expenses happen. Instead, they pull the funds from their meager savings or fledgling Contingency Fund. While certainly not as damaging as going into debt, their actions keep them forever stuck in a financial rut. They just cannot seem to get ahead. While they might handle the problem a bit differently—and, might I say, much more intelligently—the underlying problem is the same as it is for those who go into debt to survive, which is failing to set aside money for unexpected, irregular, and intermittent expenses.

If you see yourself in any of these scenarios, you are not alone. I have a strong suspicion that most people face this challenge because they do not accurately identify their necessary expenses. They allow their regular monthly expenses to grow to equal their income and then there is nothing available for expenses that are unexpected, irregular, or intermittent.

The antidote for selective amnesia is to find a reasonable and practical way to make every expense a recurring monthly expense—even expenses of which you're not currently aware.

The Freedom Account

To treat my own case of selective amnesia, I developed something I call a Freedom Account. It is a simple, personal, money-management tool that makes unexpected, irregular, and intermittent expenses as ordinary, predictable, and necessary as your rent and grocery bill. A Freedom Account eliminates financial surprises.

I have written about the Freedom Account in previous books and repeatedly in my newsletter, Debt-Proof Living (formerly Cheapskate Monthly) because the Freedom Account is the heart and soul of debt recovery and debt-proof living. It is a reasonable and practical way to eliminate what many people feel is their only defense against financial emergencies: credit cards.

Like a Christmas Club Account

Perhaps you once had a Christmas club account or knew someone who did. Many banks, and even schools, offered Christmas club accounts as a way to encourage people to save for their Christmas shopping. The plan was relatively painless because you saved just a little bit throughout the year. You decided how much you would save and then authorized the club to automatically take that amount out of your paycheck or bank account before you ever saw it. You planned ahead to save for Christmas.

The fun was in forgetting about it. You knew this sneaky thing was going on behind the scenes, but you took pleasure in pretending you didn't notice. You didn't miss the money because of the same mysterious law that lets you disregard expenses that are unexpected, irregular, or intermittent: out of sight, out of mind.

The reward for faithful membership in the Christmas club was that big check that came in the mail right around Thanksgiving. Even though you knew you were contributing a little bit at a time, it was great fun to experience the joyful surprise. The check was always bigger than you thought it would be, and you felt somehow noble or righteous because this check was tangible proof that you'd done the right thing—you had anticipated the expense of your Christmas shopping. Contrast that feeling with how you have felt in the past when you had to shop with credit cards and you carried a big load of new debt into the next year.

Creating a personal Freedom Account takes the simple principles and joyful rewards of a Christmas club and applies them to all the expenses that will come but do not recur every month. It also makes a provision for those expenses that have a high likelihood of occurring.

I promise that if you start a Freedom Account, build it gradually, and manage it diligently, you will experience a freedom in your financial life that you have not known before.

It will be a gradual process, but eventually your Freedom Account and Contingency Fund will switch places. The Freedom Account will become your first line of defense against emergencies and unexpected expenses, while the Contingency Fund will guard you from financial ruin in the event of the mother of all emergencies: the temporary loss of your income.

Before heading into specific instructions, we need to be very clear regarding the definition of "unexpected, unpredictable, and intermittent expenses." These are expenses that do not recur every month. Your mortgage payment, car payment, telephone bill, and grocery bill do not fall into this category because they are regular expenses that you deal with every month.

Step-by-Step Instructions

Setting up and then maintaining a Freedom Account is simple. But let me caution you to do it exactly as outlined below. I've tried variations and shortcuts, and I can assure you they will not work as effectively or as consistently as these simple steps.

Step 1: Make a list of expenses you do not pay on a monthly basis. This will be the most challenging step in the process. Let me encourage you to start with the obvious and work your way to the more remote. For example, if you have an automobile, maintenance and repair are irregular expenses that many of us ignore until something goes wrong.

Using your check registers for the past twelve months, your credit card statements, your tax return, or, if all else fails, your memory, make a list of expenses you do not pay on a monthly basis. These might come quarterly, every six months, or annually. They may occur so sporadically that you have no idea when they'll pop up again, if ever.

The past year or two will be the best indicator of the future. Remember, you are searching for expenses that do not recur on a monthly basis. If you already pay a portion of your property taxes every month, that does not qualify for the Freedom Account. If you pay your life insurance premiums every six months, that does qualify.

Once you have a reasonable list (it will probably not be complete, but that's okay—you can add and adjust later), do the math so you end up with an amount for each expense that represents 1/12 of the total projected annual expense. You will first have to reach an annual figure for a particular expense, then divide it by 12 to come up with a monthly amount.

Following is an example of five typical Freedom Account categories:

auto maintenance/repair	$765/year ÷ 12 = $64 per month
life insurance	$520/year ÷ 12 = $44 per month
clothing	$480/year ÷ 12 = $40 per month
property taxes	$600/year ÷ 12 = $50 per month
vacation	$800/year ÷ 12 = $66 per month
Total	**$264 per month**

124

Step 2: Open a second checking account. I'm assuming you have a checking account already, so open another one at the same bank or credit union. Order checks for your new account. You can save a bundle if you order from a printer, not the bank. Try Checks Unlimited (www.checksunlimited.com, 800-210-0468) or Checks-in-the-Mail (www.checksinthemail.com, 800-733-4443). Have your checks personalized as usual, but add a special line above your name that says "Freedom Account."

Consider carefully the different types of accounts available. If the bank or credit union offers an account with check-writing privileges that also pays interest once you reach a minimum balance, consider it seriously. If a $500 or $1,000 minimum balance is required, check if you can convert to the interest-bearing account once your account reaches that level. An account that limits the number of checks you can write in a month, say ten, will work just fine.

For this to work, you must have two active checking accounts. Your regular checking account will continue to accommodate your monthly expenses and typical day-to-day needs. You will continue to deposit your paychecks and other income into your regular account.

Do not accept overdraft protection, ATM privileges, or a debit card for your Freedom Account. This is not that kind of bank account, and having those add-ons could easily tempt you to use this account in ways for which it was not designed.

Step 3: Authorize an automatic deposit. At the time you open the account, request an automatic deposit authorization form (some banks call this an automatic money transfer form) and instruct the bank to transfer the monthly total of your irregular expenses (in the example above it is $264) from your regular checking account into your Freedom Account on a specific day of the month. Think carefully about this. The selection of your transfer date is very important because, once established, you can be sure the bank will never forget to make the transfer, nor will they ever be late.

Step 4: Use a notebook or a file on your computer and/or smart phone to manage your Freedom Account. As far as the bank is concerned, you have a second checking account. But you are going to treat your new Freedom Account as a collection of subaccounts.

Prepare one page per subaccount (the categories you created in step 1), similar to the following illustration. Include five columns labeled date, description, in, out, and balance. Fill in the title of the account, and enter the amount to be deposited into that subaccount in the upper right-hand corner. Use the page to record deposits and payments for a particular expense.

Let's go through the auto maintenance and repair subaccount in the illustration to understand how the Freedom Account works in real life.

May 5 was the launch date for this Freedom Account. The first deposit was made on that date, and $64 was added to this particular subaccount. The same deposit was made on June 5, which brought the balance to $128. Two more months went by with the same $64 deposit, bringing the balance in this subaccount to $256 on August 5.

On September 1, it was time to get the oil changed, so our account owner took her Freedom Account checkbook to the place she always has her car's oil changed, wrote out check #101 to Jiffy Lube for $19.95, wrote the entry into the subaccount book when she got home, and did the math to come up with a new balance of $236.05. Regular monthly deposits occurred again on September 5 and October 5, bringing the new balance to $364.05.

Have you ever noticed how car trouble seems to come in waves? Some insist it comes in threes, but I'm not so sure about that. Nevertheless, it always seems to hit when you least expect it.

On October 15, our account owner had to buy two new tires. But because she had the cash available and didn't have to rely on whatever shop she could find that would take the only credit card she could use, she shopped around. She found the best deal at Sam's Club, so she wrote check #102 accordingly, entered $132.25 in the out column, and calculated the new balance of $231.80.

The next day the battery died, requiring a replacement to the tune of $45.87. As you may have already predicted by looking ahead

$ per month _66_

Vacation

$ per month _50_

Property Taxes

$ per month _40_

Clothing

$ per month _44_

Life Insurance

$ per month _64_

Auto Maintenance and Repair

Date	Description	In	Out	Balance
5/5/2013	Opening Deposit	64		64.00
6/5/2013	Deposit	64		128.00
7/5/2013	Deposit	64		192.00
8/5/2013	Deposit	64		256.00
9/1/2013	Ck #101 - Jiffy Lube		19.95	236.05
9/5/2013	Deposit	64		300.05
10/5/2013	Deposit	64		364.05
10/15/2013	Ck #102 Sam's Club		132.25	231.80
10/16/2013	Ck #103 A-1 Battery		45.87	185.93
10/17/2013	Ck #104 Joe's Big Tow		45.00	140.93
10/17/2013	Ck #105 Al's Electric		98.44	42.49
11/5/2013	Deposit	64		106.49
12/5/2013	Deposit	64		170.49
1/5/2014	Deposit	64		234.49
2/5/2014	Deposit	64		298.49
2/10/2014	Ck #110 Trak Auto		22.50	275.99
3/5/2014	Deposit	64		339.99
4/5/2014	Deposit	64		403.99
5/5/2014	Deposit	64		467.99
6/5/2014	Deposit	64		531.99
6/28/2014	Ck #115 - 50,000 Mi Srv		300.00	231.99
7/5/2014	Deposit	64		295.99
8/5/2014	Deposit	64		359.99
9/5/2014	Deposit	64		423.99

on the form, the battery wasn't the problem after all, evidenced by the fact that the next day, October 17, the car died and had to be towed by Joe's Big Tow for $45. But does our account owner panic? Not at all. The auto maintenance and repair subaccount is properly funded and is handling expenses just the way it should. Later that day, October 17, the real problem is discovered, requiring another payment of $98.44 to the electrical shop for a new alternator. After three days of car trouble, is our account owner stressed? No. Car repairs and maintenance are a part of life. She has the money in place for such an occurrence.

The next four months are trouble-free, so the balance grows. In February, the account owner decides to save a few bucks by changing her own oil, writes out a check for $22.50 for enough oil for four changes, and calculates the new balance of $275.99.

Things continue to go well. The balance grows, and on June 28, more than enough is in the account to cover the 50,000-mile service on the car. She makes a few phone calls and finds that the prices for this kind of service, which is required to protect the warranty, vary greatly. She selects the best deal, has the work done, and pays for it with $300 from her Freedom Account. How freeing to know that the money is in place, ready to go.

To me, it is still amazing the kind of freedom and peace of mind that a simple $64 monthly deposit set aside for a specific purpose can bring to one's life.

Step 5: Make a deposit every month without fail. Once a month, deduct the amount of your Freedom Account deposit ($264 in our example) from your regular checking account register just as if you'd written a check for that amount. Because the bank will transfer that amount, you must treat this as a regular monthly expense the same way you treat your rent and car payment. Don't even think about forgetting, because the bank never will. You will have a mess on your hands if you bounce your own automatic deposit.

Making automatic deposits is going to feel weird in the beginning. You won't like recording a big debit entry in your regular checkbook because it feels like you're throwing money away. You're spending but not getting anything in return. But nothing could be further from the truth. You are managing your money—controlling your money instead of letting it control you.

Other Irregular Expenses

Any potential expense, including those that are not as predictable as auto maintenance and repair but have a way of hitting you over the head when you can least afford it, qualify for the Freedom Account.

Insurance Deductibles Subaccount

An excellent way to keep insurance premiums low is to carry higher deductibles. But what happens if you are in an auto accident that requires you to fork over your $1,000 deductible? Ouch! Solution? A subaccount.

This subaccount should grow until its balance is equal to the annual deductibles of your health, homeowners, and auto insurance policies. If you are nervous about raising your deductibles without having the funds in place to cover them, fund the subaccount first. Then you'll be in a good position to increase your deductibles in exchange for lower premiums.

Imagine the peace of mind you will have knowing that the deductibles are there, ready to be used if necessary, and drawing interest in the meantime. That is freedom. Once your subaccount reaches the amount you determine is adequate to cover your deductibles, you can divert future deposits into some other subaccount.

Clothing Subaccount

You cannot imagine how many families do not consider clothing when asked to list their expenses. Ironically, I have noticed that those in the worst financial shape are often the best dressed. Where does that money come from? I can only assume that many people load huge clothing expenses on credit cards or write checks using funds that were supposed to pay for groceries or utilities.

With a Freedom Account, clothing becomes a monthly expense. You may want to set up a general clothing account for the entire family or separate accounts: his clothes, her clothes, kids' clothes, or some combination thereof.

Christmas/Holiday Subaccount

Probably nothing in the world throws more of us into a debting depression than approaching the month of December. Every January you say that this year you are going to save a little bit every month for Christmas. And do you? This year will be different. Your Freedom Account is the perfect way to join your own Christmas club.

Dream Subaccounts

What do you hope to have enough money to do or be someday? Perhaps you'd like to take a class, redecorate the master bedroom, go on a special trip, start a stamp collection, or take up skiing. If you are like most of us, these things remain a dream to be fulfilled "when we get some extra money"—which is usually never. Well, not anymore.

The Freedom Account enables you to turn those dreams into achievable goals. Let your mind run wild. Insert new pages into your Freedom Account notebook and title them accordingly: redecorate master bedroom, room addition, John's woodworking tools, Caribbean cruise. Maybe you won't be able to start funding these accounts right now, but little by little you will find it possible to fund more and more pages in your Freedom Account.

One added benefit of a Freedom Account is that it is a fabulous marriage tool. By having individual subaccounts, both partners can manage their own money without feeling a need to sneak around or wallow in self-pity.

Unscheduled Income

You receive unexpected and unpredictable money all the time, such as rebate checks, tax refunds, freelance payments, and gifts. It may be only a dollar here or ten dollars there, but what happens to it? You put it in your pocket and it is absorbed into your daily spending so fast that you hardly remember getting it. Larger amounts, such as tax refunds and consulting payments, usually go into the checking account with the intention they will be used in some special way. Before you know it, however, they are gone too, but who knows where?

The Freedom Account is a wonderful solution to the case of the vanishing funds. Make it a habit to deposit unscheduled income—big or small—into your Freedom Account. Selecting the subaccount to which it will be credited suddenly gives new meaning to surprise money.

Let's say, for instance, that you misjudged your federal tax withholding, and you end up with a refund of $1,000. If you put it into your regular account, it will disappear as it slips through your fingers via the ATM machine or the latte shop. But if you immediately put it into your Freedom Account, you decide which goals to nourish.

A word of caution: You may be tempted to think of your Freedom Account as a savings or investment account. You may find yourself skipping your true savings in favor of funding your Freedom Account. But it is not a savings account. This money has been committed for a specific purpose and is meant to be spent. Prepare yourself, because this new account will give new meaning to the term ebb and flow. That's the way it's supposed to work. It is strictly a financial management tool. This is what money management is all about. By following these basic instructions and then customizing your Freedom Account to reflect you, your family, and your lifestyle, you will become a very skilled personal finance manager.

I heard from a man who diligently set up and funded his Freedom Account. However, his hesitation to use it became his downfall. In the beginning, when he had a minor auto repair, rather than using his Freedom Account as he should have, he thought he would be especially good and fund the expense from his pocket money. I can understand his way of thinking—that paying for the expense from his general fund forced him to leave money in his Freedom Account. But he kept doing it. Each time the righteous feeling he got from not using his Freedom Account prompted him to do it again.

Eventually, the expenses he was funding outside the account, for which he'd already set aside the money, became more than he could pay from his regular account. He had come to see his Freedom Account as some kind of sacred investment, and he couldn't bring himself to use it. Instead, he put irregular expenses on a credit card, thinking he could somehow pay it off in the grace period and still be the "good boy" who was not touching his Freedom Account. By the time I heard from him, he was all messed up and was on the verge of dumping the whole idea as totally unmanageable.

Clearly, the problem is that this man refused to use his Freedom Account in the way it was supposed to be used. Do not let this happen with you. You created your Freedom Account to pay for things. Of course, this does not imply that you spend wildly—that if you have accumulated $1,200 in your Christmas subaccount you must spend every last penny. That's not at all what I mean.

The point is that when Christmas comes around, you use the Freedom Account funds to cover your Christmas expenses as opposed to sneaking money out of the grocery funds. You might get away with that for a while, but I can assure you that such sloppy management will land you back from whence you've come—all mixed up and letting your emotions guide you rather than your newfound financial management sense.

Frequently Asked Questions

Q: Have you lost your mind? I don't have extra money every month to fund anything new, let alone a Freedom Account.

A: Listen to yourself. You are acting as if maintaining your auto is optional or you can skip paying your insurance if you're a little short. Do you really have a choice whether to pay your property taxes or buy clothes? You are driving a car, your taxes were paid, and you dress fairly well. Exactly how did you do that? You came up with the money somehow, and you probably have a few battle scars or credit card payments that help you remember the trouble you went through to do it.

This step is too important to pass off as something you cannot afford. I suggest you start out with the bare minimum number of accounts, limiting them to your most essential irregular expenses. You may have to reduce your spending in other areas in order to get started with a Freedom Account, but whatever the sacrifice, no matter how painful, this is one of the most important things you will ever do for yourself.

Q: Won't I incur new expenses as a result of this new Freedom Account, expenses such as fees for checks and service charges?

A: Yes, there may be some fees. However, as your total balance (the balance the bank sees is the total of all your subaccounts) grows beyond the minimum amount required, all service fees may be waived, provided you have selected an account with that kind of benefit. You will be writing very few checks from this account, so the cost of paper checks will be minimal. I suggest that you deduct any administrative charges from your most lucrative subaccount. And should the day return when banks actually pay interest on savings accounts, credit it to that subaccount as well.

Q: How do I balance the Freedom Account each month?

A: Add together the current balances of all your subaccounts. The total should match the bank statement's closing balance once you have made allowances for checks that haven't cleared and deposits not posted. Reconcile it just like any other checking account. If you've never done this, step-by-step instructions can be found on the back of your monthly checking account statement.

Q: Couldn't I create my own Freedom Account using my regular household account without opening another checking account?

A: You could, but I don't recommend it. As long as the money for your Freedom Account is sitting there in your regular household checking account, it will be too easy to comingle them. And when things get a little rocky, without that automatic withdrawal from your household account into your Freedom Account, you might be tempted to skip contributing some months. The Freedom Account should be a serious business activity, not a simple no-one-knows-if-I-do and no-one-knows-if-I-don't kind of thing.

If you're like me, you need the discipline and pressure of an automatic withdrawal. It puts everything on a businesslike, professional level. Besides, you probably won't pay yourself interest like the bank or credit union will. Record keeping is easier too when you have a monthly statement and access to canceled checks, copies of which are available from your bank.

Q: What happens if my Freedom Account gets too large? Shouldn't I be investing the money?

A: Your goal is to have a full year's funding in each of your subaccounts. That's not going to happen overnight. Also, remember that this is not an investment vehicle; this is a money-management tool. Most of your subaccounts will be self-reducing. Subaccounts for insurance deductibles or other items that may not be self-eliminating should have a cap. For instance, your insurance deductibles may total $1,000. Once you have reached the designated amount in that subaccount, discontinue deposits until you make a withdrawal. You might have a high school reunion account. Once you've funded it and have attended the gala event, you can rip that page out and adjust your monthly contributions accordingly.

If you set up the Freedom Account properly, surpluses won't be a problem. Besides, I would hardly call surplus funds a problem. You will be amazed at how financially functional you'll become once you have the opportunity to manage your money.

Q: In the beginning, when the subaccounts have low balances, what should I do if I have an expense that is greater than the current balance in that subaccount?

A: Ideally, you should find a way to open each subaccount with a larger initial deposit to cover this situation. Example: You open your Freedom Account on October 1. Your semiannual property tax bill is due on December 10. If your monthly property tax deposit into your Freedom Account is $75, you will hardly have the $450 necessary to make the payment. You will have contributed only $225 ($75 x 3) into that particular subaccount.

You should make an initial deposit into the subaccount to jumpstart the process. By contributing an additional $225 into the account on October 1 to anticipate the shortfall, the problem would be solved. As you set up your Freedom Account, you might see where a few hours of overtime or a moonlighting position for a few weeks would raise the funds necessary to launch your Freedom Account in such a way that you'll be fully prepared for the first expense. However, even if you can't manage the additional funding in the first month, don't let this become an excuse not to get started.

Let's look at another scenario. Say you have a $64 balance in your auto maintenance and repair account and you incur a $100 repair item during the first month. What should you do? Write a check out of your Freedom Account for the $64 and supplement the balance from your regular account. Do not borrow from other freedom subaccounts. While it pains me to suggest this, if you have absolutely no other way to come up with $36 (try hard—I mean really hard), it would be better this one last time to put the balance on a credit card and then pay the credit card payment from the auto maintenance and repair subaccount. I would recommend this only if the borrowed funds can be repaid within the following thirty days.

Example: Your auto maintenance and repair account has a balance of $64. Your repair bill is $100. You write a check for the $64 from your Freedom Account and pay for the balance with a credit card. By the time the bill comes, you will have made another $64 deposit into the auto maintenance and repair subaccount, allowing you to write a check from your Freedom Account to pay off the credit card in full without incurring an interest charge. Going through these steps of depositing into the Freedom Account and writing a check out of it to cover the $36 credit card bill is necessary in order to keep everything straight and your subaccount page correct.

Yes, it will take a little time to get the Freedom Account working smoothly. But don't let a little rough water in the beginning convince you to abandon such a wonderful, life-changing tool!

Q: Would it make sense for my Freedom Account to be held in a money market fund account rather than at a bank or credit union?

A: Yes, that is an excellent idea because of the greater rate of interest you can expect in a money market fund. But remember that these accounts typically have high minimum requirements. Select one that has a low requirement if you sign up for automatic deposits, such as the USAA Money Market Fund[3] (800-531-8181). There is no minimum requirement as long as you have an automatic deposit of at least $50 a month. But keep in mind that money market fund accounts have minimum withdrawal guidelines. You will not be able to write checks for less than, say, $250 (fund guidelines vary).

Freedom Account Feedback

We have no consumer debt now and a $10,000 Contingency Fund in a money market account. We will be able to pay off the mortgage in just a few more years, and we are so excited! Our Freedom Account has changed our financial life! Thank you.—Bill and Tracy

I love the Freedom Account! I set mine up this past January, and I actually have the money set aside for our property taxes. In the past, I would try to save the money and would always come up short. Then I would be forced to write a cash-advance check from my credit card. How pathetic. The first two months of having $300 a pay period transferred into the Freedom Account was really hard, but now I'm used to it. Once my car is paid off in a few months, I will set up a couple more subaccounts for household repairs and one for furniture we need. The Freedom Account is incredibly liberating! If you haven't set one up yet, do it, even if it's for $20 a month. Having the money socked away has really helped me, and my husband is very impressed by my change in behavior.—Lucy

Just this past month I was able to pay the six-month auto insurance premium instead of the usual three-month. I think I will have enough to do that on the other car by the time it is due. I love the freedom the Freedom Account has given us. We used to have to scrape by, and my husband would have to work overtime when the three-month premiums were due. Also, we had a $100 copay at the hospital when my daughter was born that I paid for with cash. Things certainly are looking up.—Jennifer

Back in February we had to replace our garage door. Actually, it needed to be replaced as early as the previous May, but we put it off because of the expense. It was our first major dent in the Freedom Account—$790—but boy did it feel good not to incur a charge of that amount. And we just paid a full six-month auto insurance premium out of the Freedom Account as well. The Freedom Account is such a great idea.—Elizabeth

I am proud of myself today. Our water heater went out yesterday. We shopped around and came up with the best water heater for us and the future. It, however, was not cheap! But when it came time to pay, we paid for it from our Freedom Account. It really felt great. Now back to the grindstone to rebuild that subaccount.—Marie

It's been more than two years since I first read about the Freedom Account. I wanted to start one, but my husband was very skeptical. One year later we officially opened our Freedom Account. It is now more than a year later, and where would we be without our Freedom Account? Even my husband loves it! At first I thought it would take forever to start adding up, but before I knew it, we had enough money to cover every "surprise" bill that appeared. It makes so much sense to have a Freedom Account because you have to pay for those bills that come every six months or once a year anyway, so why not save for them instead of wiping out your checking account? We have lots of subaccounts, including ones for taxes, insurance, auto maintenance, Christmas, and even a toy fund for my husband. It has been so nice getting the car serviced and not worrying about how we are going to pay for it. Believe me, the Freedom Account has reduced stress in this family. Thank you for such a great idea.—Virginia

9

Create Your Spending Plan

It's Not a Budget

Let honesty and industry be thy constant companions, and spend one penny less than thy clear gains; then shall thy pocket begin to thrive; creditors will not insult, nor want oppress, nor hungerness bite, nor nakedness freeze thee.

Benjamin Franklin

Okay now, where were we? Ah yes, you had just begun preparing your first monthly Spending Record (chap. 5) when we switched gears to get the Contingency Fund firmly planted into your brain (chap. 6). That accomplished, we moved on to your Rapid Debt-Repayment Plan (chap. 7). And if that wasn't enough to raise your hope meter level to an all-time high, the promise of a fully funded Freedom Account (chap. 8) filled you with more optimism and confidence than you've known since the day you finally learned to ride a two-wheeler.

By now you should be starting to figure out why your attempts to "get on a budget" in the past were less than successful. You were trying to put together your financial puzzle with only some of the pieces.

It's possible that in the past you would write down all your expenses, deduct them from your income, and to your surprise and delight, your income was sufficient to cover your expenses. Things should be okay! But that never seemed to work out. For some reason you always came up short.

Here's the problem. Your list of expenses was so far off the mark that it's no wonder you weren't hitting the target. Now that you've been able to step back and see the larger picture, the lights are starting to come on. Now you can see the gaping holes in your financial picture. And things will be different now that you have gathered together all the puzzle pieces.

It is time to take the information you learned when you tracked your spending for a full month and what you learned about your new Contingency Fund, Rapid Debt-Repayment Plan, and Freedom Account and put them together to create your first monthly Spending Plan.

The Spending Plan

A Spending Plan gives you a reasonable way to manage every bit of money that comes into your life, before you spend any of it. In a way, it is like "pre-spending" your money. Think of it this way. Your Spending Plan is how you tell your money where to go so you will never again wonder where it went.

Your Unique Format

Unlike the RDRP and Freedom Account, which are very structured and function the same way for everyone regardless of the specific financial situation, there is no single Spending Plan format that works for every situation. Therefore, I want to leave the exact layout for your unique Spending Plan to your discretion.

You may want to create your Spending Plan on your computer using an Excel spreadsheet. You may prefer to use a free web-based program like Mint or software you download to your computer like Mvelopes.com or YouNeedaBudget.com. There are many options, and you need to explore which one will work the best for you. You may want your plan to interface with your smart phone or other mobile device so you can carry your Spending Plan in your pocket. Or you may do better with the tried-and-true paper and pen. You may need a very detailed format, while others prefer to streamline and simplify.

I am going to teach you the principles of the Spending Plan and then trust you to implement them in the way that suits you best. Later in this chapter, you'll find an example of a monthly Spending Plan, one you can use as your starting point.

Fixed Monthly Expenses

Look at the Spending Record you created based on your thirty days of tracking (chap. 5). Mark each expenditure that represents a fixed monthly expense.

A fixed monthly expense occurs every month and in the same amount. These are your predictable expenses. They're not going to change, and you have become accustomed to paying them. Your rent or mortgage and car payment are examples of fixed monthly expenses. The amount you have determined you will give away each month is now a fixed monthly expense that I will simply call giving. Your Contingency Fund deposit (chap. 6) is now a fixed monthly expense. So is your RDRP total payment as well as the monthly deposit to your Freedom Account.

Let me tell you why this matter of fixed monthly expenses is so important. I doubt whether your fixed monthly expenses have contributed to your financial challenges in the past. The fixed amounts that are due every month do not take you by surprise. You're never shocked to discover that your rent or mortgage payment is due this month, next month, and every month. It's things like a busted water pipe or three wedding showers in two weeks that come out of nowhere to really mess up your money. It's human nature to get used to things that happen the same way all the time.

One of the keys to successful debt-proof living is your willingness to convert as many of your expenses—yes, even the unexpected, irregular, and intermittent ones—into fixed monthly expenses. Once you do this, in a few months you will get used to them just as you are used to your other fixed monthly expenses. And that is when you will start to understand what financial freedom is all about.

Don't panic! I know that adding fixed monthly amounts for giving, your Contingency Fund, your RDRP, and your Freedom Account to your Spending Plan at first will seem impossible. But stick with me. Try to put aside your emotions and think of this as an academic exercise. I so want for you to see how this can and will work for you.

Okay, so you have now listed on your Spending Plan form of choice the fixed monthly expenses you will have in the coming month, including rent or mortgage, giving, Contingency Fund (or savings as we called it in the 10-10-80 formula), RDRP (unless you have absolutely no unsecured debts), and Freedom Account. Good! You are making progress.

Variable Monthly Expenses

Next, look at your Spending Record and identify entries or categories that are your variable monthly expenses. These are bills you get and expenses you have every month, but the amount varies—your utility bills, landline and mobile telephones, food, gasoline, and so forth.

This is important: Your variable monthly expenses hold the key to making debt-proof living successful in your life. You have control over these expenses. This is where you have flexibility and where you can make changes to get your lifestyle down to 80 percent of your income.

Refer to your Spending Record (the one you made from your thirty days of tracking) and see how much you spent during the month on groceries—not fast food or restaurant food but just groceries.

Let's say you spent $452 on groceries in the month you tracked your spending. That is your benchmark. As you anticipate the coming month, what would you like that number to be? You may decide that $452 was too high considering you also spent $280 on fast food and another $175 in restaurants (yes, the food issue is a big one for most people in this country and a place where a lot of money leaks out undetected).

You need to come up with an amount for groceries that you will not go over in the coming month. If you spent $452 last month without any kind of cost-cutting strategy, do you think you could get that down to $425 next month? How about $400? That's a nice round number. Or are you ready to get serious about this and do all you can to knock $100 off last month's performance?

Don't get hung up now about how you will reduce your spending. Your task now is to set spending targets for each category that when added together do not exceed your average monthly income.

You are pre-spending your monthly income on paper. You are getting a feel for how things look and feel before you commit. At this point your money is like wet cement; you can keep changing things until they are just the way you want them for this month. You're in charge here, so this Spending Plan is as fluid as you need it to be.

Break It Down into Weeks

An important aspect of your thirty-day tracking was dividing the month into four reasonably equal weeks—something you can do for every month no matter how many days in that month (week 1: days 1–7; week 2: days 8–14; week 3: days 15–21; week 4: days 22–end of month).

Most people get paid once each week or every two weeks. Fewer are paid only once a month. This alone presents a challenge for many of us because most of our bills are on a once-a-month schedule. Breaking your Spending Plan into weeks will be helpful as you decide which monthly bills will be paid from each paycheck.

The key is to get this down on paper. You need a visual representation of an entire month, where your paychecks land during that month as well as the due dates for your bills.

Rework the Plan

If you are able on your first attempt to plan your spending for the coming month, including your fixed monthly expenses of giving, Contingency Fund, RDRP, and Freedom Account, so that the total of all planned spending does not exceed your average monthly net income, may I say, Hooray! Wow, that was remarkable.

And for the rest of you, it's okay. Don't get discouraged. Just go back to the drawing board and keep working at it. You may need to sharpen your pencil a few times and renew your determination to do whatever it takes to stop spending beyond your means.

Look at your Spending Plan—the one that looks like it may never balance. For each entry, ask yourself, Is this essential or optional? The way to tell is by anticipating the consequences if you remove it from your plan for the coming month. If you're looking at the $200 fast-food entry, the worst thing that will happen is that you'll have to eat at home or pack a lunch. (And the problem with that would be . . . ?)

Look closely at any item you designate optional. Is that something you can either reduce significantly or forgo for the next month or two as you get on your feet? Or perhaps you may decide to pare way back in every area rather than eliminate any spending categories.

Keep this in mind: Essential expenses are those required to preserve life, to keep your job, or to meet a legal obligation. The consequences for failure to pay essential expenses can be severe—from having your car repossessed to placing your health in jeopardy to having legal action taken against you. New clothes are optional, music lessons are optional, sports are optional, gifts and entertainment are optional. Gasoline to get to work is essential, a debt payment is essential, medications are essential, basic food and shelter are essential.

Unlike your Spending Record, which shows what happened, the Spending Plan decides ahead of time what will happen based on what happened in the past and what you want to see happen in the future. Your Spending Plan says, "I have this much money to manage, and this is how I intend to do it."

You may be way ahead of me on this, but let me point out something very important to your success in debt-proof living. Many expenses that you failed to anticipate in the past that caused you to rely on credit to get by have now become regular monthly expenses just like your rent or mortgage payment. Those are the puzzle pieces you were missing before. This is huge and explains how debt-proof living will change your life.

It is possible that when you listed your expenses in the past you did not see saving as a fixed monthly expense. Ditto for giving. In the past, if someone asked you to write a Spending Plan, more than likely you entered a monthly payment for each of your unsecured debts. Now you have just one RDRP monthly payment. (Oh, how this is going to simplify things for you.) And you have your Freedom Account to look after all your irregular, unexpected, and intermittent needs.

All the puzzle pieces are face up on the table. You know what you have, and perhaps for the first time you're beginning to see how everything fits together.

Continue Tracking

Following is an example of a monthly Spending Plan. Each of the four weeks has two columns: plan and actual. In the first column, you enter the planned amount to be spent. The second column contains how much you actually spent.

As illustrated, you will keep tracking your spending so that at the end of next month you will be able to compare what you actually spent with what you planned to spend in each category. Your fixed monthly expenses should not be a problem because, again, they are fixed. You are not likely at this point to be over-paying your mortgage or underpaying your rent. Fixed monthly expenses are what they are: fixed. They remain the same from one month to the next.

And then there are those rascally variable monthly expenses. These areas require careful attention, and you must track your spending to make sure you are not spending more than you planned to spend. Do you have any latitude? Can you change your mind in the middle of the month and rework your plan? Sure, but only to the extent that spending does not exceed earning—and I do not mean future fantasy earnings or credit but money you have now.

Refigure, Replan for Next Month

At the end of the month, write next to each amount on your Spending Plan the amount you actually spent. Add up your columns. Figure out how close you came to planning your income for the month. Where did you miss, and where did you come in under the planned amount?

Using the results of your first monthly Spending Plan, create next month's Spending Plan. Enter your fixed monthly expenses. Easy. Now look at the variables. Get serious with yourself and decide exactly what you want your money to do in the coming month. Then just lay down the law and make sure that's exactly what it does!

Each month the process gets easier. Each month you will grow more accustomed to planning your spending. And each month it will get easier to say no to unplanned spending—to anything that will add debt or slow down your progress to get out of debt.

146

Monthly Spending Plan (November)

Spending Category	Week 1 Days 1–7		Week 2 Days 8–14		Week 3 Days 15–21		Week 4 Days 22–End		Total Plan to Spend	Total Actually Spent	Total <Over> or Under?
	Plan	Actual	Plan	Actual	Plan	Actual	Plan	Actual			
giving	300	300			300	300			600	600	0
saving (Contingency Fund)	300	300			300	300			600	600	0
Freedom Account					264	264			264	264	0
Rapid Debt-Repayment Plan			161	161			161	161	322	322	0
mortgage payment			600	600			600	600	1200	1200	0
car payment	145	145			145	145			290	290	0
gasoline	50	47	50	0	50	84	50	41	200	172	28
groceries	150	172	150	127	150	166	150	172	600	637	<37>
fast food and restaurants	25	18	50	65	25	22	50	72	150	177	<27>
electricity	75	84							75	84	<9>
water, refuse			35	35					35	35	0
gas							45	42	45	42	3
telephones (land, cell)			45	0			45	117	90	117	<27>
internet					15	15			15	15	0
cable TV					35	35			35	35	0
day care	200	200	200	200	200	200	200	200	800	800	0
kids' allowance	10	10	10	10	10	10	10	10	40	40	0
auto insurance			73	73					73	73	0
medication	25	22							25	22	3
newspapers							16	16	16	16	0
entertainment	50	31	50	0	50	65	50	20	200	116	84
miscellaneous	140	142	140	109	140	10	140	54	560	315	245
Total	$1,470	$1,471	$1,564	$1,380	$1,684	$1,616	$1,517	$1,505	$6,235	$5,972	$263

average net monthly income:	$6,000
amount plan to spend:	$6,235
total spent this month:	$5,972
<over> or under plan:	$263
<over> or under income:	$28

The Envelope Method

An option you may want to consider as you learn a new way to manage your money is the envelope method. As you may have guessed, this method uses ordinary envelopes—one for each spending category on your monthly Spending Plan. You cash your paycheck and divvy up the money among the envelopes as stated on the plan.

Now you spend from the envelopes, which you are not carrying around with you but are keeping in a very secret and safe place. When an envelope is empty, you don't spend any more on that category until the next fill-up.

You can either retain your regular household checking account for payments that must be mailed or buy money orders from the post office or other source. Yes, it is a pain, and it takes time to stand in line to buy a money order. But you cannot bounce a money order and you cannot overdraw an envelope. If you have demonstrated that you are not yet able to manage a regular checking account responsibly, you should consider the envelope method to help you grow up financially.

Managing Day to Day

Creating a monthly Spending Plan is one thing. Managing it, your Contingency Fund, your Rapid Debt-Repayment Plan, your Freedom Account, and your money too will be quite another. It can be overwhelming at first, not because any of this is unreasonable but because it is new.

In the beginning, you may feel overwhelmed as you move from your old ways of spending all you have and then using plastic to finish out the month. The transition period may be challenging, particularly if you are behind in your bills or facing expenses that are greater than the money you have to work with. While I cannot anticipate every possibility, I will tell you that you can do this. You can start with small steps (but please push yourself to the maximum effort possible). For example, if you simply cannot save and give 10 percent in the first month, give and save something. Make it 5 percent, then next month push it to 6, then 7, and so on.

You may be thinking that this sounds like way too much work. But living in debt is much more trouble. If you compare debt-proof living to the way you have been letting your money run wild, it is work. However, if you're reading this, it tells me you are looking for a better way. Compared to having no system, debt-proof living does require time and effort. However, you will see that the time and effort debt-proof living takes once you have your system up and running are minimal. Once you get things in order, the system will run so smoothly that you'll wonder how you ever got along before.

On Your Way to Financial Freedom

I wouldn't be surprised if you have a tiny headache by now. The fact that you are still with me shows your determination and commitment to take charge of your finances. Good for you. And now you deserve a little break from the present to visualize the future.

Imagine where you will be one year from today if you are diligent to follow the debt-proof living method you've learned to this point. You will have a respectable Contingency Fund, and you will be funding your own financial emergencies from your Freedom Account.

I'm going to project a few other things as well. Because you will have become a conscientious giver, you will be blessed in ways you cannot even imagine right now. I believe your income will have increased while your expenses will have decreased. You will be on your way to living financially free—the reason you picked up this book in the first place.

The day will come, and sooner than you think, when your Contingency Fund will reach the goal you have set. So you may be asking, "Can I stop saving money then?" No, never! Forever you must pay yourself 10 percent. It's part of your Spending Plan—part of your financial life now. And as you continue to save, you will move up the savings levels.

Savings Level 1: Contingency Fund

When you save money, you are building a wall of protection between you and the edge. The first level of your wall is your Contingency Fund. Every dollar you place in that account is another brick that will keep you from tumbling over the edge. And each time you dip into your Contingency Fund to cover emergencies, you have to replace the bricks. Every month, as your fund grows, you add more and more bricks to stand between you and financial crisis.

Once you have accumulated $10,000 (or your designated amount) in your Contingency Fund, you will stop contributing 10 percent of your net income to that account. It is time to move your savings to the next level.

Savings Level 2: Boost Your Freedom Account

Your Freedom Account has been up and running all along, but it's possible you have been funding only the first two or three subaccounts.

You will move to savings level 2 as soon as your Contingency Fund is at goal. In savings level 2, your 10 percent savings becomes an additional deposit into your Freedom Account to give it a second source of funding. You should stay at level 2 until each of the subaccounts in your Freedom Account is funded adequately up to one year in advance.

If, for example, your property taxes are $3,000 a year, you would want a balance of at least $3,000 in that subaccount. Likewise, your Christmas or holiday subaccount should have a balance equal to what you intend to spend on that in the coming year.

In savings level 2, you get the opportunity to fund all the sub-accounts you have designed but that may have been inactive because you were unable to increase your monthly contribution to include them. Once you reach the fully funded goal, you are ready to move on.

Savings Level 3: Finish Your Rapid Debt-Repayment Plan

At savings level 3, your 10 percent savings should go to speed the process of getting debt-free, so it becomes a second source of funding for your Rapid Debt-Repayment Plan. For example, if your 10 percent savings is $400 a month and your regular monthly RDRP payment is $339, once you enter savings level 3, you put $739 toward your Rapid Debt-Repayment Plan. Now you're cookin' with gas, my friend!

Once you complete your RDRP and you are debt-free, you go right on to savings level 4.

Savings Level 4: Investment Portfolio

By the time you reach savings level 4, you will have your Contingency Fund in place, your Freedom Account will be fully funded for at least one year in advance (imagine how wonderful that will be!), and you will be free of all unsecured debt. Wow, you made it! And now the fun begins.

In savings level 4, you begin building wealth for yourself, your family, and your future and retirement. You have so many options at this level. For example, with your 10 percent savings you can:

- accumulate a down payment to buy a house, or . . .
- prepay the principal on your present mortgage(s) so you can own your home sooner and not have to pay a ton of interest on that mortgage, or . . .
- start building an investment portfolio of stocks, bonds, and mutual funds, or . . .

- create a combination plan in which you are both prepaying your mortgage and investing

Savings level 4 is where you will be for the rest of your income-producing life.

Frequently Asked Questions

Q: Nice theory, but I need 100 percent of my paycheck just to get by. I cannot save 10 percent. What should I do?

A: Saving 10 percent of your income is the goal. If you can't start with 10 percent, start with 5 percent. Still can't do it? Even if it's $5 a week, that's enough to get your Contingency Fund up and running. Now start reducing your expenses dramatically until your lifestyle fits within 80 percent of your income. You will discover soon enough that saving is addictive, and I mean that in a good way. It becomes a habit that brings you contentment and a sense of joy and purpose.

Q: I can't do both, so which should I work on first, a Contingency Fund or a Freedom Account?

A: You can do both if you start out small. It costs nothing to set up your Freedom Account. Prepare the subaccount pages and determine the monthly deposit required for each. This exercise will clear the fog and give you a boost because you are taking steps in the right direction. If you cannot begin funding both, the Contingency Fund should come first. As expenses come up that would normally be paid from your Freedom Account, it would be better to cover them from your Contingency Fund than to use credit. If you do this, you should quickly repay your Contingency Fund so you do not lose ground.

Q: I contribute to my employer's 401(k) retirement plan. Can I just make this my Contingency Fund?

A: No, because retirement accounts are not liquid in the sense that you can make arbitrary withdrawals. But that's only one problem. Cashing a retirement account can be very expensive because of the penalties and taxes. Your retirement account is really a frozen asset that is out of reach for now. If you cannot build a Contingency Fund under your current circumstances, consider reducing your 401(k) contributions temporarily to free up the money to build your Contingency Fund. It is so important to your financial freedom that I want you to consider it mandatory for you to do this.

Q: Isn't it dumb to let $10,000 sit in a bank when it could be invested in mutual funds or stocks and bonds?

A: No, not when you consider that this is primarily an emergency fund, not an investment. If you become suddenly unemployed, you want to have the funds available and intact. There are a variety of safe places to put your Contingency Fund where it is immediately available, safe, and still earning the highest rate of interest currently available.

Q: It does not make sense to me to put any of my money into a Contingency Fund while I am in debt and paying double-digit interest to credit card companies. Shouldn't I use all my available money to pay my debts first, then start saving?

A: If you do not have some kind of emergency fund, you'll be forced to use credit if your car breaks down or your water heater fails. If you keep following that pattern, you'll never get out of debt. If, on the other hand, you diligently build this wall of protection level by level, one brick at a time, you will be able to repay your debts quickly while building a Contingency Fund and a Freedom Account. You can keep your promise to incur no new debts and still keep your boat afloat. And you will be well on your way to reaching savings level 4.

10

Debt-Proof Your Attitude

Your Most Powerful Tool

You cannot tailor-make your situations in life, but you can tailor-make your attitude to fit those situations.

Zig Ziglar,
See You at the Top

Attitude, the way you respond to life and its circumstances, is more important than anything. It is more important than the past, than struggle or success, than education or experience. It is more important than how much money you have, how much you owe, what you would like to do, or where you would like to go.

While I have not seen them in person, I've seen pictures of the cables leading to the top of Half Dome in Yosemite National Park. Family and friends who have completed the climb tell me the final ascent up the sheer granite surface of that majestic landmass is by far the most challenging. The cables are there to make sure climbers reach the top safely and with a modicum of ease. However, I understand the term *ease* is terribly relative.

Once you begin the last leg of the journey and finally see the cables, you stand there, tilt your head to the sky, view the final hundred yards or so that lead to the top, and experience terror like you've never known. You realize you have no choice but to finish the trip.

At that moment, you are more thankful than you could ever imagine for the cables that will help you pull yourself to the top—not only to a spectacular view but also to the feeling of accomplishment the likes of which you cannot begin to fathom from your current vantage point.

We need to erect cables in our lives so that when we face the difficult climbs on the journey—and they will come, you can count on it—the cables we need to make it to the top will be there waiting to help us overcome our fears and self-defeating attitudes.

How to Overcome Quitting Points

All of us have faced quitting points in our lives—those times or situations that become so overwhelming or challenging that we simply quit. No matter what you call them—brick walls, insurmountable obstacles, complete surprises, or financial crises—if you don't erect cables ahead of time, you most likely will continue to give in to defeat.

Be Prepared

You can erect cables for your financial circumstances by memorizing a list of the reasons you will not give in to debt. If you drill them so deeply into your mind that you could repeat them in your sleep, you will be able to hang on to them when you feel weak and vulnerable. Here are some examples:

- I don't choose debt because it makes assumptions about the future.
- It is wrong for me to spend money I do not have.
- There is always a way out; I will not stop until I find it.
- When I step out in faith, I unleash God's power in my life.
- I trust even when I do not understand.
- I do the right thing even when I don't feel like it.
- This credit card company doesn't really care about me the way this glitzy brochure indicates; they are looking for a new sucker.

Crash Through

Another way you can erect cables is by identifying your unique quitting points and then figuring out how to crash through them. What past circumstances and situations caused you to throw in the towel and turn to credit as the easy way out? Perhaps it was Christmas or vacation or your fickle feelings of dissatisfaction when you saw what others had that you wanted.

Once you identify your quitting points, you can prepare to deal with them. You have to do this ahead of time, not at the moment you come face-to-face with the overwhelming desire to quit. People who set out to climb Half Dome are notified before they leave camp whether or not the cables are up for the summer season. Experienced hikers would never set out on that seventeen-mile trek without the assurance that the cables are in place and ready to go. Long before they need them, those hikers are already counting on the cables to be there when the going gets tough.

It takes practice to crash through your quitting points. Let's say you identify the holidays as a time when you are likely to give in to credit. Year after year, even though you say it will never happen again, you end up shopping with your credit cards, promising yet again that "this will be the last time ever." It's July or August and you've still not paid the bills from last year even though the gifts have been long forgotten and the season is but a foggy memory. The load of debt has become a pile of resentment and something you'd rather not think about. Now is the time to practice crashing through that quitting point, because next Christmas will be here before you know it.

Make a commitment way ahead of time as to how much cash you will spend and promise that you will not go over that amount. Spring or summer—when the holidays are not breathing down your neck and robbing you of your good sense—is the time to practice crashing through that quitting point. Anticipate, prepare, shop early. There are dozens of things you can do to get in shape for that particular quitting point.

Perhaps your quitting point (or that of someone you love) comes in monthly cycles—if you know what I mean. You have three weeks of every month to practice crashing through the difficult time you know is on its way. Anticipate those feelings of defeat and sadness. Practice rejecting attitudes of defeat and purposely replacing them with appropriate thoughts and behaviors. Know exactly what you will do even when you don't feel like it, when every emotion in you suggests that a trip to the mall—credit card in tow—will make you feel better. Gather all the determination you have to crash through the quitting point. Each time you do, it will get easier to do it the next time. Soon it will become a habit on which you rely, and then you will begin to experience tremendous progress.

Watch Your Attitude

We have the freedom to choose our attitude in any given circumstance. We can alter our lives and avoid quitting by changing our attitudes. That is an amazing concept and one that should fill you with confidence and joy.

When it comes to debt-proofing your life, I believe 10 percent is about the money you have and 90 percent is about your attitude toward it. How else could I possibly explain the amazing financial feats of people like Vikki and her husband, who not only survived but also thrived during a very difficult financial season. Here's their story:

After twenty-four years of service, my husband learned his job was in jeopardy. So we sat down and worked out a six-month plan. We lived by it religiously.

First, we took all the money from our regular savings account, which was enough to pay off two credit cards. We took those payments and added them to the next highest balance credit card bill and paid it in full in two months.

We tackled the next largest credit card bill. We increased its monthly payment by the amount we'd been paying toward the other bills each month plus $50 more, which we really didn't have to spare.

We did not go out to eat, to the movies, or rent videos. We altered our seams and hems to extend the life of our clothes. The adults went on a diet (we needed to shed some pounds along with the debt).

We went through our house and assessed every single belonging. If it hadn't been used in a year, it became part of our huge garage sale. We made $2,500, which we immediately paid toward the next credit card account.

We called the credit card company and asked them to lower the interest rate. They said no; we said adios. Then they agreed and lowered it to 7.9 percent for six months. Our big payment (plus $50 every month) began to make a huge impact.

On January 29, no more job. We also learned the same day there would be no unemployment benefits or child support from our granddaughter's parents. Wow. A triple whammy.

We sat down again and went over what was left to pay. At this time, excluding the mortgage, we still owed about $30,000. We were scared but decided we could do it.

We went through the house, garage, and attic again and purged. We had another garage sale. We made another $1,400, which was enough to pay off the last credit card.

The next debts in line were the doctor, dentist, and optician bills. We made arrangements to pay as much as we could on a weekly basis.

To our complete amazement, my husband got an unexpected severance package, so we paid off all our outstanding unsecured debts. We split the remaining amount into three: one-third into the checking account for monthly expenses, one-third into a contingency account, and one-third into savings.

On May 1 we were completely debt-free except for the house. We even paid past-due property taxes. We rolled the 401(k) account into an IRA. We closed all the credit card accounts (and will never, never have another one, by the way) and had three months' living expenses in the bank.

I reopened my home business, which generated food money. I used every trick in the book to get our grocery bill at rock bottom.

We made it. We stuck to our plan. We are debt-free, fat-free, and much, much wiser. We are patiently waiting and excited to know what our next employment opportunity will be.

We can learn so many lessons from Vikki's story, but I believe the most important is about attitude. She and her husband, upon learning that his employment situation was on shaky ground, had a choice. They could fall into a deep funk, or they could see this wake-up call as the opportunity to rise above their circumstances. They could plan a pity party complete with whining, blaming, complaining, and a long list of all the reasons they were doomed, or they could pick themselves up and make a plan for survival. They could quit, or they could keep going.

Out of all the possible reactions, this family chose happiness. Instead of labeling their situation a disaster, they turned their situation into a launching pad, and their positive attitudes became the fuel to ignite a season of financial accomplishment.

Don't Plan to Quit

When you keep credit cards with a just-in-case attitude, you are planning to quit. I have seen this happen many times. Someone will consolidate all their credit card balances into a new home equity loan (HEL) or put them on a new low-interest credit card, leaving the previous cards with a $0 balance. The problem? They keep those credit cards handy "just in case" or justify the available credit as a cushion if things get tight. As reasonable as that might sound, it is nothing but a sugarcoated plan to quit.

As long as you leave yourself escape routes, you may find it difficult to summon the strength, stamina, and courage to crash through your quitting points. Endurance is counter to our have-it-all-now culture, but it helps us build hope and the courage we need for those times when the situation appears impossible.

Stop Whining

When we find ourselves in challenging financial situations with our backs against the wall for any number of reasons, it is easy to default to victim status, which is often the first sign of quitting. Oh, how easy it is to start whining, blaming, and complaining. Although that does nothing but make the matter worse, for some reason resorting to self-pity is, in some sick way, comforting. Unfortunately, that attitude is also self-defeating and destructive.

As long as you see yourself as a victim, things will not change. Your attitude will bring you to your quitting point. You will never fix your problems if you blame others for your circumstances. Whatever your situation, regardless of the details, you are accountable. You are responsible.

You can either give in to your circumstances or rise above them. You can remain in your misery or climb out of that rut and look around. You can reward your whining, blaming, and self-pity with your full attention, or you can completely ignore yourself when you slip into that debilitating mode. You can choose thoughts that support your misery or those that lead you to action and a solution. You can keep living in denial, or you can find the courage to face the truth. You can dig your pit of despair a little deeper, or you can make the commitment to do whatever it takes to turn your financial life around. The choice is yours.

Debt-Proof Your Attitude

The single most significant decision you make on a daily basis is your choice of attitude. It's the difference between letting life happen to you and making it happen. Debt-proofing your attitude is the difference between letting your financial situation control your life and taking control of your finances.

Every morning when you wake up, you put on your attitude of the day, whether you do it consciously or simply by default to whatever your emotions hand you. Allowing your emotions to dictate your attitudes can be dangerous because emotions are fickle. They cannot be trusted. They will lie to you. That is why you consciously need to choose happiness, contentment, joy, optimism, trust, love, peace, and confidence while rejecting fear, denial, anxiety, pessimism, anger, and resentment.

Happiness is a choice. It has nothing to do with what you have. If you do not choose happiness, more money will just magnify who you already are. If you are bitter, more money will only intensify your bitterness. If you are greedy, more money will only make you even more self-centered and selfish.

If you choose to embrace your situation as an opportunity to experience God's power in your life, you will choose happiness.

You have to want what you already have or more will never be enough. Purposely choosing to be content is an important ingredient in debt-proofing your life.

Take Control of Your Mind

In the same way you can take control of your actions, you can control your thoughts.

162

You cannot allow your feelings to guide your actions—particularly your financial decisions—or you will spend your life on an emotional roller coaster. If you make your financial decisions based on what feels good, watch out.

The way to take control of your mind is to choose good thoughts and positive attitudes and banish every thought and behavior that is contrary to them.

When I have difficulty falling asleep, it's usually because I have overwhelming thoughts racing through my mind. I've discovered a way to get rid of them. (Actually, this works well any time of day, not only as a way to get to sleep.) I visualize my thoughts written on a chalkboard. Just as quickly as those thoughts appear on the board, I start erasing.

Typically, I make one or two end-to-end passes on the chalkboard in my mind, and I'm either sound asleep or ready to replace those thoughts with what I know to be right and positive.

File this silly technique away in your anti-debt tool chest and reach for it whenever negative and destructive thinking begins to crowd in or when you are threatened by waves of desire. It really does work well.

Counter Destructive Attitudes

Let's say your neighbor just came home with a brand-new SUV. You are overwhelmed by feelings of desire and envy. There was a time when you would have begun immediately to find a way to get a new car too. But things are different now. You have a new set of values. You no longer make financial decisions impulsively. The car you have is paid for and meets your family's current needs. But still those feelings bubble up.

Just as soon as you recognize them, counter them. Replace those destructive attitudes with thoughts of your Freedom Account and the way you are committed to the cash purchase of your next vehicle. Think about not making huge monthly payments, not paying triple insurance premiums, not paying $400 for the annual registration fee, and not forking over $600 for that 50,000-mile tune-up.

A good way to counter negative attitudes is to replace them quickly with positive ones. Here are some examples:

- I never have enough money. I am so thankful for a regular paycheck.
- It's not my fault. Even though I wasn't 100 percent to blame, I take full responsibility—I will find a way through!
- This is too difficult. This is challenging!
- I work hard, so I'm entitled to have what I want. I work too hard to let money leak out of my life.
- I want it now! Waiting builds my character.
- Maybe I'll win the lottery. I'd rather save that $2 (or $10) a week than throw it away on the lottery.
- It won't matter just this once. Even the little things add up.
- If only I had more money, then everything would be okay. More money is not the answer—managing well what I have is the secret to having more.
- If I didn't have to worry about money I'd be happy. I choose to be happy regardless of my present circumstances.
- I'll never get out of this mess. I can do all things because God strengthens me.
- They wouldn't give me the credit if they didn't think I can handle it. I have the confidence to make my own financial decisions.

Build Your Offense

I'm not much of a sports enthusiast, but I do know that the best defense is a good offense. I can't think of a better way to describe this matter of debt-proof living. You dare not wait for a surprise attack by some overwhelming desire to go back to your old way of living. You need to build your offense ahead of time so you have it handy as a defense and a prevention.

Slippery places are situations, events, or locations where you could easily trip and fall, financially speaking. For example, you might be at the mall, where you could easily slip into an old habit of shopping mindlessly and running up a lot of debt before you take time to analyze what's going on.

As you debt-proof your attitude, you need to identify your slippery places and then devise a counterattack—a specific behavior to counteract the potential negative effect on your commitment to debt-proof your life.

I have identified lots of slippery places in my life. I realized early on that there were some behaviors I could eliminate from my life. For others, like going to the grocery store and department stores, I've come up with alternatives to my thinking as well as purposeful behaviors that help keep me from falling.

You want an example, don't you? Okay, I will tell you. I engage in self-talk. I sit myself down and give myself a little talking to. "Do you really need it?" Then I make myself answer honestly. Sometimes it's yes, but most of the time I have to admit it's a no, which kinda puts an end to the whole thing.

Mail order catalogs are one of my most slippery places. I can need absolutely nothing, pick up Renovation Hardware's newest and greatest catalog, and in the time it takes to flip a few pages have about 157 urgent and critical needs. My original antidote for this slippery place was quite gentle. I made a deal that as long as I followed a few new rules, I could "shop" to my heart's content.

As I went through a catalog, I allowed myself to order anything and everything I wanted. I would fill out the order forms for all the items I just could not live without, including the order numbers, color codes, sizes, prices, shipping and handling, and tax. Once I came up with the total, I would write that amount on the outside of the return envelope, indicating the amount of the check I needed to enclose. I would also write the mailing date—one week in the future. The deal was that I could order whatever I wanted as long as I waited a full seven days and I could pass a simple test: I had to remember everything I ordered without opening and reading the order form.

It makes me laugh to admit that all the times I did this, never once did I carry through. I would either forget about the order altogether and find it months later or fail my test of remembering what in the world I had wanted. Clearly, my joy was in the shopping, not in actually acquiring all that stuff.

Curiously, the exercise was so tedious, the rules so confining, that my catalog problem has all but disappeared. Now I go through my mail next to a recycling bin and toss the catalogs without even a glance.

This technique works for online shopping as well. I can load up an online shopping cart so fast it would make your head spin. I make a note of the total charges, then vow to return in a week to finish the purchase. But I don't. It almost makes me laugh to think of all the shopping I get out of my system without suffering the financial consequences.

Jump-Start Your Attitude

Getting off to a good start in the morning sets the tone for the whole day. There are lots of ways to select your attitude before one selects you. Read a verse from the book of Psalms or Proverbs first thing in the morning. Ask God to renew your mind. If you have access to the internet, log on to my website at DebtProofLiving .com. I log on every day to share what's going on in my mind. We can help each other with our attitudes.

Come up with your own unique attitude starters. Make a list so you can refer to them often. Here are some ideas:

- Today I am grateful for . . .
- The small sacrifices I will make today pale in comparison to the more worthy goal ahead.
- Today is the tomorrow I worried about yesterday, and all is well!

- Nothing can happen today that God and I can't handle together.

Keep an Arsenal of Alternative Activities

I'm the first to admit that spending money is a lot of fun. It feels great to buy all kinds of stuff and pretend that money is no object. It's particularly enjoyable to spend someone else's money—the way it feels when you use a credit card instead of cash.

When I was going through particularly challenging times while getting out of debt, I purposely came up with alternative activities that didn't have such negative consequences, activities I could do instead of shopping whenever that urge came over me, activities that were at least as, if not more, pleasurable. My alternative activity of choice has become—you're going to laugh—ironing. I am not kidding, and I cannot believe I am actually admitting this.

I have an unusual respect for textiles, and I thoroughly enjoy ironing them. For me, there is something soothing about the sound of a good steam iron gliding over high-quality cotton or linen. I find the activity to be calming and pure joy. I love how ironing offers instant gratification. I enjoy how ugly wrinkles simply disappear under the weight and steam of an iron and with them whatever urge I had to spend my brains out on stuff I probably don't need and will not likely remember once I unplug the iron and go on about my day. When my old defeating attitudes and destructive thoughts start to crowd my mind and insist that I throw caution to the wind in favor of an all-out shopping binge, I often iron instead. It works for me.

You would do well to come up with your own arsenal of alternative activities so that when you get the urge to go back to your old ways you'll be able to deal with it quickly, logically, and responsibly.

Choose to See Things in a Different Way

Of all the techniques to debt-proof your attitude, this might be the most difficult but also the most rewarding: choose to see things in a different way. It is difficult because you may have to confront attitudes and beliefs you've had all your life.

Some years ago my husband, Harold, and I desperately wanted off the car-leasing treadmill. We'd repaid our unsecured debts, and we wanted to free ourselves from car payments.

We'd been leasing cars, two at a time, for far too many years. But how to stop? Each time a lease ended, we had no money for a down payment on another car. We always owed more than the car was worth (because of over-mileage penalties and the like), so we did what any typical car salesman recommends today. We "rolled over" any remaining balance into new leases on bigger and better cars—models that elevated our minimum standard ever higher. But finally we said, "Enough! No more leases!"

Our plan to get out was drastic. With the cash we had—$4,000— we would buy the best car we could find for that amount, and we would continue saving to buy a second car with cash. In the meantime, we would become a one-car couple. This was possible since we share an office and followed each other to work anyway.

Understand that for more than twenty years we'd always supported two late-model, high-end, leased vehicles. Every marketing campaign's dream consumer, I had bought into the myth that I was what I drove. Having my own car gave me freedom and spontaneity. But for now, we would share.

The best we could find for the money we had was a 1986 Chevrolet El Camino. At the time it was nine years old—a major step down as far as I was concerned. I consoled myself, however, in the temporary nature of the situation and that it was worth the trade-off: no more car payments!

I tried to hide just how miserable I was. After all, for twenty-two years I had driven my own car. I hadn't needed to check with anyone or ask permission. Now I had to ask my husband to drop me off or ask to use the car. I hated the feeling of dependence and my loss of freedom. I wanted to control the radio and decide when to get in the fast lane. I wanted to select the parking space. All my little quirks and control issues didn't have an outlet. Now I had to compromise, but mostly it felt like I had to give in.

After about three months of this miserable arrangement, it came down to this: I could either change my attitude or go stark-raving mad. Choosing the former (mental institutions are expensive), I sat down for a heart-to-heart talk with myself.

I said, Oprah has a driver. She never concerns herself with mundane things like parking spaces, pumping gas, car washes, and oil changes. Her driver takes care of everything. You too have a driver. You no longer have to concern yourself with mundane things like parking spaces, pumping gas, car washes, and oil changes. Your driver takes care of everything. You can talk or sleep; you can listen to music or read. Your driver is always available and makes your transportation needs his top priority. What's not to love about this?

I then moved to the financial ramifications of not having a car of my own: no car payment, no additional insurance, no annual registration and licensing fees, no biannual smog inspection (California thing), no maintenance and repair on a second car, no worrying about parking tickets for forgetting to move it on street-sweeping days, four less tires to replace, fifty-two less car washes each year. The list got longer and longer, and my conclusion was clear: I am a blessed woman.

My attitude changed in a heartbeat, and it remains that way to this day, by choice. We are still a single-car couple, and I do not want now, nor can I ever imagine wanting, the responsibility or expense of owning a second car. It works for us.

One of the most powerful debt-proofing tools you have at your disposal is your attitude. It can become your best ally or your worst enemy. You hold all the cards. It's up to you.

11

You Deserve Some Credit

Credit Reports, Credit Scores, Credit Repair, and Credit Counseling

> Although it's true that improper use of credit can be disastrous, credit properly used can enhance your life.
>
> Liz Pulliam Weston,
> *Your Credit Score*

f the mention of a credit report

a. makes your blood run cold,

b. produces heart palpitations,

c. causes profuse sweating of the palms, or

d. gives you an overwhelming urge to skip this chapter . . .

congratulations! You are perfectly normal. Most of us would prefer just about anything to a face-to-face encounter with our credit report.

Many people are so afraid to know what's in their credit report that they choose denial over reality. As long as they don't know for sure what's really in that file, the possibility remains that it's not that bad.

Many people simply do not understand what a credit report is, that they really have one, where it is, who can look at it, or why it matters.

Some naively trust the supreme credit bureau in the sky to have their best interests at heart. These folks believe that, because they pay their bills on time, their credit report is automatically a mirror image of such exemplary behavior.

Unfortunately, in this electronic age, opting out of the credit reporting system is not a possibility. We have to learn how to make it work most effectively for us.

Having credit and being creditworthy are not synonymous with having debt or being in debt. Credit is a good thing; debt is not. When it comes to your personal credit, if you prepare and prevent, you won't have to repair and repent.

Credit Reports

To understand a credit report, you must first know about a credit reporting agency (CRA), also known as a credit bureau. A CRA is a profit-making company that gathers, compiles, and analyzes credit information about individuals and then offers it to banks, mortgage lenders, credit unions, credit card companies, landlords, and employers so they can determine the creditworthiness of a customer. There are hundreds of them, but the big three are Equifax, Experian, and TransUnion.

Every adult has a credit report (also called a credit file from pre-computer days when credit information was actually stored in file folders). Think of yours as a rap sheet containing information that may or may not be true. Compiled by a credit bureau from information received from untold sources, your report is a list of allegations others have made about the way you conduct all aspects of your life, which could include things that are not of a financial nature (i.e., judgments, tax liens, and other matters of public record).

Whether you are married, separated, divorced, or single, your credit file should contain information about you only. Information about others, including your spouse, will appear only where that person is legally obligated with you on an account.

You should review your credit report at least once each year. By law, you are entitled to receive one free credit report from each of the big three CRAs each year, provided you order your credit reports from AnnualCreditReport.com. This is your opportunity to assess their contents, to make sure there are no discrepancies, and to determine if the information is factual. If you find something wrong, you have the right to dispute it. Instructions on how to file a dispute will be included with the report. While each credit bureau produces a different style of report, Experian's is the most user-friendly.

Credit bureaus are allowed (but not required) by law to report your negative information to potential creditors and others who want to know about you. The result of that can be devastating, all the way from unreasonably high interest rates to losing out on a great apartment or job to being turned down for insurance coverage.

While it might feel like those ugly blemishes will remain forever, they cannot. The law provides for specific time limits.

Bankruptcies. Up to ten years from the date of the last activity on the bankruptcy filing. Bankruptcy is the single worst thing you can do to your report.

Past-due accounts, charge-offs, collections, tax liens, judgments, and lawsuits. Up to seven years from the date of entry even if the damage is reversed or the account is brought current and/or paid off, which should also appear on the report.

Inquiries. Up to two years from the date of inquiry.

Exception. All negative information, including bankruptcies, lawsuits, paid tax liens, accounts sent for collection, and criminal records, will show up indefinitely in the future under these conditions: when you apply for $150,000 or more of credit or insurance or if you apply for a job with an annual income of at least $75,000 and your potential employer pulls a credit report.

Credit Scores

Fair Isaac Corporation tightly controls the technology that weighs different factors found in a person's credit report. The result is a three-digit number known as your credit score. In the same way you have dozens or more credit reports out there somewhere, you have many credit scores as well. The FICO score, which ranges from 300 to 850, is the one that most lenders use and the one you should care about. It tells a lender, landlord, or insurer the statistical chances he has of getting repaid should he choose to do business with you.

Fair Isaac licenses its highly secret technology to the CRAs, who then add their own programs and statistical data to produce customized credit scores under names such as Beacon, Empirica, and Scorecard. While credit scoring is not regulated or standardized, one thing everyone agrees on is that the higher the score, the lower the lender's risk.

It is difficult to say what's a good or bad score since CRAs have different criteria and lenders have different standards for how much risk they will accept. A credit score that one lender considers satisfactory may be regarded as unsatisfactory by other lenders for comparable situations.

A credit score is like taking a snapshot at a moment in time. Once the shutter clicks, that exact picture cannot be duplicated. Your credit score is calculated by taking a snapshot of your credit history plus all contributing factors at a single moment. It does not reflect an average, nor will it be the same tomorrow. Your credit score is a fluid number—it's always fluctuating. When a score is requested, the computer determines the score, reports it, and then forgets it. You could request your score from all three CRAs and MyFico.com on the same day, get four different scores, repeat the process tomorrow, and get another set of scores that could be altogether different.

Why You Should Care

Credit scoring is no longer just for determining what interest rate you will pay on your car loan. It is seeping into many areas of life. Insurance companies use it to determine risk and set premiums, landlords use credit scores to evaluate potential tenants, and employers use credit scores in the application process as a character reference.

A credit score to some people shows the way you take care of important things in your life. The problem is that people with bad or even mediocre scores wind up paying disproportionately higher and even burdensome rates.

Contributing Factors

Fair Isaac technology considers many factors when determining a credit score, some of which are kept secret. These are the fifteen factors they've disclosed:

1. payment history
2. amounts owed
3. length of credit history
4. pattern of credit use
5. types of credit in use
6. utilization rate
7. how long at current address
8. debt-to-income ratio

9. late payments

10. income

11. age

12. occupation

13. type of residence

14. how long you've had the same phone number

15. recent inquiries

Utilization Rate

Expressed as a percentage, this is the ratio between your available credit and the amount of that credit that you are using at any given moment. For example, if your credit limit is $2,500 and you have an outstanding balance of $250, you are using 10 percent of your available credit. In this case, your utilization rate would be 10 percent. In the world of credit scoring, the lower the utilization rate, the better. Generally, to maintain a good credit score, one's utilization rate should never be higher than 30 percent.

Reason Codes

Credit scores come with reason codes for why the score was not higher. Reason codes vary from one CRA to another, but these appear to be the most common:

- Your credit card balances are too close to the limit.
- You have too many accounts.
- You don't have enough accounts.
- Your accounts are too new.
- You don't have a "healthy mix" of accounts.
- You've had too many inquiries.
- You are unstable.

How to Get Your Score

Every CRA has its unique score to sell to you. Remember, you can get free copies of your credit report every twelve months, but not your credit score. You must pay for that. As I said earlier, most lenders who will be considering your score use the FICO score issued by the Fair Isaac Corporation. Therefore, if you are going to check your credit score, I suggest you check FICO because it is the one most widely accepted and respected. Simply go to MyFico .com to obtain a copy of your credit score.

Every adult has his or her own score. Potential lenders will average the scores of a married couple applying for credit.

What You Can Do to Improve Your Score

If you have a low score, you should take a look at your credit report to make sure it contains no erroneous negative information. If the information is negative but true, unfortunately, you will just have to ride it out. From here on out, make certain you pay your bills on time, stop applying for new credit, and pay down the credit you have.

Don't go crazy trying to get a perfect score. If you can stay around 760, you will be just fine.

Credit Repair

You cannot change the information in your credit report if it is true. However, if there are errors, you have every right to correct them. I would not recommend that you hire a service to do this. Credit repair companies are notorious for being shady at best. This is something you can do yourself.

The first step in repairing your credit report is to know exactly what's in it. Don't assume everything in it is correct. Nearly 70 percent of all credit reports contain some piece of information that is incorrect, obsolete, or no longer verifiable. Federal law gives you the right to challenge that information, no matter how serious or minor, through a process called disputing.

It is very important that you follow these strict guidelines when disputing any item in your credit report:

1. Make a detailed list of the items you believe to be false, inaccurate, incomplete, or obsolete.
2. Complete a request for reinvestigation dispute form and return it to the CRA that issued the report.
3. If you do not receive a response within six weeks, send a follow-up letter.
4. Keep excellent records and a good paper trail.

If after review you cannot prevail in having the item removed from your credit report, you have the right to submit your side of the story, provided it does not exceed one hundred words. This explanation will stay on your credit report until you ask for it to be removed. Anyone having access to your report will be able to read it.

How important could a one-hundred-word explanation be to a potential employer, mortgage lender, or landlord? It's impossible to know for sure, but it can't hurt.

Credit Counseling

Credit counseling is a service that helps people in serious financial peril avoid bankruptcy. Credit counseling is not charity; it is an industry.

Reputable credit counseling firms are nonprofit organizations, a designation that can be confusing. "Nonprofit" does not mean the company is run by volunteers and is not allowed to make money. On the contrary, nonprofit organizations can operate very much like a for-profit corporation. They can charge for their services and build up millions of dollars in cash reserves. They can pay handsome salaries, and their executives can drive fancy company cars and operate out of luxurious offices. They can advertise and participate in slick marketing campaigns.

Credit counseling is intervention in the form of confidential counseling and negotiation with the client's creditors in an attempt to freeze penalties, reduce interest, and create a monthly debt repayment plan that is mutually beneficial to all involved.

Counseling can also include help with rent and mortgage issues, transportation needs, student loans, and bill paying. Some counseling organizations offer educational programs to help their clients learn how to manage their money well, live within their means, and embark on the road to financial recovery with an excellent chance for success.

Creditor-approved repayment plans are administered through the counselor's debt-management program (DMP). While enrolled in the DMP, the client makes a single payment each month to the counseling organization, which then distributes payments to each of the creditors.

Credit counseling is a severe remedy. It is not the right choice for everyone. Effective as it can be, credit counseling is not a clever way to reduce high interest rates. Think of credit counseling as chemotherapy—it offers an excellent chance for recovery but is certainly not a treatment you would choose if you had any other choice.

To consider credit counseling, you need to be experiencing some or all of the following: You have past-due bills, you cannot make the minimum payments on your credit card accounts, you are borrowing from one card to pay another card, you are using credit for necessities such as groceries and gasoline, you have a damaged credit report, creditors are calling, and you have an overall feeling of despair.

Credit counseling itself typically won't hurt your FICO score, the one most used by lenders. The scoring model sees any mention of "counseling" as a neutral entry. It neither hurts nor helps your score. However, the way a potential lender, landlord, or insurer sees credit counseling as it relates to the risk they may take with you cannot be predicted.

You can get an excellent overview of what credit counseling is all about by visiting the website of the National Foundation for Credit Counseling (NFCC) at NFCC.org.

Debt Negotiation

Debt negotiation involves cutting a deal with a creditor to make a one-time cash payment that is considerably less than the amount owed.

Debt negotiation is not a regulated profession, so there are no rules. Anyone can call himself a debt negotiator. Most debt negotiators require their clients to deposit huge sums into their equally unregulated company "trust accounts" before negotiations can commence. There are no guarantees. And the horror stories I've heard from well-meaning people who thought they could beat their debts would break your heart.

If by some stroke of luck you can negotiate with a creditor to accept less than the principal balance in exchange for calling the debt forgiven, don't think it's over for you yet. The law requires that creditor to report the amount you did not pay back to the IRS as ordinary income. You will owe taxes on it upon your next filing.

Debt negotiation is so problematic that it should be seen as a last resort, and only after you've given reputable credit counseling your very best effort.

12

You Are Worth What You Saved

Discover Your Net Worth

Financial security may be a long way off but as you begin to take control of your financial future, you'll find that many rewards accompany the sacrifices along the way.

Jonathan Pond,
Your Money Matters

There's a basic rule of life that goes like this: Before you can get where you want to go, you need to know where you are.

The most beautiful road map with all the scenic routes and best views clearly marked can be perfectly accurate, but if you can't pinpoint your current location, it's not going to do you a bit of good.

In the previous chapters, we've worked hard to create your financial road map. We started with the principles and values. We outlined and developed the basic elements. It's a beautiful map, if I do say so myself. But until you have a good sense of where you

181

are in relation to the "map," you'll have difficulty staying on course and measuring your progress.

A simple device will tell you exactly where you are today and will also serve as a measuring device so you'll be able to gauge your progess in the months to come.

The Net Worth Statement

A net worth statement is a document that tells the difference between the value of what you owe and what you own.

A net worth statement shows your financial condition at a certain point in time. It shows how much money would be left right now if everything you own was converted into cash and used to pay off all that you owe.

Your net worth statement is an important tool because it helps you:

- check and measure your financial progress and how you are doing with reaching your financial goals
- make decisions about acquiring assets and taking on liabilities in the future
- estimate how well-off your family would be if you were suddenly taken from them
- determine your need for life and property insurance
- estimate what your income will be during your retirement

A net worth statement does not care about income. In fact, there is not even a place to record your annual salary. A net worth statement doesn't care how much you spend on food, clothes, or education.

What your statement reveals is how much of your hard-earned income you have been able to hang on to. It confirms the belief that it doesn't really matter how much money you make. You are worth what you save, not what you make. What matters is what you do with your money.

A net worth statement contains two categories: assets and liabilities—what you own and what you owe. When you deduct what you owe from what you own, the result is your net worth.

Assets

Your assets are your material possessions—everything from cash to investments, clothes to cars. Even those things you are in the process of paying off and do not yet own outright are considered assets.

Assets are divided into two categories: appreciating assets and depreciating assets. Appreciating assets are things you own that become more valuable over time. Everything else is depreciating.

Investments such as retirement accounts and stock market holdings are considered appreciating assets because they have the likelihood of increasing in value over time. Savings and cash come under the heading of appreciating assets, as does real estate. Certain collectibles appreciate, but be careful here. You want market confirmation of the values you set for your appreciating assets. You may believe your Beanie Baby collection is worth a lot more than what you could realistically sell it for next weekend.

Depreciating assets lose or decrease in value over time. Clothes, furniture, cars, boats, and electronics fall into this category.

On your net worth statement, list each of your appreciating assets and a corresponding value. For example, if your home would sell for $200,000 on today's market, list your home as $200,000 under your appreciating assets. This is also where you will include the current value of your retirement accounts, certificates, stocks, bonds, and mutual fund shares. Use actual cash figures for cash on hand and in checking and savings accounts.

Include money owed to you as an asset but only if you are certain of repayment. For example, if you lent $1,000 to a friend at 8 percent interest and he has already repaid $300, enter $700 under appreciating assets. Do not include potential interest you will earn.

To find the current value of your investments, look for market quotes in a current newspaper or check the day's financial markets online. You can get the current day's value for each of the stocks and mutual funds you own by simply typing in the ticker symbol, which you can also look up online. Various websites, Yahoo Finance, for example (http://www.finance.yahoo.com), let you track your portfolio values. Of course, if you have an online account like eTrade, it's all done for you.

Other possessions such as cars, big screen TVs, boats, clothes, and household goods are depreciating assets because they are becoming less valuable with time. Unless your car is a rare collector's item (in which case it would be an appreciating asset), it is worth less today than it was yesterday. In fact, if you bought it new, it was worth 20 percent less the day after you bought it due to depreciation.

It is customary to group assets into categories such as real estate or personal property, which would include your clothes and household goods. Some experts suggest an estimate of $10,000 current market value for personal property including furniture, clothes, tools, and all other household items of a typical two-adult household. You may wish to use that figure or determine your own. If you have a lot of valuable furniture, jewelry, or collectibles, you can list them separately.

Liabilities

When it comes to a net worth statement, debt is debt. We make no differentiation between secured and unsecured debt. Any amount you owe another person or entity is accounted for under liabilities. These are obligations such as mortgages, home equity loans, car loans, automobile leases, student loans, personal loans, court-mandated child support (up to one year's worth), leases, and contracts for things such as wireless devices and gym memberships—anything for which you have an obligation to pay. Following is a net worth statement showing both assets and liabilities. The example compares two nonconsecutive years for illustration only. You should prepare a net worth statement at least annually.

A Net Worth Statement

	As of July 31, 2010	As of July 31, 2014
Assets—Appreciating		
cash in checking account(s)	12	1,808
savings account	0	10,000
401(k) and IRAs	804	2,765
house on Elm St.	132,000	175,000
stocks, bonds, funds	0	575
antique grand piano	12,000	15,000
Total Appreciating Assets	$144,816	$205,148
Assets—Depreciating		
personal property	10,000	10,000
2009 Chevy truck	24,000	16,000
2004 Subaru	4,000	1,000
jet ski	2,300	750
Total Depreciating Assets	$40,300	$27,750
Total Assets	$185,116	$232,898
Liabilities		
home mortgage	122,000	112,000
home equity loan	0	5,000
student loans	32,000	30,000
credit card balances	18,900	2,000
loan from parents	4,000	0
past-due utility bills	223	0
jet ski	745	0
doctors	1,900	0
hospitals	545	0
truck loan	23,000	17,000
Total Liabilities	$203,313	$166,000
Net Worth	-$18,197	$66,898

Net Worth

Subtract your total liabilities from your total assets. The result is your current net worth.

Your net worth tells a story. It doesn't lie; it doesn't deceive. The last number, the bottom line, reveals how much of your income you've managed to keep. If that is a negative number, you've managed to spend more than you've earned, relying on credit to fill in the gap. Or you can think of it this way: You've been spending all you earned plus a lot you haven't even earned yet.

What you see on your net worth statement is your financial condition as of today. If you are discouraged by what you see, let me encourage you. You have control over this situation. As helpless or hopeless as you may feel right now, the truth is that this is a picture you can change beginning now.

Take another look at your net worth statement. Focus on one of your debts, like a credit card debt. Imagine that you will reduce that balance by $5 when you send your payment tomorrow. That will immediately increase your net worth by $5. Five dollars here, 10 dollars there is the way to get on board with changing your financial picture.

Perhaps the most important thing you can learn from this chapter is this: Reducing debt increases net worth dollar for dollar. A repaid debt is a good investment.

Your Assignment

Just as soon as practical, prepare your net worth statement. Do this work as accurately as possible. Inflating assets or conveniently excluding liabilities only hurts you. You need to know where you are so that you will be able to measure how you are doing as you begin to debt-proof your life.

You will be creating a benchmark against which to measure your progress. That will have a positive effect on your determination to become a better caretaker of your money. It is going to be exciting to plot your financial growth each year or, for the more diligent types, each quarter or month. Even your smallest efforts to repay debt and save money are going to get your attention when they will show up in black and white.

13

The Proper Handling of Hazardous Materials

Credit Cards, Charge Cards, and Debit Cards

> Yep, I love credit cards. Properly handled, they can ease your way through life. Improperly handled, they can ruin your financial life.
>
> Howard Strong,
> *What Every Credit Card User Needs to Know*

Many things we live with, rely on, and enjoy—things such as automobiles, prescription drugs, pesticides, and candles—are intrinsically dangerous. They have the potential to harm. We would be horribly misguided if we didn't take necessary precautions to prevent potential disaster. But that doesn't mean they should be banished from our lives. Instead, we learn how to handle them properly and then take extra precautions so we don't hurt ourselves and those around us.

We don't let kids play with matches. We keep highly flammable items stored safely and choose not to decorate the Christmas tree with lighted candles. We wear seat belts, obey traffic laws, stay on the right side of the highway, and teach our kids to be defensive drivers. We lock up prescription drugs and keep harmful pesticides and cleaning products out of the reach of children.

The same is true of "plastic"—credit, charge, and debit cards. They can be highly dangerous if handled carelessly or very useful tools when we treat them appropriately and with respect.

Every adult, or family, needs one good, all-purpose, well-chosen, and equally well-managed credit card—to be handled with all the care of a highly dangerous yet powerful tool. With that privilege comes the responsibility to know and fully understand everything about the consumer credit industry and how to play its game. We need to know why the industry exists, how it functions, the designs it has on us and every member of our families, and the ways we can use that industry to our advantage.

I do not advise living completely plastic-less. That is not realistic these days. Have you tried to buy an airplane ticket or rent a car with that roll of twenty-dollar bills in your pocket? It's almost impossible.

A credit card, by federal law, provides a number of benefits to you as a consumer. It will protect you if you use it to order something by mail, phone, or online and the item does not show up, for example. Used wisely, this tool will give you interest-free credit just long enough to transfer funds to pay a bill or get reimbursed for business expenses. But consumer credit is serious business, something that should not be considered lightly. Like a rope, you can use it to help you, or you can turn it into a noose and hang yourself. I intend to help you use it as a tool.

Why Consumer Credit Companies Exist

All consumer credit companies—whether they offer credit, charge, or debit cards—exist for a simple purpose, and it's time we get it out in the open. They are in it for the money! There is nothing wrong with that. I am quite fond of the capitalistic, free-enterprise system myself. Still, I want to arm you with the knowledge you need to make the choice that is right for you so you can participate in this industry in a reasoned way. Then, if the powerful industry snatches a lot of your hard-earned money, you will at least know that it happened by your choice, not theirs.

Three Types of Plastic

Basically, there are three types of plastic available: credit cards, charge cards, and debit cards.

Credit cards. A credit card creates high-interest loans by allowing the cardholder to buy now and pay later, over time, with small monthly payments. Generally, there is no annual fee for a credit card, and the interest is waived if the entire balance owed is paid during the grace period.

Charge cards. This plastic carries no provision for incurring debt because it requires the cardholder to pay the balance in full each billing period. A charge card is a pay-as-you-go device, and many require an annual fee. American Express is one example of a charge card, although the company has added related accounts that allow for a revolving, interest-accruing credit balance. Charge cards are pretty much disappearing because, sadly, most people use plastic because they don't have enough money to pay for things in cash and it's unlikely they'll be in any better shape a month from now when the bill comes due. A charge card requires that the entire balance be paid down to $0 each billing cycle.

Debit cards. A debit card looks much like a credit card but offers electronic access to your bank account. A debit card often doubles as an automatic teller machine (ATM) card. It is not a credit device. Your usage is not reported to the CRAs. When a purchase is made, the purchase amount is deducted as if a check had been cleared against the account.

While any one of these three choices of plastic fulfills the basic need for electronic access to funds, there are pros and cons for all three. The decision of which is best for you will depend greatly on your specific situation and lifestyle. Your needs may change with time as your financial picture changes. It is important that you know the differences among the three, the strengths of each, as well as the pitfalls.

Credit Cards

Of the three types of plastic, the credit card is by far the most widely used. More advertising and marketing schemes are devoted to credit cards, and that makes them the most complicated and difficult to manage.

More people are tripped up by credit cards than by any other type of plastic. Still, the credit card offers the wise consumer the best deal possible—all the benefits of plastic without any of the costs. To achieve that end, however, you must become adept at nibbling the bait without getting hooked.

If you—now or in the past—have had a consumer debt problem, most likely the culprit was this slick invention known as the credit card. There is a high price attached to the so-called convenience of having things now and paying for them later. According to US Courts.gov,[1] there were close to 1.3 million personal bankruptcy filings in 2012, 90 percent of which were the result of excessive credit card debt. Still, the average American receives twenty credit card offers each year.

The Credit Game

When you signed that credit card application and accepted a credit card—or two or ten?—you agreed to participate in a kind of game. It is a one-on-one competition in which your opponent writes the rules. You even agreed that he could change those rules at will. Worse, your competitor isn't interested in helping you learn how to play the game. He prefers that you remain ignorant—always paying, never questioning. Consumer ignorance drives the consumer credit industry.

The only way you can turn the tables and win the credit card game is to level the playing field. First, you have to figure out what the rules are, find out what's in your opponent's game book, and then develop your own winning strategy.

A credit card company's goal is to develop each of its cardholders into a "revolver" (industry lingo for someone who carries a balance from month to month). The company's success is found when it can get consumers hooked on credit and over their heads in debt. Credit card companies reluctantly tolerate those of us they call "deadbeats"—cardholders who always pay their balances in full and do not pay interest and fees. The practice of letting deadbeats off scot-free, however, is showing early signs of disappearing. Several companies are testing an annual deadbeat fee of $25 to $35 for cardholders who are not carrying their weight. There goes the no-fee feature if this practice is allowed to take hold.

Unfortunately, most credit card holders live in a fantasy world, choosing to believe the following credit card myths:

- Credit card companies want to make my life better.
- Consumer credit is a socially acceptable way to bridge the gap between my inadequate income and the amount of money I need to live on.
- The credit card company would not give me a credit limit I could not afford.
- My credit limit is my money. I'm entitled to spend it any way I choose.
- I trust the company to deal fairly with me, so I don't need to understand the terms and conditions of my credit card account.

- An increase in my credit limit is a reward for good behavior. It's a merit increase.
- It is not possible to live without consumer credit.

The Ideal Customer

Credit card companies are always looking to develop and add excellent customers. Their ideal customer is one who:

- has a perpetually revolving balance and considers that monthly payment an ordinary and necessary expense
- carries a balance that is higher than he could reasonably repay in a single month
- makes only the minimum required payment each month
- always pays on time
- accepts and then spends up to credit limit increases

No matter your debt-proof living level, whether you are in the process of getting debt-free or you are in full prevention mode, you must think of a credit card as a loaded gun—it is good to have when you need it but not something you should treat casually. You don't make false moves, act recklessly, or treat it lightly. It is something that commands your respect.

Debt-proof living strategies are rigid when it comes to the care and use of a credit card. There's no latitude if you intend to play the game and always win. Follow the rules without compromise and your credit card will enhance your life without out-of-pocket expense. Slip up and you'll find yourself in a lot of financial trouble.

The DPL Rules of the Game

You need one good all-purpose credit card. The card you choose should meet the following criteria:

- *No annual fee.* You should not have to pay a fee to use a credit card.

- *Twenty-five-day grace period.* This is the time between when you use the card to rent a car, secure a hotel room, or place an online order and when interest begins to accrue. It is important to note that if you carry a balance from one month to the next, you forfeit the twenty-five-day grace period. Interest begins to accrue immediately on any new purchases added to that card.

- *Wide acceptance.* The card you choose should be one that is accepted in most places.

- *Low interest.* While it is your intent never to pay interest on a credit card because you will be paying the balance, if any, in full during the grace period, sometimes things happen. If you do pay interest, you want it to be as little as possible.

If you use a credit card, ideally you will never pay fees or interest. Therefore, the interest rate will be lower in priority when selecting a good all-purpose credit card. Most likely the card you select will be either a Visa or a MasterCard since these are accepted in the greatest number of places.

If you have multiple credit cards on which you carry balances, do not cancel those accounts at this time. The company could increase your interest rate to the maximum or even require that you pay the entire balance now. You do not want to run those risks.

Instead of closing a card you will no longer use but on which you carry a balance, close it "emotionally." Put the card away in a place you will not have easy access to. Or go ahead and cut it up into pieces—whatever it takes for you to stop using it! When you have paid the balance in full, make a determination based on the credit score information in chapter 11 on whether to close the account. You need to keep that healthy gap between your total available credit and the total credit balances you are carrying, if any.

Once you are completely free of consumer debt, closing all but your one all-purpose credit card on which you never carry a balance or even come close to the limit during your grace period will likely improve your credit score, not lower it. Just keep in mind that closing multiple credit cards at the same time could do a number on your credit score, and not in a good way! A more reasonable way is to close one every six to eight months.

What You Need to Know

If you are now, or once were, a well-established revolver, you have been targeted by the industry as a very desirable customer. You will continue to receive unsolicited invitations, preapproved applications, and prequalified credit card offerings in the mail. There are probably three in your mailbox right now.

Every credit card account operates according to specific terms and conditions. Some of these are disclosed at the time you complete the application; others are written on the monthly statement. Never forget that what the big print giveth the small print taketh away, and that is true of both the application and the monthly statement.

If you don't fully understand everything or information is missing, call customer service. Here's a rundown of what you need to know about your credit card account:

- annual percentage rate (APR)
- monthly interest rate (punishment for late payment)
- punishment fee for going over limit
- grace period guidelines
- fees for cash advances
- balance transfer guidelines
- billing method basis
- statement closing date

Once you know the rules and the consequences of breaking them, you'll be less likely to slip up. You'll find a way never to incur late or over-limit fees and learn how to pay the least interest possible—hopefully none. Read your statement carefully every month. Scrutinize every square millimeter, and question any charge or entry you do not understand.

Take Control of the Credit Limit

It is potentially dangerous to have a credit limit of an amount more than you could reasonably repay in a single month. However, given the way you must play the credit score game, it is likely you will want a larger limit as needed to achieve a consistently low utilization rate.

It is important to note that large amounts of available credit (not debt but available credit) appearing in your credit report can be seen as a negative because potential lenders look at not only how much debt you have but also how much you could incur in a short period of time. You always have to be aware of the delicate balance you must maintain between available credit and outstanding balances, available credit and income level to ensure a good credit score of 760 or greater.

Leave Home without It

This rule applies particularly to those who are still paying off unsecured debt and those who are newly debt-free. Going back to living on credit can be so tempting at times that just carrying the card can present an overwhelming temptation to use it. Instead, keep it in a safe place—a bank deposit box or home safe. You can even freeze it in a block of ice—any place that it is safe from you.

As an alternative to carrying the card, record the number, expiration date, and toll-free number of the company (you will find this on the back of the card) in your address book or wallet. If you have a true emergency, you have what you need to get authorization by phone.

A Word of Warning

Never use a credit card to buy something because you do not have the money right then to pay for it. The credit card industry desperately wants you to adopt this mentality. For them, this is the way to huge profit margins; for you, it is financially deadly.

They want you to make the purchase today on impulse and then find you cannot pay for it within the grace period. They know (and can prove it statistically) that if you don't have the money today, you are not likely to have it twenty-five days from now. Even if you do, once you have put that must-have purchase on credit, statistics show that you are less likely to use your cash to pay for the purchase, choosing instead to roll it over.

Let's say you are absolutely sure beyond a reasonable doubt that you will have the money and that you will use it to pay for this purchase you're about to put on credit. Great. So what's the rush? Force yourself to wait the few days until you do have the money. As a bonus, you'll give yourself the gift of time—time to think and time possibly to change your mind.

Don't Be Late

Just because you mailed your payment on time doesn't mean it won't be late. Take Capital One, for example, where sorting the mail is no simple task. According to Bankrate.com, the Virginia-based credit card issuer sorts and processes anywhere from 100,000 to 600,000 customer payments each day. It takes about three hundred employees and a number of machines to make it happen.[2]

There are any number of things that can happen to delay your check on its journey to being processed the day it is received—if it is received. Remember, you are depending on something called the mail to get your payment to the processing center. Only after a payment is physically posted to an account is it no longer considered "in the mail." Being late will mean a double whammy: you will have to pay interest and the late fee. It will be a triple whammy if the interest plus the late fee plus the balance puts you over your credit limit. Then you'll get socked with an over-limit fee as well.

Setting up electronic bill pay, where your bills are paid directly from your bank account, or auto bill pay, where you give a one-time authorization and then don't have to worry about whether your payment is made on time, is a great way to stay out of trouble. It's safe, convenient, and cost effective. Just think of all the postage you won't have to pay if you go electronic.

Pay Early

If you carry a balance, making your monthly payment early in the billing cycle (even before the stated due date on the billing statement) will save you money. Why? Because most credit card issuers use the average daily balance method to figure monthly interest or finance charges.

That means the big computer at your credit card company records your current balance at the end of every day in the month. Then on the last day of the billing cycle, it adds the balances for the previous thirty days and divides by thirty to get the average daily balance. That is the figure upon which you pay interest.

What Difference Does It Make to Pay Early?

Date	Activity	Balance	Date	Activity	Balance
4/1/2013		2,500	4/1/2013		2,500
4/2/2013		2,500	4/2/2013	$400 payment	2,100
4/3/2013		2,500	4/3/2013		2,100
4/4/2013	$32 purchase	2,532	4/4/2013		2,100
4/5/2013		2,532	4/5/2013		2,100
4/6/2013		2,532	4/6/2013		2,100
4/7/2013	$117 purchase	2,649	4/7/2013		2,100

Date	Activity	Balance	Date	Activity	Balance
4/8/2013		2,649	4/8/2013		2,100
4/9/2013		2,649	4/9/2013		2,100
4/10/2013	$52 purchase	2,701	4/10/2013		2,100
4/11/2013		2,701	4/11/2013		2,100
4/12/2013		2,701	4/12/2013		2,100
4/13/2013		2,701	4/13/2013		2,100
4/14/2013		2,701	4/14/2013		2,100
4/15/2013		2,701	4/15/2013		2,100
4/16/2013		2,701	4/16/2013		2,100
4/17/2013		2,701	4/17/2013		2,100
4/18/2013		2,701	4/18/2013		2,100
4/19/2013		2,701	4/19/2013		2,100
4/20/2013		2,701	4/20/2013	$32 purchase	2,132
4/21/2013		2,701	4/21/2013		2,132
4/22/2013		2,701	4/22/2013		2,132
4/23/2013		2,701	4/23/2013	$117 purchase	2,249
4/24/2013		2,701	4/24/2013		2,249
4/25/2013		2,701	4/25/2013		2,249
4/26/2013		2,701	4/26/2013	$52 purchase	2,301
4/27/2013		2,701	4/27/2013		2,301
4/28/2013		2,701	4/28/2013		2,301
4/29/2013	$400 payment	2,301	4/29/2013		2,301
4/30/2013		2,301	4/30/2013		2,301

Total Daily Balances: $78,964
$78,964 ÷ 30 = $2,632 avg. daily balance
$2,632 x .015 = $39.48 interest due
New Balance: **$2,340.48**

Total Daily Balances: $64,948
$64,948 ÷ 30 = $2,165 avg. daily balance
$2,165 x .015 = $32.47 interest due
New Balance: **$2,333.47**

Notes: previous balance $2,500; annual interest rate 18%; monthly interest rate 1.5%

The schedule on the left side of the illustration shows the $400 payment being made at the end of the billing cycle, just before the due date. Payment is made on time. The schedule on the right side shows the same beginning balance and monthly activity, but the timing is reversed—payment is made early in the billing cycle with purchases delayed until the end of the cycle. That immediately reduces the average daily balance, so more of the payment goes toward the principal.

There are two reasons you should get into the habit of paying credit card bills early. First, you will avoid incurring horrendous penalties for being late if there are mail delays, and second, you'll pay less interest so more of your payment goes to reduce the principal.

Don't Fall from Grace

Many credit card issuers are nibbling away at interest-free grace periods. If you do not carry a balance from month to month but depend on those interest-free days, a change from a twenty-five-day to a twenty-day grace period could be very expensive. Some companies are doing away with grace periods altogether. That means that even if you pay in full, the clock starts ticking the minute you make a purchase.

Death to Cash Advances

Interest rates on cash advances can be very steep (27 to 33 percent, sometimes more), plus there's an outrageous cash-advance fee. There is no grace period on cash advances, so the company begins charging interest the day the money is taken out. Taking into account the high interest plus the horrible fees, some issuers are effectively charging more than 30 percent for cash advances. That is ludicrous. What's worse, most issuers now reserve the right to allocate a customer's payment toward any portion of the balance with lower APRs. That means if you take a cash advance, it will continue accruing big interest until you get the lower APR balances paid in full. Don't even think about cash advances on a credit card.

Watch the Mail

Credit card companies reserve the right not only to write the rules but also to change them whenever they like. Even if you have a fixed rate of interest, the law allows the card issuer to change the terms—including the interest rate—with only fifteen days' notice. That notice may arrive on a postcard or a scrap of paper in your monthly statement. The only thing "fixed" means is that the interest rate is not tied to an index the way variable-rate cards are.

Always read your statement each month because this is where you will likely be notified of a change. Another reason to watch the mail: Your account could be sold to another company, which means you will have to abide by a new set of terms and conditions, perhaps even a different interest rate and method of determining minimum monthly payments. You will be notified, but you might think it's junk mail. If you don't like being sold like a slab of meat, make a call to the new customer service department (the number is given in your notification). You won't be able to change card issuers, but you can put up a fuss and possibly negotiate new terms at least equal to those you had prior to the sale.

Know Where You Are

The worst thing you can do with a credit card is lose track of what you've spent and how much you owe. If you use a card (may I say that it would be better if you didn't), get into the habit of recording every transaction the same way you record checks that you write. You've spent the money, so write your credit purchases in your checkbook as if you wrote a check for that amount. Include the exact amount of the purchase and deduct it from your bank balance.

Take a look at the checkbook register of one of my newsletter readers. Frank sent this to me to show me how he treats credit card purchases. Whether he writes a check or makes a credit card purchase, he records the item and deducts the full amount from his current balance.

Check #	Date	Transaction Description	Payment	Deposit	Balance
101	5/1/2013	electric co.	65.38		1,184.62
Visa	5/1/2013	gasoline co.	13.60		1,171.02
Visa	5/2/2013	store no. 1	35.88		1,135.14
102	5/3/2013	telephone co.	19.00		1,116.14
103	5/4/2013	cable co.	25.00		1,091.14
Visa	5/4/2013	clothing co.	76.00		1,015.14
Visa	5/5/2013	store no. 2	15.75		999.39
104	5/6/2013	water co.	35.00		964.39
Visa	5/7/2013	vitamin store	61.20		903.19
Visa	5/8/2013	computer store	56.00		847.19
Visa	5/10/2013	gasoline co.	12.95		834.24
105	5/10/2013	church	100.00		734.24
Visa	5/13/2013	car repair	75.10		659.14
Visa	5/13/2013	Visa Total		346.48	1,005.62
106	5/13/2013	Visa Statement/ Balance	346.48		659.14
107	5/15/2013	cash	100.00		559.14
Visa	5/17/2013	gasoline co.	13.75		545.39
	5/18/2013	paycheck		800.00	1,345.39
Visa	5/20/2013	airline	175.00		1,170.39

When Frank receives his monthly credit card statement, he matches it to his checkbook. In this example, Frank verified that the eight purchase amounts totaled $346.48—the exact amount his card company said he owed for the month.

Notice that on May 13, after he made sure all the transactions he was charged were correct, he wrote "Visa Total" and entered $346.48 as a credit. He had to do this reverse action so that when he paid the Visa bill in full by writing check 106, he didn't end up deducting his credit card purchases twice (simply a debit/credit function required to make everything balance).

Of course, when Frank receives his monthly checking account statement, he will need to ignore all Visa entries—both debits and credits—he's made to manage his credit card use, but that should be simple to do. Then he can reconcile his bank statement without a problem.

There's something important about writing down credit card transactions as they occur. It's called reality and keeps you from slipping into denial.

Specialty Credit Cards

Among the hundreds of credit cards available, there are two specific types we need to discuss: affinity cards and rewards cards. Both types of cards usually require annual fees, and that pretty much puts them out of the running to qualify as the one good all-purpose piece of plastic you need to own.

Affinity cards. Affinity cards are marketed to a group of customers with a common bond, such as membership in an organization. You might have a credit card issued by your college alma mater for example. Typically, a small portion—emphasis on the word *small*—of the fees you pay to the credit card company for your affinity card goes back to the organization. You are not going to find a no-annual-fee affinity card. If you justify the fee by saying you are supporting the organization, you are really fooling yourself. You'd be better off to stick with a no-fee card and send the organization a donation occasionally.

Rewards cards. These are probably the most misunderstood of all credit cards. Consumers are often willing to pay annual fees and make frequent use of the card because they believe they are getting paid to do so. The most popular of the rewards cards is Discover card, which has no annual fee and rebates 1 percent of annual purchases. Here are my objections to the Discover card method.

First, Discover is not a card I would classify as being accepted in most places, so it doesn't meet that criteria of an all-purpose piece of plastic. Second, if 1 percent of your annual purchases is significant, you need to rethink why you are putting so much stuff on a credit card throughout the year. Statistics prove that you will spend at least 23 percent more simply because you have the credit card mentality when it comes to paying for things.

The second most popular rewards card is one that earns frequent flyer miles. Cards that earn miles almost always charge a significant annual fee of $50 to $85 or more. Here's the problem. You get one mile for each dollar you charge to your credit card. It takes a minimum of 25,000 miles to get one round-trip airplane ticket, and even that comes with a lot of restrictions. You have to put $25,000 of purchases on this single credit card to get enough miles to do anything with them. That means each dollar you charge on that card is worth one cent toward a plane ticket. By that calculation, one round-trip ticket is worth $250. That's a pile of required charging just to get a $250 benefit (remember, you had to pay at least $50 just to get the credit card), and that's assuming you will rack up $25,000 in credit card purchases in a twelve-month period. The companies involved know for certain you will tend to justify charging in order to collect miles.

Another problem is that often the miles expire—you don't have an unlimited time frame in which to redeem them. This is a marketing ploy designed to create a sense of urgency. Of course, each situation varies, but typically the miles expire after two or three years. The cardholder who is paying $50 to get something for nothing now must also charge at a high rate in order to collect enough points to turn this rebate fiasco into something useful.

I recommend that unless you earn miles by traveling a lot in addition to putting the cost of said travel on the rewards card (meaning you travel at least 50,000 miles a year on the same airline), you are far better off to go with a no-fee, non-reward card and then shop for good airfare deals when you do want to travel.

The rewards card industry is growing and changing on a daily basis. Just remember that when all the smoke clears, the reason for the rewards plan is to increase the credit-granting company's bottom line—not yours. They are not in business to give you free gasoline or free plane tickets or a rebate check at the end of the year. They are in business to turn a huge profit, and if returning a minuscule portion to the customer is the way to do it, that's exactly what they'll do. It is not reasonable to think these companies would give away more than they receive.

If, in spite of everything, you are able to make a rewards program work for you, and you are not incurring debt to get the rewards (it can be done—I've seen it from time to time), bless you. Just remember that the company is banking heavily on the statistics that say one day you'll charge more than you can repay in a single month, and then they'll cheer because they have you as an interest-paying customer.

Charge Cards

A charge card differs from a credit card in the following ways:

- There is no stated spending limit.
- The balance, if any, must be paid in full within thirty or sixty days, depending on the charge card (which can be thought of as interest-free credit). There is no rollover privilege or opportunity for debt on a charge card.
- There is an annual fee of $55 to $300, depending on the card.

Because of the strict limitations, a charge card is simple. You charge; you pay in full when the statement arrives. It's difficult to play games with a charge card. Without a purchasing limit, one might fear going nuts in the first month or two and spending beyond one's ability to pay in full. If that happens, which surprisingly is not that common, it won't happen again. The card will be canceled, and the cardholder will quickly learn a difficult lesson.

One drawback with a charge card is the lack of choices. American Express charge cards, Chase Ink Bold business, and Diners Club are becoming relatively rare among American consumers today.

Another drawback is the fact that American Express is still not accepted as widely as Visa or MasterCard.

Debit Cards

Debit cards are issued by your bank and are tied to your bank account. Most debit cards double as an ATM card, and banks have gone to great lengths to replace all generic ATM cards with Visa- and MasterCard-branded debit cards. It is to the bank's or credit union's advantage to have its customers swiping debit cards all over town. They want to become involved in every consumer purchase, not just the larger ones that consumers have been trained to pay for with a credit card. Debit cards allow banks, credit unions, Visa, and MasterCard to get in on the little purchases too, provided they can train their customers to use the debit card for those smaller purchases.

Swipe fees cost merchants, who must pay the debit card's issuing bank. But in the end, it's the consumers who pay when merchants raise prices to cover swipe fees. New legislation (as I write, some laws are pending while others have been recently enacted) means that banks are making less off retailers (12 cents per swipe instead of 21 cents), but they'll turn to consumers to make up for it. Think more expensive bank accounts, higher debit card fees, and higher minimum balances.

Two Ways a Debit Card Works

There are two types of debit transactions, and both are housed in the same card. Your old ATM card limited you to online, also known as PIN-based, transactions at some gas stations and grocery stores that had PIN machines where you would punch in your secret code. Then, as if by magic, a new debit card showed up in the mail with either a Visa or MasterCard logo on it and you discovered you could use it to buy things just about anywhere that Visa and MasterCard were accepted.

If you have a debit card with a Visa or MasterCard logo on it (and if things are not confusing enough already, Visa calls it both an ATM card and a Visa check card, and MasterCard calls it a MasterMoney card), there are two types of transactions you can make with it: debit (PIN-based) and credit (signature-based).

When paying for a purchase, the clerk will ask, "Debit or credit?" When you reply, "Debit," it becomes a PIN-based transaction. You are required to enter your personal identification number (PIN) after the card has been swiped. With PIN transactions, funds are withdrawn from your checking account immediately at the time of the transaction. When you reply, "Credit," it becomes a signature-based transaction. Signature transactions do not require your PIN, but you must sign a slip to accept the transaction.

With signature transactions, funds are held in your checking account until the transaction posts to your account in one to three days. The only thing a signature-based transaction (the one that happens if you reply "credit" when using a debit card) has to do with credit is that it is processed in the same batch of transactions as those made with credit cards.

Banks are pushing the use of debit cards because the transactions are cheap to process. It costs a bank five times more to process a paper check than a debit card transaction. As banks convert customers to debit cards, they reap huge profits on overhead savings alone.

Merchants love debit cards too. Even though they pay a fee every time a card is swiped, they do so willingly because they know a customer who shops with plastic impulsively spends more than one using old-fashioned cash or even a checkbook.

A Visa- or MasterCard-branded debit card looks just like a credit card and works like one wherever those cards are accepted. The merchant or retailer does not know the difference. You can purchase an airline ticket with a debit card provided you have the cash in the bank to cover the purchase. A debit card will also work to rent a car at most places with this specific warning: The agency is going to place a hold on the account for at least $500. This means you will not be able to go below this amount in your checking account until your rental car tab is settled. That could ruin your trip and cause a lot of checks to bounce if you've not properly prepared.

A debit card differs in several significant ways from its cousins, the credit and charge cards.

There is no annual charge for a debit card; however, some banks charge various use fees. Be sure to check the details of all charges and fees should you select a debit card as your plastic of choice.

Unlike a credit card or charge card, a debit card does not enjoy the same protection against theft or fraudulent use. With a debit card, you are responsible for a maximum of $50, provided you report the loss or fraudulent charges within two to four days. If you wait longer, you could be responsible for up to $500. If you don't notice anything wrong until after sixty days, the total of your loss would be your responsibility. These provisions seem to vary from card to card, which only adds to the confusion. Check with your own issuer to learn the specifics of your fraud protection, if any.

Debit Card Hazards

There is a hidden danger with a debit card that has the potential of wiping out its benefits: Banks do a hard sell for an overdraft protection feature when a debit card is attached to a checking account. This protection provides that in the event the account holder overdraws the account, the overdraft is automatically covered by a draw against a line of credit. Of course, the bank makes this sound like wonderful protection for the account holder. While it will prevent the embarrassment of bouncing a check, it is a sneaky way to get the customer to incur debt.

Overdraft protection does not simply cover the exact amount of the overdraw. Rather, the bank dumps money into the account in increments of, say, $200. Because this is actually a cash advance, interest accrues immediately and at a hefty rate. Plus, the penalty fees for overdraft protection can be significant.

Suppose you have $150 in your checking account. You find a terrific sale the same day you have haircut appointments for the family. You swipe your debit card a couple of times to the tune of $151 for the day. What's a buck? you reason (if you even realize what you've done). That is not, however, the way the big computer in the sky looks at your misdeed. Without flinching, your overdraft protection feature sends $100 to your account, and you begin paying interest at that moment on the entire $100, not just the $1 you needed to stay above water. Considering the fees, interest, and the possibility that you'll go ahead and spend the rest of the $100 rather than pay it back immediately, that could be the most expensive $1 you ever spent.

Human nature being what it is, most people will not immediately go through the steps necessary to pay back the entire $100. Believe me, financial institutions count heavily on human nature. I have actually received letters from people who swear they have no unsecured debt, all the while failing to see the $4,000 balance on their overdraft protection account as exactly that: a pile of debt! I can only conclude that overdraft protection has some kind of virtuous ring to it, and consumers pride themselves on paying dearly for this kind of insurance.

Some banks now allow customers to overdraw their accounts using an ATM machine. The machine knows you have no money in your account; however, it is set to allow you to make a withdrawal, and the moment you do, you are slapped with an overdraft penalty—and without notification.

The Trouble with Debit Cards

True or false? A Visa or MasterCard logo on your debit card means you have the same consumer protection as you do with a credit card. If you answered true, you are wrong. The basic difference between a credit card and a debit card is in the way it works, not the way it appears (remember, debit cards are designed to mimic credit cards in appearance). This is important, so read it carefully.

If the money comes directly out of your bank account each time you use the card, it's a debit card. If you get a monthly statement from your issuing bank listing your transactions and showing how much you owe, it is a credit card.

Credit cards are regulated under the Fair Credit Billing Act, a federal law that protects consumers against unscrupulous merchants and card thieves. Consumers can dispute charges and even refuse to pay if a merchant is unwilling to make good on its goods or services.

Debit cards, on the other hand, are regulated under the Electronic Funds Transfer Act, a weaker law that does not confer the same level of protection.

Some banks, and even the MasterCard and Visa organizations, offer consumer protection plans (for example, they will replace the money in your account if a thief somehow gets ahold of your PIN and steals money from you), but these are voluntary and can be withdrawn at any time. They are not required by law to do this. And debit cards do not carry other protections that credit cards must by law.

Let's say you buy an airline ticket. The airline goes bankrupt before you make the trip. If you paid with a credit card, your credit card issuer takes the hit and credits back to you the cost of the ticket because it failed to deliver to your satisfaction the goods or services you paid for with that credit card—not because they think you are such a great person and want to help you out but because they are required to by federal law.

But if you paid for that airline ticket with a debit card, you are out of luck. You paid for it with your money, so now it is you against the airline. Sure, you can file a claim through bankruptcy court and stand in line with all the airline's other creditors. But, believe me, you'll be way, way, way at the back of the line.

What if a crook gets your card? If it's a credit card, you're protected. You report the theft, your account is closed (the law says you pay the first $50, but most credit card issuers waive that), a new account is opened, and the theft—no matter how large—becomes the credit card company's problem.

But if your debit card gets into the hands of a crook, the entire contents of your bank account are at risk. If you notify the bank in a timely manner (the law says not later than two days), it must rectify the mistake or not charge you for withdrawals made by someone else. But here's the kicker: You must prove it wasn't you. That can be difficult if the perpetrator used your card number and PIN to clean you out. Or went on an online shopping bender.

The idea behind a debit card is a good one. It's a convenient way to pay without creating debt. But there are other ways to do that. Write a check, pay with cash, or in the case of a major purchase in which consumer protection may become an issue, use a credit card. Paying the balance in full to avoid going into debt will not forfeit your protection under the law.

If you feel you must have a debit card:

- Have your debit card account at a bank or credit union where you have no other accounts. Keep the balance low to limit your exposure to fraud.
- Watch your account closely and report any problem immediately. Remember, a thief doesn't need your card, only your name, address, card number, and expiration date to go on a shopping spree.
- Limit your debit card use to minor purchases such as groceries, gasoline, etc. Use a credit card for major purchases and anything that involves a promise to deliver such as an online transaction or a mail-order purchase. You'll be protected if something goes wrong.

The Right Plastic for You

Each type of plastic—credit cards, charge cards, and debit cards—has its own pros and cons when it comes to owning one good all-purpose piece of plastic. When making the decision, you should take into account your current and specific situation.

If you are not yet debt-free but are aggressively working on your Rapid Debt-Repayment Plan, you would probably be better off sticking with whatever you have until you become debt-free. At that time you can reassess your situation.

A charge card has a decided benefit for the person who carries no debt but feels insecure about inviting temptation. If you don't want to deal with the temptation and don't mind paying an annual fee to be freed from it, a charge card might be the best way for you to go.

It is possible to turn any credit card into a charge card provided you exercise the discipline outlined in this chapter's credit card rules. You must repay the entire balance, if any, during the grace period and never incur fees or interest. Exercise this kind of personal discipline and financial maturity, and you will have the best of both worlds: the benefits of plastic with no annual fee and no interest charges.

There was a time, and not that long ago, when I would have scoffed at the person purposely choosing to pay an annual fee for a charge card. From time to time, readers would write and tell me they carry an American Express card and willingly pay for it because it keeps them on the straight and narrow. The balance must be paid in full every month; there is no other option. My reply was always curt yet playful. For half the fee I'd be happy to babysit them and apply all the pressure needed to make them pay the balance in full during the grace period if they would switch to a no-fee credit card.

But things have changed drastically in the past few years. Credit card companies have pulled in all the slack. While in the past one could be even fifteen days late with a full-balance payment and not incur penalties, such a slipup today comes with a hefty late fee and interest on the full amount. Even the most straight-shooting consumer is human. Things happen. It is very easy to slip up and end up paying far more than the $55 annual fee on a charge card.

So I admit to having a change of heart. I believe that for many people the freedom from worry of a slipup might just warrant the fee required for a charge card. It certainly eliminates many hassles.

Debit cards are by far my least favorite type of plastic. The fraud protection is, at best, shaky. But beyond that, there is the temptation to use a debit card with a certain level of abandon—to purchase everything under the sun by swiping instead of writing a check or using cash. It becomes far too easy to empty your bank account than if you actually had to write out the checks and think about what you're doing. I would rather see you use a credit card or charge card as outlined above than to choose a debit card.

Obtaining Your Card

The following should help you locate whatever type of card you choose.

Credit cards. To find a current list of no-fee and low-interest credit cards, visit IndexCreditCards.com.

Charge cards. For an American Express Green Card ($0 introductory annual fee for the first year, then $95 a year), go to American Express.com. For Chase Ink Bold ($0 introductory annual fee for first year, then $95 a year), see creditcards.chase.com. Information on Diners Club (annual fee of $95 a year) can be found at Diners ClubUS.com. If you go with a charge card, select the American Express Green Card. Don't let your ego lead you astray into gold or platinum status. For no additional benefit, you will have to pay a much higher annual fee.

Debit cards. Contact your bank or credit union if you do not already have a Visa- or MasterCard-branded debit card but have decided this is the best choice for you. Treat your debit card with all the respect of a credit or charge card and you will not fall into the temptation of seeing it as easy access to your cash in the bank.

The Do-It-Yourself, Consumer-Protected, No-Fee, Hassle-Free, Totally Brilliant "Debit Card"

What if I told you there is a way you can have a fully functional debit card without any of the problems and hassles mentioned above. You'd say, "Mary, this is brilliant!" Well, get ready because that's exactly what I have for you.

Step 1. To do this, you need a credit card with a $0 balance. This should be a MasterCard or Visa that has no annual fee.

Step 2. Transfer money into this account. Do this by check or on-line as you would if you did have a balance and were simply sending in the money to pay it off. This will result in your account showing a credit balance. If you send in $500, you will see a credit balance of -$500 on your next statement or online when you check your account.

Step 3. When you shop online, at a store, or visit a restaurant— anywhere you normally depend on your debit card because the money comes straight out of your bank account—use this DIY "debit card" instead.

Step 4. In two or three days, the amount of your purchase will show up on your account as a charge. Your credit balance will be reduced by that amount with no fees or additional charges. If your purchase was for $3.73, your $500 credit balance will be reduced accordingly to $496.27.

Step 5. Watch your account as you would any account. If you see a fraudulent charge, you have all the protection of federal law that regulates credit cards. Call customer service.

Step 6. When your credit balance runs low, deposit additional funds.

Step 7. If you need to get your credit balance refunded, call customer service with your request. By law, they must send it to you in full within seven days of your request.

There you go. And, yes, it is brilliant.

14

Don't Jump from the Frying Pan into the Fire

Debt-Consolidation Loans

Consolidation won't make your debts magically disappear, but it can help you get a handle on them if you use it in the right way.

Gerri Detweiler,
Debt Collection Answers

Consolidating debts is being widely touted these days as a life preserver for those who are drowning in debt.

Here is the way debt consolidation is supposed to work. You add up the total of all your consumer debts (credit card accounts, installment and personal loans) and pay them off with the proceeds from a new loan—either a new credit card or a home equity loan—that has a lower interest rate and a monthly payment that is less than the total of the previous payments.

In theory, debt consolidation is a terrific solution for a burdensome debt situation because it shortens the time you stay in debt and reduces the associated costs. In practice, debt consolidation usually offers an express lane from the frying pan into the fire.

Debt consolidation does not refer to a single type of loan but rather to any plan whereby the lender hands you a lump sum of money to pay off your smaller loans, leaving you with one single debt. A debt-consolidation loan can be either secured or unsecured. It can be a new credit card onto which you transfer all the outstanding balances from your other credit cards; a home equity loan; a loan from a retirement account, such as a 401(k); a new loan from a finance company; or a personal loan from a friend or family member.

Debt consolidation is not a panacea. On the contrary, it often represents a much more costly and eventually difficult situation than the problem it was supposed to relieve. I am not at all thrilled with the whole idea of debt consolidation for the following reasons.

Debt Consolidation Represents a Detour

Of course, there are occasional exceptions, but for the most part, debt consolidation represents at best a lateral move. It doesn't pay down debt but only moves it around. It makes your debt situation more comfortable, but it doesn't put you any closer to getting rid of the debt. Many times it does just the opposite—it reduces the payment but extends the payback time so far into the future that the debt grows considerably because of the interest that piles up.

I received a letter from Michele, who wrote with a question on debt consolidation. It seems she and her husband have a $25,000 home equity loan at a whopping 15 percent interest and a $3,900 signature loan at 23 percent with the same household finance company. She explained that the interest rates are so high because when they took out these loans years ago, their credit history was, shall we say, less than pristine.

She went on to say that the lender approached them with a pre-approved offer to combine both loans into one new loan at a fixed rate of 13 percent, extending the payoff time to twenty years. The lender was even willing to increase the loan to give them a little breathing room or take that well-deserved vacation or add on to the house. She wanted to know if this was a good deal, since the monthly payment would drop considerably.

Before I even looked at a single number, I had my suspicions. I don't believe there is a lender on the face of the earth who would approach a current customer with an offer for a new loan deal that wasn't in the financial interest of the lender. What lender would volunteer to rewrite or consolidate debt if it benefited only the borrower?

That fact alone should be a clear signal that someone is about to go for a ride. Then add on the fact that the lender wants to lend even more money to this family, and you can see the proverbial handwriting on the wall.

After reaching into the tool chest at my website, DebtProof Living.com, and pulling out the loan comparison calculator, I was able to come up with comparative figures the lender didn't happen to mention to Michele.

I learned that given their current loans and payment schedule, they would pay $31,951 in interest on the home equity loan and $1,264 in interest on the signature loan, or a total of $33,215. The proposed consolidation loan, on the other hand, would, over twenty years, require interest of $52,360. The lender stands to increase his profit by more than $19,000 in this deal. Clearly, if Michele were to fall for this, she would be taking a major detour on her journey to becoming debt-free by tapping into her home's equity and paying even more interest.

Debt Consolidation Prevents Personal Growth

When we keep putting Band-Aids on difficult financial situations, it is nearly impossible for us to learn the tough lessons about what got us to this point in the first place. For example, if you have ten credit cards, all of which are maxed out, and you transfer those balances to a new credit card that promises a lower monthly payment, you have in fact told yourself that new debt is the solution for old debt. That's wrong. The solution for old debt is to discover what prompted the situation to escalate to this point and then to do whatever it takes to repay the debt—not simply move it around to a more comfortable position.

Debt Consolidation Has a Doubling Effect

If you've ever lost ten pounds and gained back twenty, you'll easily recognize this danger.

Consolidation is a good theory. Transfer all your credit card balances with high interest rates to a single new credit card with a lower rate of interest. Your one monthly payment is now lower than the total of all your individual credit card payments. However, this is when the trouble begins.

If you are like most people, you look at the credit cards that now have zero balances and you feel a certain sense of delight. You're quite proud of yourself because it feels like you're debt-free (you aren't really, but you enjoy pretending). You know for sure that you will never use those cards again (yeah, right), but do you close the accounts? No. You think that just in case you have some unforeseen emergency it would be nice to have the financial cushion these credit lines represent. You also reason that if you close them and then end up needing them in the future, you'll have to reapply and go through that needless hassle. (I know you well, don't I? That's because I know myself.) You may even feel a bit like a savvy financial counselor as you instruct yourself to put the cards in a safe place so the balances will all remain at zero.

The truth is that regardless of whether those cards are in your wallet or stashed in the bottom of a vault in another city, available credit will haunt you. In the beginning, you'll be terrified that you will have a reason to use some of it. Unfortunately, the feeling will go away quickly.

Before you know it, an "emergency" will show up, and that will be the beginning of the end. It is a strange thing how the availability of credit creates emergencies. And it does so in record time, particularly if you don't have clear and concise personal criteria in place for what constitutes an emergency.

I can't begin to tell you how many people I've heard from over the years who did the credit-card-balance-transfer thing—or took out a home equity loan to pay off all their credit card balances—and managed to get those credit card balances back up to their all-time high. And then they had double the debt to contend with—the consolidation loan plus all the credit card accounts.

When looking at a debt-consolidation loan, you cannot focus all your attention on the monthly payment. It is quite likely that while the monthly payment is less, the interest rate will be higher and the payoff time longer. You must look at the big picture, comparing the total amount of interest to be paid as well as all terms and conditions.

So is there ever a time when a debt-consolidation loan would be in order? Theoretically, yes. However, it is becoming more and more difficult to make it work—not only because of our weak human nature but also because of the credit industry. By the looks of the average person's mailbox, low-interest credit card deals are quite plentiful. But don't be fooled; carefully read all the terms and peruse each and every bit of fine print before you decide to apply.

Even the low-interest, fixed-rate cards are not all they appear to be. First, the interest rate may be fixed but only for a specific period of time. What happens at the end of the first year? If the rate climbs significantly or then becomes a variable rate tied to an index, watch out. Other offerings have very attractive interest rates and terms, but you need to pay careful attention to their penalties for paying late. Many deals provide that if you are late even one time during the introductory period (and that means missing the deadline by even five minutes), the rate immediately shoots up five or six percentage points. If you make that mistake twice, the rate on some of the more popular deals can go to 29.99 percent or higher. Clearly, that kind of deal makes a beneficial consolidation attempt nearly impossible.

If you are able to find a better deal and you can qualify to consolidate your debts in a less costly account—and you've done your homework and understand every aspect of the deal—make sure you cut up all the other credit cards as you pay them off. Even though you have "closed" the accounts as far as using them is concerned, they will be reported to the CRAs as having zero balances. Many open lines of credit will not necessarily help your credit score. You should proceed to systematically close the accounts at a rate of one every six to eight months.

Cutting the cards will go a long way to putting to rest the idea that those lines of credit are available to you and may very well help you clean up your credit report. Remember that in some cases, like qualifying for a real estate loan, too much available credit becomes a negative.

Debt-Consolidation Safety Rules

1. Do not tap into appreciating resources such as home equity or a retirement plan to consolidate or pay off consumer debt. It is not wise to use appreciating assets (your home equity and retirement plan are both growing in value) to pay for depreciating goods and services.

2. If you can successfully switch your credit card balances to a lower-interest credit card, keep paying the most you can each month. Never allow yourself to see the minimum payment as appropriate.

3. Completely close the paid-off accounts. Do this over a period of time, closing one every six to eight months to incur the least negative impact on your credit score. You must call the company with your instructions to close the account and follow up in writing. Do not consider the matter closed until you see on your credit report, "Closed at customer's request." These companies do not want to lose you, so be prepared. Breaking up is hard to do.

4. Do nothing to add to your total debt load. Used properly, a debt-consolidation loan should lighten your debt load, not create an opportunity to increase it. It should put you in a more favorable position, not further behind.

Instead of looking for shortcuts that may turn out to be costly detours, stop using the plastic, get busy putting together your Rapid Debt-Repayment Plan (chap. 7), and stop thinking of new sources of debt as the solution for existing debts.

15

A Home of Your Own

Mortgages and Home Equity Loans

The benefits of homeownership for families, communities, and the nation are profound. It is through initiatives to further grow homeownership that we empower individuals and families by helping them build wealth and improve their lives.

Elizabeth Dole, former US Senator

Homeownership is more than a financial decision. Sure, those monthly payments represent forced savings, and of course you anticipate that over time your home will gain in value and produce a profit. But it is definitely more than that—much more.

Homeownership is a state of mind. A home is a place where you can enter, close the door, and know that all others must wait for an invitation. It's a security blanket not often found with a rental agreement.

A home represents that one place on earth you can call your own, where your kids can put down their roots. It's probably your only hope for a rent-free retirement in which no one will be able to take your home away from you.

Regardless of the way property values rise or fall, if you ever wonder whether you would be better off just renting a place so the landlord can take care of everything, remember this: Mortgage payments come to an end, but rent goes on forever. Homeownership is a good thing and would be out of reach for 99.99 percent of the people in this country were it not for the home mortgage.

From its inception, the home mortgage was designed so that people would pay it off just slightly ahead of retirement. To this day, it is reasonable to believe that thirty years is time enough to repay one's home mortgage. Yes, one would think.

Homeownership versus Mortgage Ownership

Something changed in the seventy years between 1929, when Bill and Agnes McAulay refused to buy a car until their mortgage was paid in full, and 2011, when Jen and Travis Harris bought their first home. Not only are the Harrises stretching beyond reason simply to make their monthly mortgage payments on time, but they also hold absolutely no hope of living long enough to pay the mortgage off. What changed between then and now is our definition of homeownership.

To Bill and Agnes, owning their home meant owning their home. To Jen and Travis, owning their home means owning a mortgage on their home. Owning a home used to mean having a paid-in-full note and an unclouded title. It meant making significant sacrifices until the larger goal was reached. Now it means 360 payments, wondering if and when to refinance, unbelievable amounts of interest, and home equity lines of credit. Then, just when the equity starts building and the payments become not just manageable but comfortable, homeownership invariably means trading in one home for something bigger and better and picking up a fresh new batch of even larger payments.

The difference between owning a home and owning a mortgage depends on your way of thinking. If you start planning to reach the goal of owning your home outright, you can do it. But you're going to have to take things into your own hands. You're going to have to run the show.

Make Your Mortgage Work for You

Avoid Prepayment Penalties

Whenever you are shopping for a mortgage of any type, you want to make sure it is not subject to a prepayment penalty. In the 1970s and 1980s, it was not uncommon for a mortgage to carry some kind of stiff financial penalty if the borrower paid it off more quickly than originally prescribed. Thankfully, nowadays, prepayment penalties have mostly disappeared from home mortgages.

Prepay the Principal

The key to rapidly repaying your mortgage is to prepay the principal. Each month, you have a required payment. Much of that payment is interest; only a small amount is principal. That's why you can make $896-monthly payments on a $125,000, 7.75 percent, thirty-year mortgage for two and a half years and still owe $122,000. You've paid more than $25,000 but reduced your debt by only $3,000. When you prepay the principal ahead of schedule—even by a little bit—it dramatically affects the eventual total cost of the mortgage. That's because each month you pay interest on the remaining balance, which by all rights should be dropping, if only a little.

There are a couple of painless ways you can do this. The tactics will net you a tremendous amount of interest savings and bring your mortgage-free day much closer. However, beware of the following one that works but doesn't make good sense.

Avoid Biweekly Payment Schemes

Years ago, a very smart person figured out that if you paid one-half of your mortgage every two weeks instead of the whole thing once a month, in a year's time you would end up paying one extra payment. You see, if you make one payment a month, you make twelve in a year. But if you make one every other week, biweekly, you make twenty-six half payments in a year or the equivalent of thirteen monthly payments. So far, so good.

A problem arose, however, because mortgage companies were not set up to deal with half payments and a biweekly payment schedule—nor were they required to—the way that credit card companies are able to receive and process any amount at any time. Some banks would return the partial payments as "cannot be processed," while others would just hold the half payment pending the arrival of enough money to make a full payment as required by the mortgage documents.

The desire of consumers to participate in this trendy, new, fast-pay method, combined with the entrepreneurial spirit, produced middleman companies who began selling the biweekly mortgage theory. Simply put, these companies would collect the half payments for a fee and then see that the equivalent of twenty-six half payments were sent to the customer's mortgage holder each year.

Eventually, many lenders saw the demand for this alternative payment schedule and the money to be made by allowing customers to make biweekly payments. I imagine they didn't like the idea of a middleman company collecting all that gravy. So with personalized letters that included the homeowners' potential savings, some banks and mortgage companies tried to get customers to sign up for a special program that would convert the monthly payment schedule to a biweekly one, at a cost.

228

In the case of one major lender, there was a stipulation that the borrowers would allow the lender to deduct the equivalent of one-half payment from their checking account every two weeks for a one-time setup fee of $340 plus a $2.50 service charge for every withdrawal.

Even late-night television infomercials hawked biweekly conversion schemes but presented them as a complicated issue the typical homeowner was not qualified to handle.

Why did so many consumers fall for these biweekly servicing schemes? Marketing pitches can be powerful persuaders, and many people bought into the idea of simplicity, savings, and service. Becoming accountable to a middleman disciplined them to make those biweekly payments.

However, paying even one cent of your hard-earned money for the privilege of a special prepayment plan of any sort is a complete waste of money. Mortgage companies offering this for a fee should be ashamed of themselves.

The practice of mortgage prepaying is excellent, and here is a way you can do it yourself without having to seek permission or sign a contract. And you can change your mind at any time if you want to stop doing it. Again, without a penalty or permission.

Use a Do-It-Yourself Plan

First, divide your monthly mortgage payment by twelve. For example, a mortgage payment of $1,200 divided by twelve equals $100. Every month, send $100 along with your regular monthly payment of $1,200. As long as you are paying a full payment or more, the mortgage company has to accept and process the entire amount (the only exception would be if you have a prepayment penalty clause in your contract, which is rare). As a precautionary measure, I suggest you write a separate check for the additional amount with "principal prepayment" clearly written in the memo area of the check along with your account number. Now there will be no question as to your desire for the disposition of this extra amount.

If you fear you are not disciplined enough to make this additional partial payment each month, authorize your lender to automatically withdraw it from your checking account once a month. Virtually every lender will do an electronic transfer for free, but you have to ask.

With this alternative to the mortgage company's biweekly payment schedule, you will pay the equivalent of thirteen monthly payments each year because you are paying an extra one at a rate of 1/12 each month. Sound familiar? That is exactly what you would be doing if you paid twenty-six biweekly payments in a year.

The power of principal prepayment never ceases to amaze me. Every dollar you invest into the prepayment of your mortgage is a dollar well invested, simply because it represents a guaranteed return on investment. No investment is as sure as a repaid debt.

If that $340 or $375 initial fee (whatever your mortgage company charges to convert your mortgage to a biweekly payment schedule) is something you really want to pay, pay it to yourself. Jump-start your new payment plan with an initial prepayment plus that amount. Every dime of it will go toward your home and not the bottom line of a middleman or mortgage company.

The tremendous savings of interest and hastening of one's mortgage payoff date result from paying the equivalent of a thirteenth payment each year. Your mortgage company will not accept less than a full payment at any one time, but they will accept a payment that is greater than what you've agreed to pay each month. That is the key—and the reason you never want a mortgage with a prepayment penalty.

An important feature of this do-it-yourself mortgage prepayment plan is flexibility. Let's say you find yourself in the unemployment line. Of course, you have your Contingency Fund and Freedom Account in place, so you will not panic. However, it might be in your best interest to pull back on every optional expense and carefully conserve your funds. If you have agreed to a formal biweekly conversion of your mortgage, you are pretty much stuck. You might be able to go back to monthly payments, but it will be a hassle, and it will undoubtedly result in an "unconversion" fee. Besides, this situation could be temporary, meaning you'd want the option to return to the highly beneficial biweekly plan at a later date.

Administering your own prepayment plan lets you retain the option of going back to monthly payments any time you want. You also retain the flexibility to prepay much more than just 1/12 of a payment each month. Say you receive a dividend payment or some other type of unexpected amount. You can choose to add that to your mortgage prepayment check. No amount is too small, and every cent of it will go toward your future. You could even calculate what the payment would be if your loan was amortized over fifteen years rather than thirty, increase your payments accordingly, and then reap all the benefits of a fifteen-year mortgage. Yet, you have the freedom to go back to the thirty-year schedule if necessary without seeking permission or going through any kind of conversion process.

Pay Down or Pay Ahead?

Some time ago, we refinanced our mortgage. The transaction closed in December with the first payment due in February. Rather than take a month off from making payments, we made an unscheduled payment in January to reduce the principal right off the bat. We were very careful to write "principal prepayment" on the check.

We received a detailed statement that correctly reflected the starting principal balance and showed that we had made an unscheduled payment, and it was credited in its entirety to reduce the principal.

The next day another statement arrived showing that the mortgage company had reversed the previous transaction and applied the total amount of that unscheduled payment to the February payment. Huh?! Why did they do that? The lady in customer service said someone must have assumed we wanted to "pay ahead" rather than "pay down."

My explanation is just one word: interest. Applying that unscheduled payment to pay down the principal was not profitable for the lender. That's a chunk of money they cannot collect interest on for the next fifteen years. Prepaying the principal saves huge amounts of interest and shortens the payback time. This one transaction will save us more than $4,000 in interest, and we'll own our home three months sooner. On the other hand, applying it to the February payment put most of it into the lender's pocket in the form of interest.

There are two common reasons that borrowers send extra money to their mortgage companies:

1. *To pay down the principal.* When you pay down the principal, your loan balance goes down. But you still have to make the next scheduled payment. Let's say you make your regular mortgage payment in April plus three extra payments. You enclose a note that the additional payments are to pay down the principal balance. You will still have a payment due in May and June and July as scheduled.

2. *To pay the account ahead.* On the other hand, let's assume you sent those three extra payments because you are going to Europe for the summer and want to pay all your bills in advance before you leave. In this scenario, you want to pay ahead. You'll be back before the August payment is due.

   If you are not clear how you want the extra funds handled, the lender might assume you want to pay down the principal balance. You head off on your trip assuming you've made your mortgage payments. Of course, you don't get the late notices because you're not around. You arrive home only to learn that your home is in foreclosure for failure to pay. You cannot assume the mortgage company will automatically pay your account ahead if you do not send clear instructions. Nor can you assume they will know to pay down the principal balance.

Some lenders will simply return additional payments if it is not clear how they are to be handled. Others automatically apply additional sums to future payments, defaulting to the lender's benefit.

When you make prepayments on your mortgage, always enclose clear instructions. And make sure you also include your instructions on the check itself. But don't leave it there. Follow up in a couple of weeks to make sure the transaction was handled per your instructions. And don't be surprised if your lender is not easily persuaded to pay down. Unless you have a prepayment penalty clause in your mortgage (doubtful), you have every legal right to pay down your mortgage.

Refinancing Your Mortgage

Refinancing is tempting, particularly if you have a relatively high interest rate. Let's say you could refinance and reduce the interest rate by a full 2 percent. Sounds like a great deal, right?

Maybe . . . but maybe not.

What about fees? There will be some, and even if they are rolled into the new loan, you need to know what they will be so you can make a wise assessment.

And now for the real test: How does the total payoff in your present situation compare with the total payoff of the refinance you are considering? Unless the interest on the refinance is significantly lower—and assuming that your goal is to own your home outright as soon as possible—it's not worth it.

Let's say you are twelve years into a thirty-year mortgage. Your original loan was $100,000 at 8.75 percent interest with monthly principal and interest payments of $787. You've made 144 of those babies—216 to go. If you stick with what you have, you still have $169,992 to pay (216 x $787) including the interest on the remaining principal ($85,400).

You look into refinancing. The lender says you can easily get a new thirty-year loan for $100,000 (or more if you want) at 6.75

233

percent interest with total fees of $3,000, which can be rolled into the principal (you would actually be borrowing $103,000). You can pay off the old mortgage, put about $10,000 in your pocket, and reduce your monthly payments by $118 to $668. Wow, it sounds pretty good. But how does that stack up?

With these terms, the refinance will be $668 x 360 months or $240,480. The refinance, even with lower payments, is going to cost you an additional $70,488 in the long run. The reason is simple. You've already paid back a good chunk of your current mortgage and you've reached a level where more of your monthly payment is going toward the principal. If you refinance to a new thirty-year mortgage, you start over with new big interest payments. Instead of owning your home in eighteen years, it's going to be another thirty years. Bad deal.

There is a way you could make this refinance work for you. Borrow only the amount necessary to pay off the original mortgage ($85,400), pay the $3,000 in fees up-front, and choose a fifteen-year term. Let's see how that changes the big picture.

You refinance $85,400 at 6.75 percent for fifteen years. Your new payback of $756 x 180 months equals $159,120. Add the $3,000 you paid up-front, and the total payback comes in at $162,120. Now that's a good deal! Your payments are about $30 less each month, but more importantly, you reduce your total payback by over $7,500 and own your home three years sooner (in fifteen years instead of eighteen). Elect to keep making your old payments of $787 and you'll pay it off in fourteen years and save another $3,200.

If you are considering a refinance, make sure you look at more than just the monthly payment. Find a good loan calculator with an amortization schedule. I have the perfect one in our members' area at DebtProofLiving.com. You can plug in the information on your current mortgage to see where you are and your total payback at this point. Now you're ready to consider a refinance—one that makes sense because it's good for you!

Do your homework. Don't rely on a loan broker to decide if refinancing is right for you. You have to understand that a broker (or even the loan officer at the bank) has something more than your best financial interests in mind. (You do know about commissions, right? Not that there is anything wrong with earning a commission, in the same way that there is nothing wrong with you looking out for your best interests!) If refinancing your mortgage will not improve your big picture—the total payback—don't even think about it.

Home Equity Loans

Home equity loans are quite dangerous for this one big reason: You can lose your house for nonpayment.

If anyone had told the typical homeowner in the 1940s that second mortgages—then viewed as a major cause of human misery and financial ruin—would one day be a hip way to pay off credit card debt, send Junior to college, give Buffy the wedding of her dreams, or take the family on a Caribbean cruise, they would have been too stunned to respond. But that is exactly what has happened.

This type of loan got a spiffy new name in the 1980s—the home equity loan (HEL)—and it rocketed in popularity when it became the only game in town for the consumer seeking tax-deductible interest payments. Unfortunately, a second mortgage by any other name is still a second mortgage.

Locked up in your house is a beautiful pot of tax-free money, reachable only if you sell and move out. This money represents all the profits you've ever made on the homes you've owned.

A home equity loan does not unlock some big cash drawer in the sky with your name on it in the same way you would have that money at your disposal if you sold and moved. A home equity loan simply grants you the temporary use of these funds. Essentially, a

HEL allows you to rent your equity, placing you under heavy-duty restrictions and requirements for the privilege.

Home equity deals come in two varieties: loans and lines. In either case, the homeowner is allowed to borrow up to 80 percent of the home's current market value minus the balance on the mortgage.

Home Equity Loan

The home equity loan (HEL) is the traditional second mortgage. It generally comes with a fixed interest rate, and you get all the money in one lump sum to be repaid over five to fifteen years.

Home Equity Line of Credit

The home equity line of credit (HELOC) is the most dangerous of the two types of home equity loans. Typically, the line of credit is open-ended, meaning the amount of money available to you changes with the current market value of your home. As your equity increases, so does the amount of money you can borrow against it.

Once the loan is approved, the borrower receives the equivalent of a checkbook, not the proceeds of the loan. You simply (simplicity is one of the main problems with the line of credit) write a check to tap into the equity. You then pay interest on only the portion you have drawn out, not the entire amount available.

In theory, the HELOC sounds too good to be true—a way you can have your cake (own the property) and eat it too (spend the equity). In reality, it offers the same temptations as a dozen low-interest credit cards. Both closed- and open-ended home equity loans still let you ruin your financial life—just more slowly and, some financial-adviser types might argue, more intelligently than with credit cards.

I am generally opposed to both types of home equity loans but especially to the line-of-credit variety. First, it feeds the myth that the equity in your home is a liquid asset. Having those funds so readily available (essentially you are walking around with the sum total of your home's equity in your pocket calling out to you the way money has a way of doing) makes you feel as if this is your money and you can spend it any way you please. A home equity line of credit brings new meaning to the idea of money burning a hole in your pocket.

If you resist, you might begin to fear that your spouse will find something to spend it on. You could quickly lose control and go through the entire wad in a week and a half. If you are the one who cannot rest as long as all that money is there to be spent, your spouse might be the one filled with paranoia.

When eventually you give in and spend it (and you will, trust me), even if it is for the most reasonable and noble cause, the vicious cycle will have begun. You make regular payments, but because nearly all of the payment goes to pay the interest, you don't make a dent in the principal. Then when those unrelenting payments become a financial strain on what used to be your barely-making-ends-meet-every-month situation, the temptation to tap further into the equity will be there staring you in the face.

The equity in your home is one of your most precious assets. For most of us, it is the only appreciating asset we have now or possibly will ever have in the future. Borrowing against your home's equity to pay down credit card balances, finance a fabulous family vacation, or purchase new furniture may not seem like a big deal if you are young and believe you have all kinds of time to prepare for retirement. But when you tap into your home's equity, you are not only reducing its overall value but also severely retarding—and in the case of the line of credit, wiping out completely—that important feature called compounding growth. You are, in essence, killing the one financial asset that is actually growing.

Spending the equity in your home as quickly as it appears essentially eliminates the prospect of ever owning your home outright. It guarantees you will have mortgage payments or rent for the rest of your life. If you use that equity to pay for things early on in your life, it and all the offspring it should have reproduced are not going to be there when you deserve a rent-free retirement. When you reach into your home's equity, you are, in fact, tearing a hole in your safety net. Never underestimate the worth of a rent-free retirement.

But It's Deductible!

Unfortunately, many people are drawn to the concept of a home equity loan because the tax deductibility of the interest has a righteous ring to it. Let's face it. This option qualifies as secured debt and shoves this kind of loan into the semi-intelligent category. But the benefit of tax-deductible interest is highly overrated.

Say you owe $1,000 on your home equity line of credit and your interest rate is 10 percent. If you pay the loan off in one year, you will pay $100 in interest. If you are in the 28 percent tax bracket, you will save $28 (28 percent of $100) at tax time if you itemize your deductions. So after you factor in your tax savings, the amount of interest you actually paid was just $72.

The point is that you still had to pay $72. Many equity borrowers assume that because the interest is tax deductible, the tax savings not only wipe out the effect of paying interest but also in some way reward them with cash back. Here's another way to look at it. The after-tax interest rate on the 10 percent home equity line of credit was merely reduced to 7.2 percent. Big whoop.

Bottom line: You do not want to find clever ways to create tax deductions. Of course, you want to take all the deductions to which you are entitled if you have taxable income. But even the best deduction cannot erase the tax you must pay to create the deduction.

Let's say you are in the 28 percent tax bracket. For each dollar of deduction you have, you receive a 28 cents reduction in the amount of money on which you must pay taxes. But here is the fact you dare not miss. You still had to pay out the $1 to the property tax collector, the banker, the mortgage lender.

If you are really bent on having lots of deductions, I'll make you a deal. You send me all your dollars, and I promise to send back to you 50 cents for each and every one of them. You don't even have to file a return or wait for April 15. What do you think about that deal? (I'll be watching my mail.)

What Lenders Want You to Know

If you have eyes toward a home equity loan, the lender is going to do all he can to convince you that the line-of-credit type is better than the straight second-mortgage variety for the following reasons:

Flexibility. You can draw down as much or as little of the line as you want and pay interest on only the amount you actually use.

Easy access. You have either a checkbook or an ATM card that allows you access to the equity in your home.

Lower interest rate. Compared to the interest rate on a credit card account, the interest rate on a home equity line of credit is significantly lower. Because of its variable-rate feature, it is also lower than its cousin, the fixed-rate home equity loan.

What Lenders Don't Want You to Think About

What the lender will fail to point out are the negatives that come packaged with a home equity line of credit:

The temptation. No matter how you slice it, a line of credit has "easy money" written all over it. Just knowing all the money is available brings decorators, travel agents, and car dealers out of the woodwork.

Lightweight repayment. Home equity lenders are particularly anxious for repayment to be done at a leisurely pace and over a long period of time. They don't want you to repay too quickly or they lose their passive income stream.

Variable interest rate. This may seem like a nice feature when interest rates are low, but what happens when the cycle takes a turn

239

and inflation kicks in? Remember, when the rate increases (and you must assume that it will), the entire amount you owe will be subject to the increased rate, not just the amount you withdraw in the future.

Annual fees. While a home equity loan does not have annual fees (all fees, if any, are part of the origination costs), a home equity line of credit is subject to an annual fee of $50 to $150. This fee is not included in the annual percentage rate and might not seem like such a big deal—until you multiply the fee by the number of years you will have that line available. Then it becomes a significant number.

Using a HEL

While home equity loans are not ideal (what kind of debt is?), I am not entirely opposed to them. However, their purpose is very limited.

Following the principles that set intelligent borrowing apart from that other kind of debt, the proceeds of a home equity loan should be used only to create or add to an appreciating asset. That means putting the funds right back into the home—to improve, renovate, or add to it. This way the home equity loan becomes a financial investment.

Troublesome Home Loans

The dramatic increase of home values in recent years has been met with an increase in "creative" home mortgage programs. Basically, these nontraditional loans are for people who are unable to qualify for a traditional mortgage with its more reasonable terms.

Many states have instituted subsidized home loan programs designed specifically for first-time buyers. While many are good programs, there are at least two types of home mortgages that should be avoided.

Interest Only

With this type of loan, borrowers pay only the interest during the first years of the loan (usually five years). The pitch from the loan salesperson is that the property will appreciate dramatically. By the time five years have passed, the borrowers will be in a higher income bracket, and at that time they can simply refinance their very valuable home into a fixed-rate loan. Nice theory. However, the risks far outweigh the positives.

Unpredictable market. Of course, during good times it appears that home values will only increase. But real estate values rise and fall. When you have no equity in your home, if the values drop, you're stuck with a home you cannot refinance and you cannot sell.

Rising interest rates. No one knows where interest rates will be in five years. They could be double the current rate. But if you have an interest-only loan, you will have no choice. You will be forced to refinance into a loan at the then-prevailing rates. And that could be devastating to your financial situation.

In over their heads. In most cases, the purpose of an interest-only mortgage is to allow borrowers to buy a home they could not otherwise afford. That is very dangerous. An 80 percent mortgage with a 20 percent down payment represents a safety net. You would be better advised to buy a home you can afford and for which you have a down payment than to get in over your head.

125 Percent

Following the real estate crash of 2007–8, subprime loans became the bane of the home lending industry. But slowly, the low to no down payment loans have come back, as have the worst of the worst—the 125 percent mortgage. Perhaps you have seen the compelling commercials on late-night television offering loans that lend you more than the full market value of your home. The problems with such a ridiculous loan are many.

Fees. Finding out the details of these loans is not easy. I've called as both an investigator and a potential customer. I could not get any salesperson to state the interest rate or the fees involved. They will deal with you only after you have filled out a loan application and given them permission to pull your credit report. Therefore, I had to get this information from people who fell for the pitch and now live to regret it.

Interest rates on these loans are outrageous, often 5 to 10 percentage points higher than the going rate. And up-front fees can be as high as 15 percent of the loan amount.

Prepayment penalty. These loans almost always carry a stiff prepayment penalty. If you attempt to accelerate payment of the amount borrowed or pay the loan in full through refinancing or selling, you are hit with a huge penalty.

In my opinion, these companies have just one thing in mind: They want your property. The intention is to take advantage of a miserable situation (these loans appeal only to those who can least afford them), fleece you of every dime up-front, grab all the interest they can from you in the beginning while you are still hanging on by your fingernails, and then simply hang a foreclosure notice on your front door when you fall behind.

16

The Overlooked Safety Net

Disability Insurance

> A twenty-year-old worker stands a nearly three in ten chance
> of becoming disabled before age sixty-five.
>
> Social Security Administration

In addition to having health and automobile coverage, most people insure their lives so that in the event of their untimely demise—a term that for me always begs the question, Is there such a thing as a timely demise?—those who depend on their income will not be left high and dry.

Term life insurance, the insurance of choice for debt-proof living, is relatively cheap because so many people who pay for it never use it. The insurance companies invest all those premiums, make an obscene fortune doing so, and end up paying out far less than they take in.

Curiously, less than 15 percent of people who buy life insurance insure something far more important: their ability to earn a living. Face it, folks, these days, with medical technology what it is, the odds increase every day that a disease or accident that would have killed you even a decade ago will now leave you disabled—alive but unable to work.

Please do not take the absence of detailed information on other types of insurance as an indication that they are not necessary. They are. Due to space limitations, I am not going to address automobile, health, life, and homeowners/renters insurance in this book. But I do want to discuss disability insurance because of all the types of insurance that exist, this is the one you are most likely to overlook yet need the most. Failure to have it could wipe you out financially.

Your chances of becoming disabled at a relatively young age, either temporarily or permanently, are far greater than your chances of dying young. Some would argue (and I would be one) that if you cannot afford both life and disability insurance, you should decide in favor of the latter.

The debt-proof living philosophy relies heavily on being prepared for the unforeseen. That's the reason for my emphasis on a Contingency Fund, a Freedom Account, and living without debt. However, none of these provisions is going to carry you through for long periods without an income.

Just over 1 in 4 of today's 20-year-olds will become disabled before they retire.[1] Over 37 million Americans are classified as disabled; about 12 percent of the total population. More than 50 percent of those disabled Americans are in their working years, from 18–64.[2] And while most working Americans have access to Social Security Disability Insurance, it's not something we should count on receiving long term. Sixty-five percent of initial SSDI claim applications were denied in 2012.[3] Even if you were to be granted this type of financial assistance during a season of disability, can your family live on $1,130 a month? That's the average monthly benefit paid by Social Security Disability Insurance (SSDI) at the end of 2012.[4]

Why Is It So Expensive?

Disability insurance is far more expensive than term life insurance. In fact, it rivals the more expensive whole life insurance but does not offer the dubious advantage of cash values. No wonder so many people overlook this most important type of insurance.

Disability insurance is expensive because there's a much higher probability you will use it. Insurance companies operate on levels of risk. The greater the chances they will have to make payment on a claim, the higher the premiums.

With life insurance, most people underestimate their life span, so they end up buying insurance they will never use. Or they buy ridiculously expensive insurance such as whole life or universal life and then drop it the minute they go through a financial downturn. That's why insurance companies make out like bandits.

But when it comes to disabilities, people of all ages have equal risks, which means it is more likely that you will need disability insurance at some time during your earning years. If you are in a two-breadwinner household, it is likely you need disability insurance more than life insurance, given how expensive it can be to care for a disabled person. Disability insurance is not, in my opinion, the luxury item most people consider it to be.

How It Works

Standard disability insurance is straightforward. If you are disabled and unable to work as defined by the disability insurance policy, the insurance company replaces a specific percentage of the income you would have earned had you not been disabled. In the same way that health, auto, and life insurance policies have unique provisions, exclusions, and stipulations, a disability policy has all kinds of provisions that you should consider carefully. Generally speaking, the lower the premium, the greater the number of exclusions and stipulations. Consider them carefully, and never buy insurance coverage you do not fully understand.

What to Look For

A disability insurance policy is not a simple document to decipher. However, if you go over one with the following checklist in hand, you should not have trouble deciding if a policy is right for you.

Simple definition. You want a policy that defines disability very simply: a decline in income as a result of sickness or accident. A policy that gets complicated in this regard will likely be difficult to nail down when it's time to file a claim.

Guaranteed and noncancelable. This type of policy will have a fixed premium and will stay in effect as long as your payments are current regardless of health issues or other variables. Just as the policy states, you have guaranteed coverage and it cannot be canceled. Avoid a policy that carries a provision that states it is "class cancelable." That means a policy can be canceled if an entire class of policies is canceled. If a company were to cancel an entire class of occupations, say truck drivers, and you were one of them, you'd be out in the cold even if your policy was guaranteed and noncancelable.

Addresses preexisting conditions. Make sure your policy covers disabilities resulting from preexisting conditions that you disclosed at the time of application. If you had a disabling back condition twenty years ago and have since recovered, you don't want to find out a new back condition is not covered because of that preexisting situation. Make sure that if you have preexisting conditions they are clearly stated and the terms under which they will be covered are spelled out.

Waives premiums during disability period. You want to find a policy that waives the premium completely if you are disabled for more than, say, ninety days. That means that if you are disabled, your insurance provisions stay in full effect but you do not pay those expensive premiums.

Insures for your occupation. You want a disability policy that protects you against your inability to work in your own occupation. Without this important provision, your insurer will not pay you unless you can't work at all.

Payment increases. You want a rider on your policy that provides for payment increases to keep up with inflation and your income. If you bought the policy when you made $25,000 and make $45,000 when you suffer a disability, you want to make sure you are covered at the $45,000 level.

Pays until retirement. Some disability policies pay for only a specific period of time, such as five or ten years. The best policy is open-ended and continues as long as you are disabled until retirement age.

Option to purchase. If your policy includes an option to purchase clause, you will be able to increase your coverage at predetermined times regardless of your health or other factors. This is a good protection that will allow you to adjust your coverage in the event the economy experiences hyperinflation. There are riders that automatically adjust policies upward to allow for inflation, but they are very expensive. The option to purchase clause is a reasonable substitute.

How Much Coverage

I could suggest you look for a policy that would pay 100 percent of your income—and you would look forever and never find it. Disability policies pay a percentage of your current income or an average based on some stated period of time. Of course, the lower the percentage, the cheaper the premium, so it is important that you determine your absolute minimum requirement in the event you are unable to earn a living.

Your regular expenses will be reduced somewhat during a disability period simply because you won't be going to work every day. Figure how little you could get by on and then start looking for a policy that will meet that portion of your income.

Reduce the Cost

One thing you can do to reduce the high cost of disability insurance is to accept a longer waiting period or elimination period. Some policies kick in, or begin paying benefits, immediately upon a disabling event. Others have a 30-, 60-, 90-, or even 180-day waiting period. It is advisable to take the longer waiting period, resulting in a significantly lower premium, and then look to your Contingency Fund or other nest egg to cover the bills during the waiting period.

Where to Look

Even if you feel you are not in a position to take on another expense at this time, start thinking about it. I hope that soon you see this as a priority you can no longer ignore. At the very least, find out what a good disability policy would cost. Ask friends or relatives for a referral to an agent or disability insurance carrier.

The most logical place to look for disability insurance is right in your own neighborhood, so to speak. Ask if your employer offers this as a group benefit. Some employers provide a small amount of coverage as an employee benefit and allow employees to purchase more at their own expense. A call to your human resources department might turn up a very nice surprise, since group coverage of any type of insurance is always much cheaper than an individual policy.

If your employer doesn't offer this benefit, find out if any trade organizations to which you belong—or would if you were convinced they offered you something of benefit—have group disability insurance. Ask your friends, both personal and professional, if they might have a recommendation.

If all else fails, start looking at individual coverage. Your current life insurance provider may also offer disability insurance, so make that call without making any commitments. Remember, you are only shopping at this point.

Finally, if you can prove a connection to the military, you can get disability insurance through USAA with reasonable premiums. From its founding, USAA has been devoted to offering financial and insurance services to individuals and families in the United States military. While its banking services have been opened to the public, its insurance arm remains restricted and available only to people who can prove a connection. That means if your father served, most likely you and your immediate family members are eligible. You can check USAA.com for more specific information on this issue or call USAA Life Insurance Company at 800-531-8000 for a price quote. The fact that they have no agents helps to lower the premiums.

17

Student Loans, Student Debt

Paying for a College Education

Invest in yourself, in your education. There's nothing better.

Sylvia Porter,
Sylvia Porter's Money Book

College is expensive but generally worth it if you pay as you go. Paying double or in some cases triple, however, by putting the cost of a college education on credit to be paid for over the next twenty-five to thirty years borders on the unthinkable.

As you know, I am seriously opinionated about the matter of debt—unsecured, consumer debt. Hang on to your hat. You haven't read anything yet.

I do not believe that every person able to pass the entrance exam is entitled to an education at the college or university of his or her choice. Just because your son is smart enough to be accepted into Harvard, for example, does not mean he is automatically entitled to attend. There is this little matter of being able to afford it. To say otherwise would be as ludicrous as saying that because he is a good driver he's entitled to a Ferrari.

I believe that student debt has the potential to be so destructive to a person's financial life that it should be avoided if at all possible. There, I've said it.

Secured or Unsecured Debt?

Many financial experts hold to the position that student debt is secured debt. The collateral, they contend, is one's ability to earn a better living in the future because of said education. Therefore, it is not unsecured debt. Others simply acquiesce to the student loan system, advising that you borrow all you can, get through school, and then find a way to deal with the debt.

I believe student debt is unsecured debt—there is simply no other way to categorize it. It offers few, if any, realistic escape routes. If things don't work out the way you, your student, your parents, or whoever has put their neck on the line for repayment planned ("I'll get a great job and just pay it all back really fast"), you're stuck. Those loans must be repaid.

There was a time—and not that long ago—when I didn't have much of an opinion about student loans. Then I made a trip to Nebraska to speak at a women's conference. Included on my schedule for the weekend was a Friday afternoon session at a local private college to speak to the graduating students about the dangers of consumer debt and strategies to handle their student loans.

The women's conference commenced on Friday morning, and after the first session, a young woman came up to me in tears. We found a private corner to talk, and she poured out her heart.

I learned that she had graduated from the college I would be visiting later in the day. As a freshman, her plan had been to become an elementary schoolteacher, and she had felt perfectly justified in taking out the maximum student loan each semester. She didn't think twice about the future ramifications and assumed she'd pay the loans easily when she landed a good job. She figured they'd never give her loans she wouldn't be able to repay, so she didn't question the system. She was thankful for the provision.

During the four romantic years (it is a lovely, old campus), she fell in love and upon graduation married her college sweetheart, who also had aspirations of becoming an elementary schoolteacher. Her husband-to-be had nearly the same amount of student debt— nearly $70,000 between them. Upon saying "I do," her debt and his debt became "our debt."

She became pregnant within a very short time. He applied for teaching positions, but opportunities were not forthcoming. To keep food on the table, he took a job at a local factory as they awaited the birth of their first child, and her plans to become a teacher made their way to the back burner.

By the time she and I met, she was pregnant with their third child, and he was still at the factory. She said he'd long since given up his dreams of teaching in favor of staying at the factory in this tiny Nebraska town. His salary barely covered their basic living expenses even though he worked as much overtime as possible. His take-home pay, based on minimum wage, put them close to the poverty line.

She told me how her loans had been in forbearance, but payments of $400 a month were now past due—money they absolutely did not have. His loans would come due some months hence, and together their payments would be close to $900 a month. She wept as she told me there was no way out. She spoke of the strain this was placing on their marriage and the family. She said they'd considered filing for bankruptcy until they'd found out all the loans were not dischargeable—even through bankruptcy. She related that the loan counselor had informed her there were only two ways the loans could be forgiven: full payment or death.

I'm sure that during their carefree college days both of these young people didn't flinch as they signed for loan after loan after loan. What they didn't allow for in their planning was that life doesn't always turn out as we plan. Things happen. Babies are born; jobs don't pan out. Had they not been saddled by this heavy load of debt, their options would have been greatly increased. I had little to offer this woman by way of hope. I suggested that since she had a spare room and a large yard, she might consider opening a day care center. Lots of hard work? Yes, but possibly a way she could work to repay the debt in record time. She could be with her children and at the same time earn additional funds to repay the debt. I never heard back from her, but to this day her story weighs heavily on my heart.

That afternoon, as I addressed the students, I learned that most of the graduating seniors would be leaving school with heavy loads of debt. Few of them had a clue about the terms of the loan repayments. The attitude was that surely the school wouldn't allow them to get into something they wouldn't be able to handle. Many of these students, I learned, had purposely taken loans for more than they really needed so they could buy computers, cars, and pay for ordinary living expenses so they "would have more time to study." One young man was very open about the fact that he had used much of his loan proceeds to pay for an off-campus apartment and to buy a car.

After the session, one young woman—she said she thought she had about $30,000 in loans—lingered to chat. I asked about her plans for the future. She hesitated and then said that since she had a double major in multicultural studies and geography she thought she might like to be a travel agent. My blood ran cold.

First, I know that travel agents don't make the kind of money required to service $35,000 in unsecured debt (she'd picked up an additional $5,000 in credit card debt).

Second, I couldn't imagine anyone spending four years in college, selecting a fairly sophisticated double major, and then being satisfied with a job that had no advanced-education requirements. She told me she had decided to come to this particular college because the campus was beautiful and she knew she'd make lots of friends.

My advice to her was that she see this debt as a top priority in her life—that she buckle down to a very frugal lifestyle and work at least two jobs with the goal to pay the loans in full within the next three years. I followed that advice with, "And whatever you do, don't get married until it is paid." She blushed a bit and then told me she would be getting married just three weeks hence. Yes, her fiancé was a fellow graduate with about the same amount of student debt.

The director of students drove me back to the conference. With two stories fresh in my mind, I couldn't help asking her just how dependent this college is on the student loan system. Her answer shocked me. She said that 85 to 90 percent of all students (or their parents) take out student loans of some type. It is a denominational church school, and many people in the Midwest send their children to this school. It is a way they can support their denomination and know that their kids will be in a wholesome environment.

Clearly, this particular private college depends heavily on student loans—as is the case with most of these types of schools, I fear. Without the government-backed loan programs, their student bodies would disappear. I finished that conference with a very heavy heart.

Since my experience in Nebraska, I've received hundreds of letters regarding student loans. One came from a young man who had prepared to be a chiropractor. I don't know how many years it entailed, but he finished with $160,000 in student loans. He passed his state exams and entered the field only to find that he absolutely hated it. After some time of personal struggle, he admitted that what he really wanted to do was teach school. He is now teaching junior high school, living like a pauper, and trying to pay back his huge debt on a teacher's salary.

Another letter sent my stomach into spasms. This man finished law school with nearly $200,000 of student debt. His plans for practicing law (and quickly repaying the debt, of course) were dashed when he failed the bar exam three times and simply gave up.

Still another letter from a young woman told of her heartbreak. The man of her dreams had broken their engagement. She had nearly $40,000 of student debt, and he could not agree to start their marriage in the hole.

I've received countless letters from pastors who cannot pay their student loans on their salaries. Their secret struggles are nearly more than they can bear. Other letters come from people who feel the call of God to be missionaries but cannot be considered by any mission board because of the huge student loans to which they are obligated.

Going to College without Going into Debt

Lest you conclude I am opposed to higher education, let me assure you I am not! While not every person is college material, I firmly believe that every young person should be encouraged and given the opportunity to seek some type of higher education. Education is key to the future of this country. We need to encourage young people to become as educated as reasonably possible.

But I am also convinced it is possible to get an education without taking on massive amounts of debilitating debt. It takes a lot of work, planning, and even sacrifice, but it can be done. And if an education is important enough to you or your student, you will find a way to do it.

Go to a community college. There are more than 1,655 two-year community colleges in the United States—two-year, post-secondary institutions that offer certificate programs, associate of arts degrees, associate of sciences degrees, plus many other programs.[1] Even if you are anticipating a four-year degree, you can take prerequisite courses at the community college level—at an amazingly low cost.

What many people do not consider is that the first two years of any college career are packed with basic prerequisite courses. Why not pay $46 a unit at a community college (the current in-state rate in California[2]) to take the same courses the private university charges $500 for and then enter the four-year college as a junior ready to dive into your chosen field of study? This tactic alone can cut the cost of a four-year college education about in half.

Consider state colleges and universities. Many state schools offer an excellent education for a fraction of the cost of a private school, provided the student meets the residency requirements. When our oldest son went to a state college, we were astonished to find that tuition and all related costs were far less than tuition alone at the private high school from which he graduated.

Live at home. While I agree that the social aspect of college has its benefits, it is not worth going into debt to pay for room and board in a dormitory or all the related costs of renting an apartment. Living in a beautiful setting and making nice friends is not worth twenty or thirty years of heavy debt payments.

Sit out a year or two. As a parent, I understand the fear that if a student doesn't go straight to college after high school he may never make it. I suggest that an equal fear is that if he does go to college but because he hasn't a clue what he wants to do, and therefore lacks direction or motivation, the effort is completely wasted. Many times, a year or two of dealing with the real world convinces a young person that getting an education can be the path to a better job. A motivated high-school graduate willing to live frugally at home could in a matter of two years save a tremendous amount of money for college.

Start when they're babies. Parents choosing to pay for their children's college degrees should start saving when the kids are babies. That is the most painless way to pay for an expensive education. Save regularly and select the investment vehicle for these funds based on the age of the future collegian.

Up to age twelve, you can afford to be very aggressive with your college fund. Faithfully put your money away, month after month—good times and bad—into stock mutual funds. Reinvest the dividends and don't worry.

Once your child reaches age twelve, leave your mutual fund account alone but begin depositing your new savings into safer vehicles such as US savings bonds, long-term certificates of deposit, and other Treasury securities. As the college years approach, begin transferring the money in the stock mutual funds into the safer havens. Now is the time to make sure the money is safe. If you continue investing this money in the stock market, you will not have recovery time if the market takes a plunge. If those babies don't end up going to college, the funds can be easily transferred into retirement accounts.

Some states now have 529 educational accounts that allow parents to pay for their children's college educations while the kids are still young, thereby providing a hedge against rising costs. Good idea? Perhaps, but be particularly careful before you jump in. The biggest question is whether the funds are fully refundable. Life is uncertain, and should your child decide not to attend college or should something happen that would preclude him from attending school in the state you now call home, you want to make sure you can get that money back, with interest. My advice is that if you have the money, invest it wisely yourself. Then when the time for college comes, your options will be plentiful. To learn more about 529 Plans, go to SavingforCollege.com, then search for "College Savings 101" at that site.

How to Pay as You Go

Save early. Paying for college with money saved and invested is definitely the cheapest way to go because a great deal of the money you send to the college will come from interest, dividends, and capital gains. But you have to start early to get those benefits.

Use current income. Spending current income—either the parents', the student's, or a combination of both—is a more costly way to pay as you go. This will definitely require a change in lifestyle and considerable sacrifice. But when you're finished, you're really finished. The education will be paid for in full. Achieving that goal is definitely worth the sacrifices required.

Work for the school. Many private colleges give an excellent discount to the children of college employees. There are lots of jobs on a big campus other than teaching positions. Check it out. You never know what you might find. A number of colleges that I know of offer free tuition to the family members of school employees.

Seek out discounts for pastors and missionaries. Many church-affiliated colleges and universities offer significant discounts to the children of pastors and missionaries. If you fall into one of those categories (or feel a change of profession coming on), make inquiries.

Apply for grants. A grant is a flat-out gift. It is free money, and there is no requirement to repay. The most common is the Pell Grant, money from the federal government to assist low-income undergraduates. But don't get too excited. The amount of the grant will be small, at best, and will be determined by the family income. It could be as little as $200 or as much as $2,500. If the student is a displaced homemaker (a woman who has left the workplace to rear children and is single as a result of either divorce or death and requires training to return to the workplace) or a dislocated worker (anyone fired or laid off due to downsizing or a self-employed person whose business failed because of a turn in the economy), that grant applicant will receive preferential treatment. The Supplemental Educational Opportunity Grant (SEOG) is available for very low-income undergraduate students and ranges from $200 to $4,000 per year. Many states have grant programs for students who go to state colleges or universities. In addition, many colleges have their own grants based on need.

Take part in a work-study program. A federal program, work-study provides on-campus jobs for students. The college administers the jobs and supervises the workers. Once the student is granted an award, he must work until that award is earned. There is no requirement to pay the money back, even if the student does not graduate.

Look for corporate benefits. Many large corporations have an education reimbursement program for employees who qualify. This can be an excellent way for a student to get a great deal of their college costs paid for. Those seeking graduate degrees might consider a job change to a corporation with such a program before enrolling in graduate school.

Serve in the military. For those young people wishing to serve in the military, an excellent education could be a decided benefit. The military will put you through medical school, for instance, if you enter as an officer and agree to stay for a period of time upon completing your residency.

Apply for no-need scholarships. There are jillions of scholarships available that are not based on need but rather on ability or one's ethnic heritage—many of which go unawarded every year. You can find exhaustive lists online at sites such as Fastweb.com.

Apply for financial aid. Financial aid is a term the educational system uses to refer to grants, loans, work-study, and scholarships. Even if you desire to pay cash rather than accept loans, you might want to go through the financial aid process to learn if you might be eligible for grants or other aid. You need to apply for financial aid at least one year in advance. I suggest that you take a couple of aspirin before getting started, and you will do yourself a big favor if you eliminate all expectations. Learn more at Fafsa.ed.gov.

A friend, Carol Anne, had a rude awakening while going through this financial aid process when her daughter enrolled at a large, private university. She went through the long and arduous process and discovered to her surprise that her daughter was eligible for aid for all but $5,000 of her first year's costs.

Her daughter, a brilliant and highly motivated journalism student, decided to go after every possible scholarship to make up the $5,000 gap. Sure enough, she was selected as the national champion for a journalism scholarship to the college of her choice in the amount of—you guessed it—$5,000. How shocked they were to be informed by the college that her financial aid would be reduced dollar for dollar by any scholarship she won on the outside. The college said it wasn't their fault. They are required to adhere to federal regulations that require all sources of income be taken into consideration. They saw the scholarship as a new source of income.

If all else fails, go as a senior citizen. Many states have college programs for seniors. In Ohio, for example, any senior citizen can go to a state college or university at no cost.[3] The only requirement is that there be an opening in the class once all paying students have registered. Classes can be taken for full credit or audited for no credit. Ohio's seniors have the opportunity to take a single class now and then or earn a degree—even a master's or doctorate. To find out if your state has any such program, call your state's department of education and ask about programs for seniors.

If You Must Take Out a Student Loan

In the same way that most people would never be able to buy a home without a mortgage, most people cannot afford a college degree without some amount of financial aid in the form of student loans. I wish that were not the case, but it has become a fact of life. That being said, here are guidelines to follow to make sure student debt doesn't become a much larger problem for your future than if you had not gone to school in the first place.

Borrow only the amount you absolutely must have to get by. It will be tempting to borrow the full amount for which you are eligible. But that could be more than necessary. Be strong. Say thanks but no thanks. Do not accept more than you need so you can do any of a number of very foolish things with borrowed funds (all taken from the annals of my mailbox):

- invest the excess (this one always amazes me)
- buy an engagement ring (oh, puhleeze)

261

- buy a computer (the one you have is fine)
- buy a car (can you say "public transportation"?)
- live off campus (dormitory living is an education in itself)
- spring break at Daytona Beach (I'll pretend I didn't hear that)

Borrow no more for your education than you will earn in the first year working in the field for which you are preparing. For example, if you are getting your degree to become an elementary schoolteacher in a city where first-year teachers are paid $27,000, your total student debt for your education should not exceed $27,000. That's a rule of thumb you can rely on.

Begin immediately to make payments even though you have the option to defer payments until you graduate. Student loans issued by the government come in two flavors: subsidized and unsubsidized. Subsidized loans are need based and issued to families and students who can demonstrate a financial need. These loans do not begin to accrue interest until after the student finishes or leaves college. Unsubsidized loans are available to anyone and begin accruing interest the moment you cash the check. However, the government allows the interest to be rolled back into the loan and does not require payment of it until after graduation. This means you could borrow, say, $8,000 but end up owing a great deal more because of the interest. At the very least, begin immediately to pay the interest each month on all unsubsidized loans.

Repay the debt in three years. You will have opportunities to consolidate your loans into one loan so you can make a single payment each month. That's fine, but know that you can accelerate your repayment, and you should. You do not want to be making these payments for the next ten, twenty, or even thirty years. Buckle down. Continue to live like a starving student so you can get your repayment taken care of in short order.

Know the ropes. The government has over the years introduced provisions that allow for partial forgiveness of some student loans based on income, service, and other life situations. While it's tough to qualify, this is information you need to know if your name is associated with any kind of student debt.

Income-based repayment, for example, is tied to your gross household income after graduation. If it's low or you work in public service or for a nonprofit organization, you could qualify to have some of your debt forgiven. But there are requirements having to do with on-time payments over a long period of time and so forth. SavingforCollege.com, Studentaid.ed.gov, and StudentLoans .gov are information-rich sites that will help you stay on top of the laws and regulations for all things student loans.

If you as the parents or your student end up going into debt to fund a college education, do it as intelligently as possible. Know at all times exactly how much you have borrowed, the interest rate, the exact terms, and when the payments will commence. Start repaying at the first moment possible and pay more than is required. Don't push the limit by accepting the six months of grace you'll get before starting to repay your debt. Don't consolidate or rewrite the loans if doing so extends the payback time. Accelerate the schedule so you pay off the loan as quickly as possible. And, of course, never default.

A Word of Advice for College Students

Your college years will definitely be among the best of your life. Make the most of your very expensive education. Don't select a major because it sounds fun or so you can be in classes with your best friend. If you don't know what you want to do with your life, get some counseling. You may need to sit out for a few semesters until you do know.

Beware of credit cards for students. You will be amazed to find the major credit card companies hounding you to accept their credit cards. They are going to come after you with a vengeance. They will make you feel mature and responsible; they will offer you huge lines of credit, and they won't require that you have a job or even that your parents cosign—or even know. They'll try to convince you that you need a credit card just in case of an emergency or to build a good credit score. It will be difficult to say no, but I encourage you to do just that.

However, let me follow quickly by saying that if you are enrolled in college, you will have an easier time qualifying for your one and only all-purpose credit card. You need to begin building a credit history, and having one card that you manage responsibly can go a long way to giving you a good start.

IndexCreditCards.com maintains a current listing of all consumer credit cards available and categorizes them to make it easy to find the right one. Just keep in mind that when you have a credit card, you need to keep the account active by using the card regularly. You can make a $10 purchase twice a year on the card, then repay it quickly so your account returns to a $0 balance. That's enough to keep it active, you out of debt, and your credit history positive. Never roll the balance from one month to the next, and never pay interest or fees.

And now for my warning: If you accept a credit card with a big credit limit, I can guarantee you will have lots of emergencies. They'll come in the form of pizza and airline tickets, clothes and social events. Before you know it, you will have a huge debt, and then you'll be in big trouble. If you don't have the money to pay for the things you want, do not go into debt to get them. What makes you think you'll have the money next month when the bill arrives? Instead, show a little discipline and maturity: save first and spend later.

Any kind of unsecured debt is a negative thing—whether it's credit card debt or student loans. Never think of a loan as free money, as beating the system, or as getting away with something. You won't get away with anything, and just thinking that will set you up for a life riddled by debt.

Your college years are the perfect time to practice frugality— another way of saying living below your means. You don't have a family and young children depending on you. You have a lot of freedom to make your own decisions. It's a great time to practice making the right choices.

Never spend all that you have. No matter how little you have, save something for later. Learn to be content with what you have. Look for ways not to spend money—don't be obnoxious about it, just wise and conservative. The standards you set for yourself during these wonderful years will become the foundation for the rest of your life. When you graduate owing no one, your options will multiply. You'll be free to get a job, serve on the mission field, travel, go to graduate school, and on and on. The possibilities will be endless, and the world will be your oyster.

If, on the other hand, you graduate with huge credit card debt and a mega-student-loan package for which payments will become due sooner than you think, you will feel weighed down and defeated. You'll have no choice but to take the first job you can find. The carefree college years of fun and freedom will quickly fade as you face the daily grind of living from paycheck to paycheck in bondage to your creditors.

An education is a privilege, not a right. You are not entitled to attend the college of your choice. It is a privilege you must earn and something you should never take for granted. Because you will have made a huge investment in yourself, your degree will become something you value highly—not something your parents made you do.

If you leave college with a diploma and a pile of student loan debt, it could be worse. At least you have the degree. Millions of your fellow students owe huge sums for degrees they never received.

If you find yourself in the unfortunate position of having a load of student debt, take heart. You can conquer it provided you buckle down, face the monster, and put on your game face.

Whether or not you know the status of the loans you have, who the lenders are, or the terms of repayment, a few things are certain: You owe the money, the debt will not go away, the lender will find you, and the consequences for nonpayment will be severe.

The good news is that you can escape from student-debt prison. But first you have to learn everything about the confusing world of student loans.

Know Your Student Loan

Federal student loans. These loans are guaranteed by the federal government. That means the government will reimburse your lender if you default. But don't think of default as an easy way out. If you default, the government will come after you aggressively and will show no mercy. There are currently fifteen federal student loan programs, and the plans are always changing. The most common are Stafford Loans and Perkins Loans.

Private student loans. These are loans made by banks and other financial institutions without government backing. If you default on a private loan, expect to hear from an aggressive guarantee agent.

Interest. Interest is the commission or "rent" you agreed to pay on the money you borrowed. If you have a loan with an interest rate of 6.3 percent, each year the holder of your loan will add 6.3 percent of your outstanding balance (principal) to the total amount you owe.

The method of adding interest can be confusing. If your loan says interest will be compounded daily, your loan holder will add 1/365 of 6.3 percent to the balance of your loan each day. If compounded monthly, the holder will add 1/12 of 6.3 percent at the start of every month.

Interest that builds up over time is called accrued interest. All loans begin accruing interest the moment the loan is funded. Who pays that interest is the critical issue.

Subsidized. If your loan is subsidized, the government pays the interest while you are in school and during times of deferment. Subsidized loans are granted based on need. Private loans are never subsidized by the government.

Unsubsidized. If your loan is unsubsidized, you must pay interest from the moment the loan is funded. But since the lender doesn't require you to make payments while you are in school, every month the interest is tacked onto the loan balance. The interest becomes part of the principal—it is "capitalized." Even though you are not borrowing more money, the balance is growing because of the interest. Unsubsidized loans are not need based. You don't have to prove you need the money. If you can sign your name, you can get an unsubsidized loan in most cases.

There is no grace period on Parent Loans for Students (PLUS). The repayment period for a PLUS loan begins on the day after the final loan disbursement is made.[4]

How to Track Down Your Student Loan

Student loans are frequently passed from one financial institution to another without rhyme or reason. It's easy to lose track of them if you've been in school or deferment for a long time. To find out about your loans—even if you are in default—contact the Federal Student Aid Center (http://studentaid.ed.gov/data-center; 800-433-3242) or the Department of Education's Debt Collection Services Office (800-621-3115). If you have several loans, you could have as many loan holders.

When You Cannot Pay

If you're in over your head and can't make payments, don't panic, but don't hide either. It's not the end of the world. You will survive, but you must act quickly to figure out your options.

Loan cancellation. There are circumstances under which you might be able to cancel some or all of your student loans. But don't get too excited. It is not easy to qualify for cancellation. You have to meet specific conditions that depend on what type of loans you have and when you borrowed the money. You may be able to cancel some or all of your student loans if:

- You are dead. This will be of little consolation to you, but your heirs will want to know that your executor can request cancellation of all of your outstanding student loans upon your death. So can parents who took a PLUS loan for you.
- You became permanently and totally disabled after you got the loan.
- The trade school you attended went belly-up before you could complete the program.
- You serve the United States government wearing a uniform.
- You are a teacher serving certain needy populations, including low-income or disabled students.
- You do not teach but serve certain needy populations in certain capacities and certain professions.
- You perform community service in the Peace Corps, Ameri-Corps, VISTA, ACTION, or other volunteer organization.
- You work in certain healthcare professions; you are a nurse or physician in your residency and/or you agree to work in certain areas where healthcare workers are needed.
- You work in law enforcement.

To determine if you qualify for cancellation, call the Department of Education's Debt Collection Services Office at 800-621-3115. They will send you a cancellation application and instructions on obtaining necessary documentation.

Deferment. This is an authorized temporary postponement of your loan payments. Conditions under which you might be granted a deferment are:

- You return to school and study at least half-time.
- You are temporarily but totally disabled.
- You are unemployed.
- You are suffering economic hardship.
- You are enrolled in a rehabilitation program for the disabled.

- You are a parent with young children, have a very low income, or are on parental leave.

Deferments are never automatic. You must apply for a deferment directly with the loan holder. Interest continues to accrue during deferment. However, if you are deferring a subsidized loan, the government pays the interest during deferment. To obtain a deferment, contact your loan holder for an application, complete it carefully, and make sure you include all required documentation. You will have to prove your case. Follow up to make sure your request is processed correctly.

Forbearance. If you don't qualify for deferment but are facing hard times, your loan holder may allow you to postpone payment or temporarily reduce your payments. This arrangement is called forbearance. A forbearance is easier to obtain than a deferment. But forbearance is less attractive because interest will continue to accrue while you are not making payments, no matter what type of loan you have. Forbearance is attractive only because it will keep you out of default. The cost of default is much more expensive than the extra interest that accrues during forbearance.

Student Loan Consolidation

This is when a lender combines many loans into a single new loan or refinances one loan with new terms. When you consolidate, you extend your repayment period and lower your monthly payments. Consolidation increases the overall cost of the loan repayment and is rarely advisable.

Most student loans may be consolidated, but there are some restrictions. You won't be able to put your private loans into federal loan consolidation programs. A few private lenders, such as Access Group, have set up consolidation plans for private loans.

You might consider consolidation if you are so deeply in debt that you cannot keep up your monthly payments or if you can afford larger payments and want to refinance at a lower interest rate under more aggressive payment terms.

You should not consolidate if you can find any possible way to abide by your current terms. Consolidation is usually quite expensive over the long term. With most student loans, if you consolidate, you lose the subsidized feature. Also, you may lose the cancellation option if you consolidate now but later find yourself eligible under one of the cancellation provisions above.

You can consolidate your student loans only one time, so keep this in mind. The interest rate you have upon consolidation is the rate you will have for the duration.

Consequences for Not Paying

If you have not paid for at least nine months and have not arranged for cancellation, deferment, or forbearance, you are no doubt in default. If you do not reinstate your loans immediately, this is what you can expect.

Collection letters. If you have not yet received letters from your lender, don't get too comfortable. Your lender is using every legal means to find you, including contacting your past employers and your relatives. They are checking utility company records and the IRS. You can run, but don't think you can hide. It's only a matter of time.

A report to credit bureaus. A bad credit report will negatively affect your ability to buy a house, get a job, or even rent an apartment in the future.

Garnishment of tax refunds. The IRS and state tax boards can and will intercept your income tax refunds through the Department of Education's tax offset program. This is the most common method of collecting defaulted student loans.

Garnishment of your wages. Unlike other creditors who must first sue you to garnish your wages, the Department of Education and guarantee agencies are authorized to garnish your wages without a judgment.

A lawsuit. The Department of Education has forever to sue you because there is no statute of limitations. Once they have a judgment, they will move aggressively to attack all bank accounts and liquidate your assets, including your home and personal property.

Student Loans and Bankruptcy

Many students consider filing for bankruptcy to get rid of their student loans. Unfortunately—and despite the cries of bankruptcy lawyers who promise to clear the slate of all your debts—this may be more fantasy than reality. Congress has all but eliminated the ability to erase student loans through bankruptcy.

Have a Complaint?

Due to so many complaints, Congress finally responded by creating a student loan Ombudsman to help student borrowers resolve any complaints. Call 877-557-2575 or visit Ombudsman.ed.gov.

18

Building Wealth on an Ordinary Income

Basics of Responsible Investing

A faithfully kept program of savings and conservative investments can give you more money and a better life than that of your neighbors who spend everything they get.

Jane Bryant Quinn,
Making the Most of Your Money

Funny, isn't it, how the word *investment* has the ability to turn otherwise intelligent people into quivering masses of intimidation?

Perhaps you've experienced this phenomenon yourself. I know I have. For that, I believe, we can thank the investment industry. It has gone to great lengths to create the impression that investing is difficult and not something amateurs like us should attempt. Investment professionals want us to think they are working on our behalf to protect us from something that could harm us greatly. Moreover, some are all but obsessed with making forecasts. They

273

insist that unless you can time the market (predict when values will rise and fall so you can buy low and sell high), you have no business making investment decisions.

The truth is that nobody knows what's coming next year, next month, next week, or even tomorrow. Nobody. Not only are market forecasts confusing, but they can also be contradictory, misleading, and potentially expensive to those who allow outsiders who rely on them to make their investment decisions.

I do not profess to be an investment counselor or adviser. I am not formally trained in the matter of high finance, nor do I hold any Wall Street–type certifications. I do possess, however, a basic understanding of investing and the knowledge necessary to develop and manage a personal investment portfolio. I take a conservative approach to investing and stay away from risky situations.

What I know about investing I learned from reading excellent books by those who teach the fundamentals of investing, especially the book *The Sound Mind Investing Handbook* by Austin Pryor. Even if you are not yet ready to begin building your investment portfolio, I recommend you read that book—just as soon as you finish this one or you reach savings level 4, whichever comes first—so you will be ready to go when the time comes.

Two Kinds of Investors

Investors can be divided into two categories: reactive and proactive.

Reactive investors do exactly as their name implies. Their investment decisions are reactions. They do not initiate their moves but rather react to what happens. They wake up in the morning unsure of their next move because they've not yet read the financial page or logged on to their favorite stock quote website. Reactors make their investment decisions by reacting to what happens in the news or what their hungry broker recommends that particular day. Reactive investors don't have a specific plan or strategy in place.

They have a difficult time sleeping for all their worries about what the market is doing today or might do tomorrow. They are plagued by fear that they might make the wrong move, miss a forecast, or fail to time the market.

Proactive investors have a specific plan—an investment road map. They invest according to sound principles and a specific investment strategy. They don't pay attention to what the market is doing from day to day. When it comes to sleeping, it's lights out the minute their heads hit the pillow.

Is one approach to investing right and the other wrong? No. But for the beginning investor with limited money to invest, the proactive approach offers a level of safety and simplicity. As you gain experience and confidence, you will develop your individual investment style.

A friend of mine, for example, is a very conscientious investor who uses elements from both styles of investing to her advantage. She diligently follows the activities of about thirty stocks. Some of them she owns; others she'd like to own if they reach a price she is willing to pay. She's a bargain hunter and as such is blending her proactive style of investing with calculated and well-reasoned reactions. While her road map might be completely different from mine, that doesn't make one approach more correct than the other. Still, my friend didn't start out at this level. Through years of learning, patience, researching, and building a respectable portfolio, she has developed her individual investing style. She knows how much risk she's willing to take and where to go for specific advice.

This chapter is for investors with limited money who lack knowledge and experience but desire to step confidently into the investing arena. You can begin investing with as little as $25. To become a proactive investor, you need to:

- learn what you need to know about investing to get started (Don't wait until you know everything there is to know or you'll never get started.)

275

- build a strategy for how you will invest your surplus funds
- understand your tolerance for risk based on your temperament and personality type and then invest only within your comfort zone

What Investing Is and What It's Not

Investing is not magic or mystery. It is the deliberate act of putting money to work in a commercial endeavor with an expectation of reasonable gain and with the full understanding that no investment is without some level of risk.

Speculation is exposing money to high levels of risk with the expectation of a large return in a short period of time. Speculation should be left to highly experienced professionals.

Gambling is not investing but rather putting money at unreasonable risk in an effort to profit from the outcome of a game of chance.

Day-trading is tantamount to gambling within the stock market. Day-trading is the act of buying and selling stocks for a profit in the same day with no overnight holds. The risks are so high that the chances of winning are miniscule. Day-trading is highly inadvisable.

Types of Investments

There are only two ways you can invest money. You can become either an owner or a lender.

When you invest by owning, your intention is that the investment you own will increase in value so that you can at some point sell it for more than you paid for it, realizing a profit. Investments in which you own something generally have a higher risk level and also a higher expectation of return. Real estate, stocks, art, and antiques are examples of investing by owning.

When you invest by lending, your money experiences a gain in the form of interest paid to you by the individual; corporation; insurance

276

company; or local, state, or federal government that borrowed it from you. When you lend money, your risk is less than when you become an owner, but so is your reward. The risks are twofold: The borrower is unable to repay the loan and you lose your principal, or you get locked into a low rate of interest when interest rates are rising. Savings accounts, certificates of deposit, commercial paper, bonds, Treasury bills, notes and bonds, cash-value life insurance, and fixed annuities are examples of investing by lending.

When to Begin Investing

In the same way you need to be physically fit before embarking on a physically challenging activity, you need to be financially fit before you begin investing your surplus funds. Financial fitness means you're prepared for emergencies and you are debt-free. Ideally, it means your mortgage is paid in full as well. After all, "investing" in your debt offers a sure rate of return. Once your debt is paid, the interest you are now paying to your lender is yours to pay to yourself, to be invested.

If you are living paycheck to paycheck, carrying unsecured debt, and are not adequately prepared for emergencies and unexpected expenses with a Contingency Fund and a Freedom Account, you need to direct every dime of surplus to those things.

Every investment has some level of risk—there is a chance you will lose all or part of the money you have invested. It is not advisable to put any of your money at risk until you have achieved financial fitness.

Let's say you owe $5,000 on a credit card account and you have a surplus of $100 a month. If you put that $100 at risk in an investment, you could lose it, but you would still owe $5,000. If, however, you apply the surplus to the debt, you will owe $4,900 regardless of what happens in the stock or real estate markets. It makes sense to invest your money in your debts.

Once you have a Contingency Fund and a Freedom Account and you are completely debt-free, you will have a pile of money to invest each month: your 10 percent savings as well as the money you'll redirect from your RDRP. As your investments ebb and flow in value (and they will), you won't be financially devastated because you are in a strong financial position.

Things to Know before You Begin

Diversification is the opposite of having all your eggs in one basket. As you assemble and grow your portfolio, you will want to concentrate on two things: high safety and low risk. You want your invested money to be as safe as possible while exposed to manageable risk. Diversification is the way to achieve both without sacrificing your rate of return.

It would be foolish to have all your investments in the stock of a single corporation. If that company gets into serious trouble, you could lose everything in one mighty blow.

Nor would you want to have all your investments in a single type of investment. Understand that the stock and bond markets are cyclical. When one is up and prosperous, the other might be flat and lackluster. The most conservative approach to investing suggests that you should have a good mix of investments in your portfolio. Then if one section of your portfolio goes through a downturn, your entire portfolio won't suffer.

The mix of investments you determine is right for your portfolio should be in harmony with your personality type (some people are risk takers while others are naturally more cautious) and season of life. The younger you are, the greater amount of risk you can tolerate; you have time to ride out downturns and recover. As you approach the second half of life, however, and you are more likely to depend on your investments to cover your cost of living, you will want to move into lower-risk, safer positions.

Long-Term Investing

Conservative investors use a long-term rather than an in-and-out-quickly approach to investing. This philosophy provides safety and minimal risk.

If you were to view a snapshot of the stock market in this country since its inception more than sixty years ago, you would see that even with all the ups and downs it continues to show growth. My point is that if you are invested in the stock market and are committed to leaving your money there for a period of time (ten years is good; five years is minimal), you are more likely to experience growth than if you are in and out, reacting to the ups and downs. Generally speaking, as a conservative investor, your approach should be to buy and hold.

Dollar-Cost Averaging

One systematic strategy for long-term investing is called dollar-cost averaging. This requires investing the same amount of money in the same investment at regular time intervals. This approach automatically accomplishes the goal of the wise investor: buy more shares when prices are low and fewer shares when prices are high.

Let's say my strategy requires that I buy $100 worth of stock in the DPL Corporation each month. This month on the day my purchase is recorded the per share price is $5, so I add 20 shares to my portfolio. However, next month the price jumps to $7. Now my $100 buys 14.28 shares—fewer than last month when the price was down. The stock takes a plunge the following month and drops to $4 a share. The price is down, so my $100 buys 25 shares.

Over the three months, I invested $300 and purchased 59.28 shares for an average of $5.06 per share. With dollar-cost averaging, I'm happy no matter the state of the market. When the prices are low, I can buy more shares. When the prices are high, I'm making more money. That's a good investment attitude.

Dollar-cost averaging is an excellent way to gradually invest a large sum of money. It's practical, and it's neither complicated nor time-consuming.

Automatic Purchasing

Many types of investments allow you to sign up for automatic purchasing. You fill out the appropriate paperwork authorizing the mutual fund company or corporation in which you are buying shares of stock to automatically withdraw from your checking account a certain amount on a specific date each month. What was a no-brainer (dollar-cost averaging) becomes even simpler. You can truly forget about investing and allow your wealth to grow. Of course, you'll want to make sure the automatic withdrawal is covered by sufficient funds in your checking account. I do predict, however, that by the time you reach this place in your debt-proof living journey, bouncing checks will not be a problem.

Investment Options

Bonds

Bonds are relatively low-risk, high-security, heavy-duty IOUs that offer low returns and little in the way of excitement—the perfect choice for the very cautious investor. Because bonds score high in the reliability department, they can bring stability and strength to an investment portfolio. When you invest in a bond, you know upfront what your return will be because the interest rate is stated. Bonds have varying maturity dates. Some might be for three years, ten years, or even thirty years.

While it might be nice to know for sure that you will receive a set rate of interest for a long time, you should consider that the interest rate could be woefully under market during the life of the bond. The other risk in bond investing is if the bond issuer (the borrower) is not creditworthy and defaults while you are still holding that bond. Losing your principal in this way is the worst-case scenario. The way to neutralize this risk is to buy only highly rated bonds issued by creditworthy entities and to limit your activity to terms of no longer than three years.

Bonds can be sold prior to maturity in the secondary market. However, if you're locked into a long term at a below-market interest rate, you will likely have to discount the face value in order to find a buyer.

Stocks

When you purchase shares of stock, you become a part owner of a corporation. As the value of the company increases, so does the value of the shares. Many companies sell their stock only through brokerage firms.

Mutual Funds

Wouldn't it be great if we could stop worrying about understanding every little detail and nuance of investing and just hire a professional to take care of it for us? We could write the guy a check every month and forget it.

Of course, we'd need to find someone we could trust to invest our money in the kinds of companies we like. And it wouldn't hurt if he was educated, reputable, and had enough smarts to make a few excellent investment recommendations now and then.

If this investment manager was really top-notch, he'd spend all his time working just for us—doing all those Wall Street–like things investment professionals do.

Naturally, we wouldn't actually want to pay the guy, but I don't think we'd have a problem chipping in for his expenses. Basically, we'd want 100 percent of the money we gave him to go straight into the purchase of stocks or bonds—with no commissions. And let's not forget the paperwork. We'd want to make sure he did all the paperwork and just sent us a simple report once or twice a year.

Who are we trying to kid? We'd be dreaming if we thought we could find that kind of situation. Or would we?

What we just dreamed up is a very loose description of a segment of the investment industry that has exploded in recent decades: mutual funds.

A mutual fund is all the money thousands of small investors put together to form a big pool of money that gives the fund, as a whole, much greater buying power and financial advantages than a small investor would have on his own.

The money in the pool is managed by a hired professional and regulated by the Securities Exchange Commission (SEC). When a mutual fund is formed, it establishes ground rules that limit the types of investments and that protect the investors. Some mutual funds invest in stocks. Others invest in bonds or any variety or combinations determined by the goals and objectives established by that particular fund.

Austin Pryor, who is quite a mutual-fund enthusiast, says mutual funds offer twenty major advantages for beginning investors:

1. Mutual funds can reduce the anxiety of investing. It's like trusting a master mechanic to fix your car rather than attempting to do it yourself.
2. Mutual fund shares can be purchased in small amounts, which makes it easy to get started. Most funds have minimum requirements to open an account that range from $500 to $3,000; however, many funds eliminate the minimum requirements when you agree to make regular monthly deposits to build your account.
3. Many funds will set up an automatic deposit for you.
4. Mutual funds reduce risk through diversification. The typical mutual fund holds as many as two hundred stocks in its portfolio.
5. Mutual funds' price movements are more predictable than those of individual stocks.

6. A mutual fund's past performance is a matter of public record. Most funds post their daily activities in the newspaper the same way stock prices are reported. You can check on how they've fared in the past.

7. Mutual funds provide full-time professional management.

8. Mutual funds allow you to reinvest your dividends efficiently (distribution of profits to shareholders). You can instruct the fund to reinvest your profits automatically so your account will grow even faster.

9. Mutual funds offer automatic withdrawal plans. Preplanned selling enables the fund to mail you a check for a specified amount at a frequency you specify.

10. Mutual funds provide individual attention. In a mutual fund, the smallest member of the pool gets exactly the same attention as the largest because everybody is in it together.

11. Mutual funds can be used for your individual retirement account (IRAs) and other retirement plans.

12. Mutual funds allow you to sell part or all of your shares at any time and get to your money quickly. All of this can be done by phone in a quick and efficient manner.

13. Mutual funds enable you to reduce instantly the risk in your portfolio with just a phone call. You can switch funds.

14. Mutual funds pay minimum commissions when buying and selling for the pool. If you purchased the same stocks as an individual, you would get socked with huge commissions.

15. Mutual funds provide a safe place for your investment money. But remember that every investment carries some level of risk.

16. Mutual funds handle your paperwork for you. You get simple reports in the mail.

17. Mutual funds can be borrowed against in case of an emergency. I hope you won't, but the value of your mutual fund holdings can be used as collateral for a loan.

18. Mutual funds involve no personal liability beyond the investment risk in the portfolio.

19. Mutual fund advisory services are available that can greatly ease the research burden. You can check your fund's ratings on the internet by clicking on "stock quote" on any search engine.

20. Mutual funds are heavily regulated by the Securities Exchange Commission (SEC) and have operated mostly scandal free for decades.[1]

A Prospectus

A prospectus is a legal document that outlines a mutual fund's objectives, policies, performance, per share data, performance history, expenses, and how to buy or redeem one's shares. Typically, an application to open an account is enclosed in the prospectus. Anyone can request a prospectus by calling that mutual fund company's toll-free customer service number. The prospectus will be sent to you in the mail. Most mutual fund companies now have websites where you can request a prospectus as well.

Opening a mutual fund account is similar to opening a bank account. You fill out an application that includes your Social Security number, name, address, and name of a beneficiary. Then you send it in with a check to establish the account. This application also carries instructions for establishing an automatic purchase program.

Creating Your Investment Strategy

It is at this point on the subject of investing that I must defer and refer. I am simply not qualified to advise you on the specifics of the investment portfolio you need to create. What I can tell you again is that everything I know about this topic I learned from my favorite book on the subject, *The Sound Mind Investing Handbook*. I have followed the specifics of Austin Pryor's "just-the-basics Strategy" because it is simple, understandable, and simple to administer.

In his book, Pryor also provides specific fund recommendations, telephone numbers to get started, and investing models that are simple and easy to follow—models that address personalities and seasons in life. With great confidence I refer you to Pryor's excellent book as you prepare for the exciting world of investing.

Financial Planners

While not discounting the fact that I believe you should be able to develop and manage your own investment portfolio, let me say that the time may come when you need to seek more advanced advice from a professional financial planner.

A financial planner is not a stockbroker, money manager, or insurance agent with a single focus. A financial planner is a professional with the education, experience, and knowledge to provide professional guidance as you develop a coordinated plan.

While you may doubt it at this point, let me assure you that if you follow the principles outlined in this book, the day will come (and sooner than you think) when you may need a more sophisticated level of financial advice. That does not mean you've abandoned your resolve to be a proactive investor but that you've moved to a more sophisticated level and are wise enough to acknowledge your areas of weakness. You will need professional guidance from a planner you can trust.

If at that point in your journey you decide to hire the services of a financial counselor, I suggest you find a fee-based planner. The reason is simple: A commission-based planner will earn a commission on every product he advises you to purchase and/or sell. That is, in my opinion, a conflict of interest. It is only human nature to direct one's clients to the products and services that will best compensate one's own bank account. Your best interests will not be the commissioned planner's top priority.

A fee-based planner, on the other hand, will charge a flat hourly or session fee that you will agree to ahead of time. The compensation will be the same whether you follow the advice, buy everything that is recommended, or change your mind altogether. You can be reasonably confident that this planner's recommendations will be in your best interest because the conflict has been removed.

A third option is a hybrid of the previous two options. In this scenario, you hire a financial planner who charges a nominal fee for his or her services, and in exchange you receive a complete written plan. However, the planner stays with you after the plan has been created, helping you to implement all the aspects of that plan. Believe me, it is not easy to find the right insurance as recommended in a comprehensive financial plan or to purchase the correct mutual funds or other investment instruments. Having the planner on your team to hold your hand while you go through the maze of setting up your portfolio is helpful. It would not be unusual in this arrangement for the planner to earn a commission on some of the instruments involved.

The best way to find a reliable financial planner is to get a referral from a friend or relative. If you are unable to find a fee-only financial planner in whom you have confidence, contact the National Association of Personal Financial Advisors, 1-888-FEE-ONLY, or visit their website, NAPFA.org, where you can find planners who practice in your area.

When it comes to investing and financial planning, never forget who is in charge: you. Don't allow or depend on others to make your financial decisions. Seek outside advice but never outside authority.

Afterword

When everything is said and done, here's the best advice I can offer as you contemplate debt-proof living: use your common sense. Determine right now that you will do whatever it takes to live your life on less than your income.

Take all the information you've read in the preceding chapters and plant it in your mind. Ponder it, nurture it, and then trust yourself to make the right moves. Effective personal money management is not difficult. You can make your own decisions—even the difficult ones.

If you don't know exactly what to do to get started, I can help. Get a pen and small notebook. Write today's date on the first page and write down exactly how you spend your money today. Nothing complicated—just what and where. Tomorrow, turn the page and start over. Write everything down—the big things, the small things, even the embarrassing things. If you are in any kind of a financial fog, this is going to help clear it.

Every day as you track your spending, something amazing will happen—you will start paying attention. You won't be able to keep yourself from focusing on where your money is going.

Begin giving away some part of everything you receive. Do it thoughtfully, joyfully, and with all the gratitude your heart can muster. Find a place to start saving part of everything you receive. Make plans; do some research. Find out where you can open an account for your savings. Make it a top priority in your life.

As you continue to give and save, you'll begin to see your savings develop into your Contingency Fund. Now you're on your way. Take the next step and face your debts head-on. Get to work on your Rapid Debt-Repayment Plan and your Freedom Account. Develop your Spending Plan. Get it just right. Then live the plan one day, one week, one month at a time.

Don't worry about doing everything perfectly. Just get started. As long as you are managing your money according to the plan, you will begin to move toward success—one step at a time, day after day after day. At first it may feel awkward—you'll think this planning-ahead stuff is way too confining. But soon the shackles that bind you will begin to loosen. As you gain control, you'll also experience a new kind of freedom. Managing your money will become a wonderful new habit in your life.

Before you know it you will be on your way to financial freedom, prepared for whatever the future holds. You'll be confident to face any eventuality. And I will be cheering you on all the way.

I hope you will pay me a visit at DebtProofLiving.com. This is a site where you will find all the tools you'll need relative to what you have learned in the previous chapters. More than that, you're going to meet a lot of wonderful people, all of us making this journey to financial freedom. You'll find information and a place to ask questions. You'll even have direct access to my email inbox.

If you remember only one thing from what you've read, I hope it is this: Money is not just for spending. It is for managing first and then for spending. Exercise your management skills well. Persist.

You will be richer in the end.

Notes

Introduction

1. http://www.infoplease.com/ipa/A0104583.html.
2. Quarterly Report Household Debt and Credit, February 2013, Federal Reserve Bank of New York, http://www.newyorkfed.org/research/national_economy/householdcredit/DistrictReport_Q42012.pdf.

Chapter 1: Debt-Proof Living

1. Natalie H. Jenkins et al., *You Paid How Much for That?!* (San Francisco: Jossey-Bass, 2000), 15.
2. Ragnar Storaaski, PhD, and Howard Markman, PhD, 1991, University of Denver, Center of Marital and Family Studies, DU Graduate School of Professional Psychology, 2450 S. Vine St., Denver, CO 80208, 303-871-3873.
3. Median Household Income in the United States, http://www.davemanuel.com/median-household-income.php.

Chapter 2: Two Kinds of Debt

1. http://www.indexcreditcards.com.
2. http://www.bankrate.com.

Chapter 3: Caught in the Debt Trap

1. http://www.federalreserve.gov/econresdata/scf/scfindex.htm.

Chapter 4: A Plan to Debt-Proof Your Life

1. George Clason, *The Richest Man in Babylon* (New York: Penguin, 1955), 15.

Chapter 5: Where Does All the Money Go?

1. http://www.cbsnews.com/8301-505144_162-57351515/starbucks-raising
-prices-in-some-markets.

Chapter 8: Expect the Unexpected

1. http://www.federalreserve.gov/releases/g19/Current/#fn1a.
2. http://www.nerdwallet.com/blog/credit-card-data/average-credit-card-debt
-household.
3. https://www.usaa.com/inet/imco_mutualfund/ImFundFacts?action=INIT
&fundNumber=0042&fundCategory=MM.

Chapter 13: The Proper Handling of Hazardous Materials

1. http://news.uscourts.gov/bankruptcy-filings-down-fiscal-year-2012.
2. http://www.bankrate.com/brm/news/cc/19990222b.asp.

Chapter 16: The Overlooked Safety Net

1. U.S. Social Security Administration, fact sheet, February 7, 2013.
2. U.S. Census Bureau, American Community Survey, 2011.
3. U.S. Social Security Administration, Disabled Worker Beneficiary Data, December 2012.
4. Council for Disability Awareness, Personal Disability Quotient (PDQ) calculator.

Chapter 17: Student Loans, Student Debt

1. http://www2.ed.gov/about/offices/list/ovae/pi/cclo/ccfacts.html.
2. http://en.wikipedia.org/wiki/California_Community_Colleges_System.
3. http://aging.ohio.gov/information/learning.
4. http://www.direct.ed.gov/leaving.html.

Chapter 18: Building Wealth on an Ordinary Income

1. Austin Pryor, *The Sound Mind Investing Handbook: A Step-by-Step Guide to Managing Your Money from a Biblical Perspective*, 5th ed. (Louisville: Sound Mind Investing, LLC, 2008), 110–15.

Glossary

401(k) savings plan. An employee-provided, salary-deferral plan approved by the Internal Revenue Service that allows qualified persons to save and invest pretax dollars.

adjustable-rate loan. Also called variable-rate loan. The interest rate of the loan fluctuates, adjusting periodically to the moves of a key rate, such as the prime rate or one-year Treasury bills.

affinity card. A credit card marketed to a group of customers with a common bond, such as membership in an organization.

allocation. The way in which a person's savings are divided among the different accounts he or she has selected.

annual fee. The annual charge, from $35 to $400, paid by a cardholder to a credit card company for the privilege of possessing their particular credit card. Many credit cards do not charge an annual fee. The annual fee is billed directly to the customer's monthly statement.

annual percentage rate (APR). The true cost of borrowing money, expressed as a percentage. It includes interest and fees on some loans such as an auto loan. The interest rate on a mortgage or home equity loan does not include fees.

annual percentage yield (APY). Typically, APY is used when you are earning interest. It is the interest rate you earn plus the effect of compounding interest.

appreciating asset. An asset that has a reasonable expectation of increasing in value with time.

appreciation. An increase in value.

appropriate. To set aside funds for a specific use.

asset. Anything of value that a person owns.

ATM card. A plastic card that gives the owner access to the automated teller machine when used with one's personal identification number (PIN). An ATM card often doubles as a debit card.

attitude. A way of thinking or behaving.

austerity. A severely simple lifestyle.

automated teller machine (ATM). A convenient way to deposit and withdraw money from a savings or checking account any time of the day or night. (Often thought of by children as a place in a wall where Mommy and Daddy can get as much money as they want.)

automatic deposit. A deposit that is made from one's account or paycheck into an investment or other account every month or at specific intervals as directed by the account holder. Authorization is made by the account holder and can be retracted or amended at any time. It is a painless way to get into the habit of saving or investing regularly.

automobile loan. A loan from a bank, credit union, or finance company to purchase an automobile.

balance transfer fee. A charge by a credit card company to customers for transferring an outstanding balance from one credit card to another.

bankruptcy. A legal declaration of insolvency. The bankruptcy law contains several types of bankruptcy. Chapter 7 is full discharge of all of one's debts except for student loans and obligations to the IRS. Chapter 11 and Chapter 13 denote reorganization repayment plans set up and administered by the courts.

belief. A feeling of certainty about the meaning of something.

biweekly mortgage. A form of repayment. If a person makes mortgage payments every two weeks—or the equivalent of thirteen payments a year rather than twelve—he or she can reduce the term of a thirty-year mortgage by eight to twelve years.

biweekly schedule. A method by which a person pays one-half of a monthly payment every two weeks. The net result is twenty-six half payments each year or the equivalent of thirteen monthly payments. This is a fairly painless way to pay more than is required and thus reduce the time and fees associated with the indebtedness.

budget. A formula for adjusting expenditures to income.

buying power. Worth determined by how much something will buy. For instance, the buying power of a dollar today is much greater than it will be fifty years from now.

canceled checks. Checks that have been paid by the bank as directed by the checking-account holder. Canceled checks are sometimes returned to the customer for record keeping, although generally many banks and credit unions retain copies but do not return the actual canceled checks.

card hopping. The act of transferring credit card balances to a low-interest card for just the introductory period, then transferring them again to another card for its introductory period. Card hopping can be detrimental to one's credit score.

cash advance. A very expensive loan taken against a credit card's credit limit.

cash-advance fee. A charge by a bank to a customer using credit cards for cash advances. This fee can be stated in terms of a flat per-transaction fee or a percentage of the amount of the cash advance. For example, the fee may be expressed as 2 percent or $10. This means the cash advance fee will be the greater of 2 percent of the cash advance amount or $10. Banks may limit the amount that can be charged to a specific dollar amount. Depending on the bank issuing the card, the cash-advance fee may be deducted directly from the cash advance at the time the money is received or it may be posted to a bill as of the day the customer received the advance.

cash flow. Refers to the money that flows in and out of one's possession. Spending more than comes in produces a negative cash flow. A positive cash flow occurs when more comes in than goes out.

certificate of deposit. An interest-bearing receipt from a bank guaranteeing that upon deposit of a specific amount of money, at a specific point in time, a guaranteed amount of interest will be paid to the bearer along with the original deposit. CDs are available in a variety of denominations and for varying time periods. The longer a person agrees to leave his or her money on deposit, the greater the interest rate he or she will earn.

cheapskates. Those who give generously, save regularly, and never spend more money than they have.

co-branded card. A credit card that is issued through a partnership between a bank and another company or organization. For instance, a large department store may co-brand a card with a bank. The card would have both the bank name and the store name on it. Some co-branded cards are also rewards cards that provide the consumer with benefits such as extra service, cash, or merchandise every time the card is used. Also called an affinity card.

collateral. An asset owned by the borrower that is pledged and held by the lender pending the borrower's faithful repayment of the debt. Something of value such as real estate, stocks, bonds, or other assets offered as security to encourage a lender to make a loan.

commercial paper. Short-term IOUs of large US corporations.

compounding interest. The concept that money makes money. When interest is allowed to remain in an account rather than being paid out, it becomes principal. Now interest is earned on the interest. Compounding interest is what allows investments and savings to grow.

consumer credit industry. That segment of the business world that extends credit to consumers on an unsecured basis.

consumer debt. Unsecured loans offered to consumers to buy goods and services.

contentment. Being happy with what you have.

Contingency Fund. A pool of money that is readily available within seventy-two hours and is held as a hedge against emergencies such as health and safety issues or the loss of one's income.

corporate downsizing. The process by which a corporation pulls in its belt by drastically reducing overhead and expenses. Corporate downsizing is often the catalyst for massive layoffs.

credit card. A card authorizing the holder to buy goods or services on credit. (Mary's preferred definition: A small piece of plastic that has the ability to make its bearer do strange things he or she probably wouldn't dream of doing with cash.)

credit inquiry. A notation on one's credit report that indicates the person gave a company permission to look into his or her credit file.

credit insurance. Insurance that pays off all or part of a loan if the borrower dies or becomes disabled or unemployed.

credit report. A report filed by a subject's name, birth date, and Social Security number that gives an accounting of that person's credit activities and payment history. This report will help a new lender determine the creditworthiness of the applicant. Many prospective landlords and employers look at a person's credit report to get a true picture of the applicant's character.

Major companies providing these credit report services include Experian, TransUnion, and Equifax.

credit scoring. A point system lenders and credit bureaus use to assess a person's creditworthiness.

credit union. A nonprofit financial institution formed for the benefit of its members. Since there are no stockholders, profits are partially paid back to the members in the form of dividends. It offers checking accounts, savings accounts, and loan services and generally has better interest rates, lower fees, and personal service. A person must qualify to join. It is not open to the public.

daily Spending Record. A simple list showing where a person spent his or her money today. It should include every single expenditure, even the small ones.

day-trading. A form of investing that involves buying and selling stocks for a profit on the same day with no overnight holds. The chances of losing money are very high.

debit card. A plastic card that gives a person electronic access to his or her checking account. It often doubles as an ATM card and can also be used like a credit card to make purchases from vendors.

debt. Something that is owed.

debt-proof living formula. Giving away 10 percent, saving 10 percent, and living on 80 percent.

debt trap. That place where a person is overcome by too much debt. A place of bondage.

debt, intelligent. That to which the borrower is obligated in a loan transaction secured by collateral that can be repaid anytime.

debt, stupid. A debt that is not secured, has no collateral attached to it, and can be incurred with a signature alone.

dejunk. The act of getting rid of all the clutter in one's home, office, and life.

depreciate. To lose value simply because of the passing of time.

depreciation. A loss in value or efficiency resulting from usage and/or age.

deprivation. The act of withholding.

discontentment. Not being happy with what you have.

discretionary income. That which is left after all the bills are paid; money available for nonessential expenditures.

dislocated worker. Anyone fired or laid off due to downsizing or a self-employed person whose business failed because of a turn in the economy.

displaced homemaker. A woman who has left the workplace to rear children, is single as a result of either divorce or death, and requires training to return to the workplace.

disposition fee. The amount of money charged to a lessee at the end of a lease when turning in a vehicle. One should negotiate this before signing the lease and only agree to pay an acquisition fee or a disposition fee, not both. A typical charge is $200 to $400.

diversification. The practice of spreading investments among a number of different investments to reduce risk. It's the opposite of putting all your eggs in one basket. A mutual fund is an example of diversification because it invests in many different securities.

dividend. A sum of money to be distributed to stockholders.

dollar-cost averaging. Investing the same amount of money in the same investment at regular time intervals.

down payment. The up-front money required to enter into a loan.

DPLers. People actively engaged in debt-proofing their lives.

durable goods. Things that have a life expectancy exceeding three years.

entitled. A feeling that is the result of having an available balance on one's credit card account.

equity. The value remaining in excess of liabilities or loans.

f (fixed). If the letter *f* appears after the annual percentage rate (APR), the interest rate is fixed and not subject to adjustment.

face value. The original dollar value of a security as stated by the issuer. For stocks, it is the original cost of the stock shown on the certificate. For bonds, it is the amount paid to the holder at maturity (generally $1,000). Also known as "par value" or simply "par."

falling payments. Payments that fall in direct proportion to the outstanding balance, such as minimum monthly payments on credit card accounts, as opposed to mortgage payments that remain fixed regardless of the current outstanding balance.

federally insured. Money deposited into a bank or savings and loan that is covered by insurance. In the event the financial institution becomes insolvent, the insurance will reimburse the depositor.

federal tax withholding. Money withheld by one's employer and sent to the IRS in anticipation of payment of federal income taxes and Social Security taxes.

financial bondage. That uncomfortable situation in which one owes so much money to so many creditors that he or she feels like a slave.

financial calculator. A calculator that figures payment schedules and debt-payoff periods.

financial freedom. The state or condition of being free from financial pressures brought on when one lives from paycheck to paycheck and under the bondage of heavy debts.

financial security. That point in time when a person can live the lifestyle he or she has chosen, financed by the assets he or she has accumulated, without the need for additional income.

for-profit corporations. A corporation that has stockholders and the expectation of making a profit, which is then paid to said stockholders.

Freedom Account. A separate checking account into which a person deposits monthly 1/12 of his or her known irregular expenses.

frugality. That which is necessary to keep expenses less than income.

gambling. Putting money at unreasonable risk in an effort to profit from the outcome of a game of chance.

grace period. The period of time a customer is allowed to pay a monthly bill before the account begins to accrue interest. Issuers determine a grace period based on different stages in the transaction. A grace period can begin based on one of the following: (1) transaction—the actual date the customer used the card for a purchase or a cash advance; (2) posting—the actual day the issuer received the charge and posted it to the customer's account; (3) billing—the date the bill is generated for mailing to the customer.

hoarding. Saving to an extreme and to the detriment of joy and an ability to do good in the world.

home equity loan (HEL). A loan secured by the equity in one's home. Also called a second mortgage.

home mortgage. A loan from a bank or other lender that is secured by the value of one's home.

income. The money that flows into one's life.

index. A published, market-based figure used by lenders to establish a lending rate. Examples of the most common indexes are the One-Year Treasury Constant Maturity Yield, the Federal Home Loan Bank (FHLB), the 11th District Cost of Funds, and the prime rate as it appears in the *Wall Street Journal.*

indexed rate. The sum of the published index plus the margin. For example, if the index is 9 percent and the margin is 2.75 percent, the indexed rate is 11.75 percent.

individual retirement account (IRA). A personal savings account specifically designated for retirement. Anyone who has earned income may contribute up to $5,500 a year to an IRA. The money placed into an IRA may be tax deductible depending on one's income and participation in other retirement plans. Even if it is not, all money in an IRA account grows on a tax-deferred basis—taxed only when a person begins withdrawing funds.

insurance premiums. Payment for insurance coverage.

intelligent borrowing. Borrowing only when the loan is secured and the proceeds go to buy something that will appreciate.

interest. A fee a borrower pays to a lender for the temporary use of the lender's money.

interest-bearing account. A savings or checking account that earns interest for the account holder.

introductory rate. Also called the "teaser rate," this is the rate charged by a lender for an initial period, often used to attract new cardholders. This rate is charged for a short time only and is used to entice borrowers to accept the card's terms. After the introductory period is over, the rate charged increases to the indexed rate or the stated interest rate.

investing. The deliberate act of putting money to work in a commercial endeavor with an expectation of a reasonable gain and with the full understanding that no investment is without some level of risk.

investment portfolio. The entire collection of one's investments. A portfolio should represent many different types of investments, including stocks, bonds, mutual funds, real estate, security, and cash. A well-diversified portfolio is one that offers the greatest security.

irregular expenses. Any expenses that do not recur on a monthly basis.

late fee. A charge to a customer whose monthly payment has not been received as of the due date or stated deadline for payment as shown on the billing statement. This fee can be stated in terms of a flat per-transaction fee or a percentage of the amount of the cash advance. The fee may be expressed as follows: 3 percent or $25. This means that the late fee charged will be the greater of either 3 percent of the amount of the balance or $25. Late fees are a serious indication of a borrower's lack of financial integrity and show up on one's credit report for future lenders or others assessing one's character to see for up to seven years.

leasing. Renting for a specific number of years. Leasing carries a legal obligation on the part of both the lessor (owner) and the lessee (renter).

liability. A financial obligation.

lien. A legal right to claim or dispose of property in payment of or as security for a debt.

line of credit. A preapproved loan in which one can draw down as much or as little of the line as he or she wants and pay interest only on the amount he or she actually uses. A credit card limit represents a line of credit, as does a home equity line of credit in which the loan is secured by the equity in the home. If the borrower defaults, the lender can foreclose on the property.

liquidating. Turning assets into cash.

liquid cash. Money that is available right now in spendable cash. An investment in stock is not liquid. It would have to be sold to convert it to cash.

liquidity. The ability of an asset to be turned into cash. A checking account is very liquid because a person can draw out the cash at any time. US savings bonds are somewhat liquid, but it takes about three weeks to receive the cash once liquidated. The equity in a home is less liquid because of the time necessary to go through the sale and actually receive cash. Great Uncle Fred's stamp collection would have a low degree of liquidity.

living beneath your means. Spending less than you earn.

long-term investment. An investment one intends to hold for a minimum of five years.

lower-rate cards. Credit cards with amazingly low interest rates. Usually the low rates are limited to the first six months or so until the true rate kicks in.

means. Money or other wealth available to provide for one's living.

minimum monthly payment. The least amount a creditor will accept as the monthly payment on a debt. Often the minimum payment represents only the creditor's profit and does not reduce the principal.

money leaks. The ways money leaves a person's life unnoticed and unaccounted for.

money managers. Caretakers of money.

money market account. A savings account offered by a bank that pays better interest than a passbook savings account. It offers check-writing privileges and is guaranteed by the FDIC up to $100,000. It is not to be confused with money market funds that are not FDIC insured and issued by mutual fund companies.

money market fund accounts. Specialized funds sponsored by mutual fund organizations that take a person's money and make very short-term loans to big businesses, the US Treasury, and state/local governments. It's a way of pooling one's money with that of other small investors and getting a better deal on interest rates. It is basically a savings account disguised as a mutual fund. It is not insured against loss the way a money market account in a bank is insured by the FDIC.

monthly interest rate. The annual interest rate divided by twelve. Credit card companies use the monthly interest rate times the average daily balance to determine the monthly interest payment on a credit card account.

monthly Spending Record. Four weeks' worth of daily Spending Records divided into categories to reveal the money leaks and a picture of where one's money goes.

MSRP. Manufacturer's suggested retail price.

mutual fund company. A corporation chartered by a particular state that pools the money from shareholders and invests in a portfolio of securities. It is "mutual" because the fund is actually owned by its shareholders, who pay a pro rata share of fund operating expenses and receive a pro rata share of income earned and capital gains realized.

net asset value (NAV). The current value of a mutual fund share, stock share, or bond share. The net asset value of any mutual fund, stock, or bond changes daily.

net income. One's take-home pay, reflecting what's left after taxes and other items are deducted.

net worth. The dollar value of one's assets (what one owns and what is owed to them) minus one's liabilities (financial obligations).

no-load mutual fund. A mutual fund whose shares are sold without sales charges of any kind. Some no-load funds charge a small fee, usually 1 percent, for investments held less than six months.

nonrecurring expense. Any kind of expense that is a one-time charge. An appraisal fee would be an example of a nonrecurring expense of buying a home.

nonsufficient funds (NSF). Not enough funds to cover a check. In other words, the check bounced. It is illegal to knowingly write a check when there are not sufficient funds in the account equal to the amount of the check.

offers of entitlement. Preapproved or preselected credit card applications or offers.

overdraft protection. A line of credit attached to one's checking account that puts in a set amount of money at a time to cover checks written in excess of available funds. High interest rates plus significant fees for accessing funds are charged to the account.

par value. The original dollar value of a security. For stocks, it is the original cost of the stock shown on the certificate or statement. For bonds, it is the amount paid to the holder at maturity. Also known as "face value."

passbook savings. A regular savings account in a bank or credit union, the contents of which used to be recorded in a little book called a passbook.

paycheck to paycheck. Spending the entire amount of one's paycheck before the next paycheck is earned.

payoff plan. A specific written plan to pay off debt that lists payments, dates, and the date the plan will be complete.

Pell Grant. A gift from the government for one's college education that is not subject to repayment.

personal finance. One's money in one's personal life as opposed to a business.

points. An up-front fee charged by a lender that, in effect, lowers the nominal interest rate on a loan. A point equals 1 percent of the total loan amount.

portfolio. A collection of investments.

poverty. Living on less money than it takes to survive.

premium. The annual price one pays for an insurance plan as a whole.

prime rate. The interest rate a bank charges to its best or "prime" customers. Each bank will quote a prime lending rate.

principal. The amount borrowed separate from the interest.

private mortgage insurance (PMI). The insurance homebuyers must maintain until the equity in the property reaches at least 20 percent. This insurance protects only the lender in case the borrower defaults on the loan. It is sometimes confused with mortgage insurance, which is similar to life insurance.

prospectus. A legal document that describes the objectives of an investment, such as a mutual fund, including risks, limitations, policies, services, and fees. By law, a prospectus must be furnished to all prospective investors.

purchasing. Acquiring goods and services with a plan and purpose in mind.

purposeful giver. A person who does research and looks for needs so that his or her giving is directed purposefully and not in a haphazard or flippant way.

quitting points. Events or occurrences in our lives that weaken our resolve never to give up and tempt us to quit.

Rapid Debt-Repayment Plan (RDRP). A simple, powerful plan to repay rapidly one's unsecured debts.

rebate. Something given back. In the case of a grocery product, the rebate is the amount of money sent back to the consumer in exchange for a proof of purchase or some other qualifier.

repossess. To take back. Lenders repossess cars or homes they've lent money on when the borrower defaults or refuses to make payments as agreed.

resale value. The value of an asset determined by the amount of money it could bring if sold.

retirement nest egg. Money exposed to interest and growth during one's working years that becomes the security of one's retirement years.

revolvers. Credit card customers who roll a balance over from month to month, pay interest faithfully, and never quite have enough money to pay the balance in full in any given month.

revolving debt. Debt that continues from month to month, year to year.

rewards cards. Cards that allow a customer to accumulate cash, merchandise, or services based on card usage.

saving. Putting money in a safe place where it is not exposed to the risk of loss and pays only a pittance in interest—not enough to keep up with inflation.

savings bond. An IOU from the US government in exchange for a loan. US savings bonds are very safe but pay low rates of interest.

second mortgage. A second loan on a house or other real estate that is second in position to the first mortgage holder. If the homeowner gets into financial trouble and cannot pay, the lender in first position has first right to the property.

secured debt. A debt that is secured or guaranteed by something of value. A mortgage and an automobile loan are examples of secured debt. If the borrower gets into trouble, the home or the car can be sold to satisfy the obligation.

Securities Exchange Commission. The governmental department that regulates the securities industry—the stock market, bond market, etc.

security deposit. Money given up-front to a landlord or car leasing company as a promise of the renter's/lessee's faithful performance of the deal.

selective amnesia. The mental "condition" in which one conveniently forgets that Christmas, for example, is coming; then when he or she finally remembers, it's too late to do anything but shop with a credit card.

shopping. The activity of cruising through stores with a credit card, checkbook, or cash.

signature loan. An unsecured loan that can be obtained with a signature alone.

single-cycle billing. A billing method to determine interest owed on a credit card bill by multiplying the monthly interest rate by the average daily balance of the past thirty days.

slippery places. Situations, events, or locations where one could easily trip and fall, financially speaking. An example might be the mall, where one could easily slip into an old habit of shopping mindlessly and running up a lot of debt before he or she has time to analyze what's going on.

solvency. Having enough money to pay one's bills, debts, and obligations with some left over.

speculation. Exposing money to high levels of risk with the expectation of a large return in a short period of time. Speculation should be left to highly experienced professionals.

spending limit. A term credit card companies use for a credit limit to soften the idea of a loan or debt being involved.

Spending Plan. A written strategy for how one plans to spend his or her money.

Spending Record. A detailed, written account of where one spent his or her money.

statement closing date. The date on which a credit card company cuts off the billing cycle. Purchases made after the statement closing date will show up on the next month's statement.

SuperNOW account. A type of checking account that requires a person to maintain a higher minimum balance and in return pays a higher rate of interest.

Supplemental Educational Opportunity Grant (SEOG). $200 to $4,000 a year available to very low-income undergraduate students.

surplus. The amount of money over and beyond what is needed to pay all of one's expenses.

teaser rate. A low introductory rate to entice a borrower to accept a loan or credit card.

thrift. The economical management of assets and resources.

transaction fee. A fee charged for the privilege of borrowing money through a cash advance.

Treasury bills. Government issued bonds that have short-term maturities. Also called T-bills.

two-cycle billing. A billing method to determine interest owed on a credit card bill by multiplying the monthly interest rate by the average daily balance of the past sixty days.

unclutter. To simplify one's life by getting rid of the clutter and unused stuff.

unemployment benefits. Proceeds of unemployment insurance available to someone who is laid off, but only for a short period of time.

unsecured loan. A loan not guaranteed by the pledge of any collateral.

upside down. Owing more money than a collateralized asset is worth. Typically used to refer to a car loan or lease when the car has a fair market value of less than the balance due.

US Treasuries. IOUs issued by the US government in the form of savings bonds, T-bills, T-notes, and T-bonds.

v (variable). If the letter *v* appears after the annual percentage rate (APR), the interest rate is variable and subject to change.

values. Specific types of beliefs that are so important and central to one's belief system that they act as life guides.

windfall. An unexpected sum of money in any amount.

work-study program. A federal program that provides on-campus jobs for students. Money earned from the job goes to the payment of tuition and is not subject to repayment.

Index

Mary Hunt, award-winning and bestselling author, syndicated columnist, and sought-after motivational speaker, has created a global platform that is making strides to help men and women battle the epidemic impact of consumer debt. Mary is the founder of Debt-Proof Living, a highly regarded organization consisting of an interactive website, a monthly newsletter, a daily syndicated column, and hundreds of thousands of loyal followers. Since 1992, DPL has been dedicated to its mission to provide hope, help, and realistic solutions for individuals who are committed to financially responsible and debt-free living.

As a speaker, Mary travels extensively, addressing conferences, corporations, colleges, universities, and churches at home and abroad. A frequent guest on radio and television, she has appeared on dozens of television shows, including *Dr. Phil*, *Good Morning America*, *The Oprah Winfrey Show*, and *Dateline*.

Mary lives with her husband in Orange County, California.

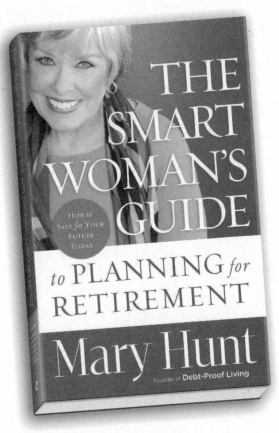

THE SMART WOMAN'S GUIDE

How to Save for Your Future Today

to PLANNING for RETIREMENT

Mary Hunt

Founder of Debt-Proof Living

"Mary Hunt takes the fear out of an often-terrifying topic. Any woman who's ever wanted to be able to retire confidently can benefit from the down-to-earth knowledge in this book."

—Liz Pulliam Weston, *MSN Money* columnist and author of *The 10 Commandments of Money*

"Simple rules of the road that cut through confusion, mystery, and misery."

—Lisa Rose, founder, First Friday Women

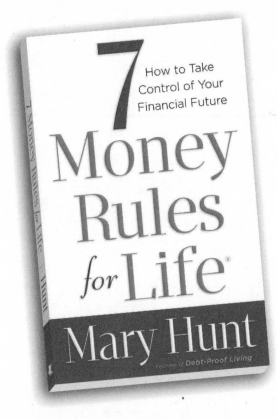

Mary Hunt, nationally syndicated financial columnist and founder of Debt-Proof Living, distills over 20 years of experience into seven simple principles that help people get out of debt and manage their money.

Debt-Proof
LIVING

Debt-Proof Living is a great big wonderful community offering help and hope to anyone who wants to learn how to manage their money more effectively. If you want to get out of debt—or stay out—and learn how to live below your means, Debt-Proof Living is the place to be.

Debt-proof living is a way of life where you spend less than you earn; you give and save consistently; your financial decisions are purposeful; and you work toward your goals by following a specific plan.

DebtProofLiving.com is the home of the debt-proof living philosophy. It is primarily a member-only website with features ranging from money management tools, articles, resources, community forums, consumer tips, recipes, and more. Here you'll find, in continuous publication since 1992, the DPL newsletter, which is published in an online format available to all members of this website.

Visit DebtProofLiving.com today to find out how you can debt-proof your life!

Be the First to Hear about Other New Books from REVELL!

Sign up for announcements about new and upcoming titles at

RevellBooks.com/SignUp

Don't miss out on our great reads!

Revell

a division of Baker Publishing Group
www.RevellBooks.com